I BELIEVE IN THE HOLY SPIRIT

To the students of St. John's College, Nottingham,
Wycliffe Hall, Oxford, and the congregation of St. Aldate's
Church, Oxford, who taught me more of what it means
to live in the Spirit.

I Believe in the Holy Spirit

MICHAEL GREEN

Victor®

ISBN 1 84291 145 7

Published by
KINGSWAY COMMUNICATIONS LTD
Lottbridge Drove, Eastbourne BN23 6NT, England.
Email: books@kingsway.co.uk

Book design and production for the publishers by
Bookprint Creative Services, P.O.Box 827, BN21 3YJ, England.
Printed in Great Britain.

Contents

Preface

This book was the first in the *I Believe* series, published during the 1970s. The series had a remarkable circulation in many countries, and a number of its volumes have subsequently been reissued in a new format. This gave the authors the opportunity to make alterations and corrections to their work, and I took that opportunity in 1984 by making a thorough revision of this book. It was not that I had changed my understanding of the Holy Spirit, but that I had gained a great deal more experience of his power in individual and Church alike. Moreover, the charismatic or renewal movement, comparatively young when the book first appeared, had matured and developed enormously in the subsequent decade.

A further revision was called for in the 1990s, in the light of the enormous changes brought about in the preceding decade, which saw the collapse of the Berlin Wall and the subsequent release of Christianity in Eastern Europe, the amazing growth of Pentecostal Christianity in Latin America, and the phenomenal spread of the gospel in China and South-East Asia generally, not to mention the developments in the Western churches. If you attempt, in your writing, to keep in step with the Holy Spirit there is always going to be need for revision!

That is why, with a change of publisher, I have now completed a further light revision of the book. The *I Believe* series was intended to take a fresh look at controversial issues in the Christian faith. It was written by scholars who had one foot firmly anchored in the Bible and the other equally firmly in the contemporary scene. Each writer sought to give an overall biblical interpretation of his subject, but to do so in such a way as to be of practical help to modern Christians who found themselves perplexed by controversy on the subject. And so in this particular book I would have been failing to meet the aim of the series had I neglected the controversial issues of the baptism, the gifts and the fulness of the Holy Spirit. Equally, in making this further revision, I have naturally had to take account of the remarkable happenings in Toronto and Pensacola.

Because the series was directed not to the scholarly elite, but to the Church at large, the authors tried to keep the style comparatively light, though the content was substantial.

I edited the series, and chose to write on the Holy Spirit myself for a very definite reason. I had, for the previous fifteen years, enjoyed the privilege of living in a Christian community where the charismatic question had been a lively issue, and where 'charismatic' and 'non-charismatic' ordinands lived together with a high degree of mutual respect. The charismatic movement did in places cause division and provoked suspicion then as now. But it was my settled conviction, and indeed my experience, that this need not be so, and that the Spirit of unity would have it otherwise. I therefore offered this book in the hope that it might embody a healing and unitive perspective on this most exciting – and disturbing – movement of our time. The three subsequent revisions have preserved that aim, to provide a bridge between those who find themselves divided by the renewal movement. It is the work of the unholy spirit to divide Christians. The Holy Spirit longs to unite. That remains the fundamental conviction behind the reissue of this book.

There has been a great deal of literature on the subject in the past forty years, and the situation on the ground has been constantly developing. Christians in many countries are becoming increasingly aware of the vibrant reality of the Holy Spirit. The suspicion with which the renewal movement was regarded in the early days has diminished, as has the stridency of charismatic claims. A whole new and virile Christian movement, the New Churches (originally House Churches), has emerged. Christianity is advancing across the globe at the rate of more than 70,000 new Christians a day, faster than at any time in history. It is therefore appropriate to take a long hard look at the person and work of the Holy Spirit.

In the first edition I acknowledged my debt of gratitude to my teacher, Professor Geoffrey Lampe, who has since died courageously of cancer; to close friends, the Revd. David Watson and the Revd. Julian Charley; to Edward England, my publisher, and to St. John's College, Nottingham, where I was at that time principal. How things have changed since then! David Watson became a household name, and then he too died of cancer with the utmost courage, to the great loss of the whole Christian world. Edward England, who inspired the series in the first place, left Hodders and started the very successful Highland Books. He has since retired, as has Canon Julian Charley. I myself left St. John's in 1975 and spent twelve happy years as Rector of St. Aldate's Church, Oxford, years which taught me a great deal more about the work and power of the Holy Spirit, his gifts, his humbling and his wonderful life-transforming power in individuals and congregations alike.

Since then I have worked for six years as a professor in Canada, for five years in evangelism for the archbishops of Canterbury and York all over the U.K. and often abroad, and in recent years as a pastor and teacher among men and women training for Christian ministry at Wycliffe Hall, in the University of Oxford. Each of these chapters in my life has given me deeper insight into the graciousness, power, and · sheer unpredictability of the Holy Spirit. It has been a wonderful joy to see a little of what he is accomplishing in the many parts of the world where it has been my privilege to visit and minister. So above all, as I put this book out afresh, I want to thank God for his inexpressible generosity in giving the Holy Spirit to us fallen human beings, to be to us both the means of grace and the hope of glory.

Pentecost 2003   Michael Green
                                        Senior Research Fellow
                                                Wycliffe Hall
                                            Oxford University

1

The Holy Spirit

The Spirit

Discounted?

The Christian Church has always had a good many professing members who are rather like those disciples at Ephesus who, when asked by Paul, 'Did you receive the Holy Spirit when you believed?' replied, 'No, we have never even heard that there is a Holy Spirit' (Acts 19:2). Of course, this group at Ephesus must have heard something about the Holy Spirit if they listened at all attentively to John the Baptist, but they did not realise that the promised Spirit was available for them; that he could make a difference to their lives. Many adherents of all denominations have been in the same state. They have, of course, heard about the Holy Spirit, but have either put it all down to typical ecclesiastical in-talk, or assumed that it was not intended for ordinary folk like themselves. For all practical purposes, the Holy Spirit could be discounted. Christianity was a matter of churchgoing, of soldiering on and trying to do one's best, and of believing in the existence of God and the historical life and death of Jesus (even if his deity and his resurrection were not to be taken too seriously).

Imprisoned in Church . . .?

On the other hand, there have always been people in the Christian Church who were very sure about the Holy Spirit. It was simple. He was the divine backer of their particular emphasis in theology and practice. A good deal has been written in recent years about Primitive Catholicism, the tendency apparent even within the New Testament period itself to domesticate the Holy Spirit, to make him the perquisite of the Church. The man who is validly baptised or rightly instituted into office in the Church is assured that he has the Holy Spirit.

. . . or Bible?

It is not only Catholic Christendom which has been guilty of seeking to domesticate the Holy Spirit in this way. Protestants have been no less anxious to do so, for the Holy Spirit is a disturbing influence. Let him therefore be paid lip service, but for all practical purposes be shut up in the Bible where he can do no harm. Let his presence attend the confessional statement of our particular brand of Protestantism. Let the bizarre and miraculous elements which the New Testament documents narrate about his activity be relegated to those far-off apostolic days: it would be very embarrassing and doctrinally untidy if the Holy Spirit were to speak to men today, or to enable miracles to be performed and men to speak in tongues not their own. The Bible, accordingly, is the safest place for the Spirit. That is where he belongs; not in the hurly-burly of real life.

. . . or theology?

There was at least this to be said for the mainline Catholic and Protestant positions. They were comprehensible and clear, if narrow and restrictive. However, since the growth of biblical criticism in the last two centuries, and the revolt against authoritarianism in the past fifty years, there has been a marked tendency to seek the Holy Spirit in other quarters. Since we can no longer be shackled by the authoritarianism of a discredited Bible and a crumbling Papacy, it is to the human spirit that we must look for inspiration. To begin with, liberal theologians thought of the Holy Spirit of God as speaking to contemporary man through those elements in Bible or Church tradition which accorded best with their own insights. Pope and Bible were dethroned, to make way for the Professor of Theology. But unfortunately he did not last very long, and his views were soon considered out of date by his successors. Why, then, should it be assumed that the Holy Spirit was particularly active in professors? Surely this was a hang-over from the scholasticism of an infallible Bible and the authoritarianism of an ecclesiastical teaching office?

... or congress?

Perhaps it would be better to seek the contemporary witness of the Spirit in ecumenical discussions, where all could contribute their special insight and the Holy Spirit would, doubtless, be found along with the majority of the votes at the end of the day? I have been to enough ecclesiastical congresses which have claimed that the voice of the Holy Spirit lay behind the votes of the big battalions to be sickened by it. It was not a habit of the Holy Spirit in biblical times to be identified with the views of the majority!

... or wider?

Often we are invited to take a broader view of the whole scene and to discover the Holy Spirit at work in Buddhism and communism, in humanism and atheism. Is it to the Holy Spirit, then, that I must assign Buddhism's denial of the possibility of forgiveness, or communism's cavalier attitude to truth and human life, or the self-satisfied man-centredness of much contemporary humanism? This broad interpretation of the person and work of the Holy Spirit is somewhat confusing, to say the least. The whole subject bristles with problems.

... in the Renewal?

Is it surprising that against a background as inchoate as this a new and virile movement should have arisen, central to whose belief is the power and reality of the Holy Spirit? At the beginning of the twentieth century there were no Pentecostals. Now they number many millions drawn from almost every nation on earth, and almost every denomination too. The characteristic emphases of this movement can be seen from glancing at some of the book titles published on the subject in recent decades. It is, first and foremost, *The Haven of the Masses*, a movement of the people; neither dominated by its ministry, nor dependent on foreign indoctrination. *They Speak with Other Tongues*, which is embarrassing and distasteful to many non-members of the Pentecostal scene. The claim that they and they alone have *The Baptism with the Holy Spirit*, in contrast to water baptism which marks the rest of Christendom, and the conversion which figures as largely in Evangelical theology as does confirmation in Catholic. *As at the Beginning* the gifts of Pentecost have been renewed to a parched Church, and *It can happen to Anybody*. For the Church of God's frozen people this is the *Pathway to Power*; individual and Church alike are *Gathered for Power*. *The Third Force* has come into the Christian spectrum, and it is a force to be reckoned with. Healings, exorcisms, tongues, prophecy are merely the spectacular tip of the iceberg, the heart of which is a living, loving, believing Christian fellowship.

What has God disclosed?

What, then, in the face of these many and conflicting voices, is the Christian to make of the Holy Spirit? Where shall we begin? It is important to remember that we are mere human beings, talking about God. And it is not possible for us to know anything at all about him unless he is generous enough to disclose himself. Without revelation we cannot say anything about the Lord who is Spirit. St. Paul makes this very clear. 'What person can know a man's thoughts,' he asks, 'except the spirit of the man which is in him? So also no one comprehends the thoughts of God except the Spirit of God' (1 Cor. 2:11). In other words, it takes God to reveal God. And Paul claims that God has done so, through the Spirit interpreting spiritual truths to men who possess the Spirit. Accordingly, the purpose of this book is to examine what the Scriptures, particularly in the fuller light afforded by the New Testament, have to teach about the Holy Spirit, and to relate their message to our own situation.

Theologians often distinguish between God as he is in himself, and God as he has revealed himself to us. It seems to me to be both useless and presumptuous to attempt to pierce the incognito of the essential Godhead. It is quite enough for me to try to grasp the way in which God has disclosed himself to us. And without too much distortion, you could say that it is a drama in three acts.

Act One: on from Eden

Act One is a long one. It lasts from the beginning of the world's history until the coming of Jesus Christ. It comprises the whole history of the people of Israel until the coming of the Messiah. The Law, the Prophets and the Writings (the three divisions of the Old Testament Scriptures) combine to teach one basic lesson. It was this. There is one God, and no runners up. That is the lesson Abraham learnt in polytheistic Ur of the Chaldees. It had to be learnt time and again by his descendants through-out the succeeding twenty centuries. Yahweh, the God of Israel, was the only deity. The other gods of the heathen were idols (literally 'nothings' in Hebrew). The downtrodden cap-tives in Egypt at the time of the Exodus came to realise that Yahweh, the only self-existent one (Exod. 3:14), was a mighty deliverer who could be trusted. The Mosaic Law underlines the fact that their whole social, religious and daily life must be gov-erned by loyalty to that one God who brought them out of the land of Egypt, out of the house of bondage. They forgot the message times without number. The Old Testament records them running after false gods, the gods of the nations round about them, whenever opportunity offered. Elijah has to drag

them back from the worship of the heathen fertility gods introduced by Jezebel. Hosea has to recall them to Yahweh, their
first love, when they have gone and committed adultery, like
Hosea's own wife, with some other 'Lord' on whom they have
lavished their worship and devotion. Jeremiah and Isaiah never
tire of reminding the people that there is one God who can save
his people, and that all other refuges are in vain. At last the
lesson got home, and in the last two centuries before Christ,
the Jewish people gave signal proof of their loyalty to the one
God. Under the Maccabeans they withstood the attempts of
Antiochus to overcome their country and shatter their religion.
Later, under Roman occupation, they maintained with unbreakable courage their strict monotheism; so much so that the Roman
governor did not even dare to bring his standards into Jerusalem
lest the medallions on them depicting the emperor should be
thought to infringe the Second Commandment. Roman coinage
struck in Palestine carried no image of the emperor. Indeed,
when Pilate produced a coin which had an augur's staff on its
obverse, it could well have cost him his job; for an augur's staff
smelt of pagan religion, and that could not be tolerated in Judea.
Finally, as everyone knows, Jewish faith in the one God who
alone was fit to govern Israel led to the Great Revolt of A.D.
66–70. It culminated in the capture of Jerusalem, and the
destruction of that temple whose empty Holy of Holies elo-
quently proclaimed the greatness of God whose name was too
holy to mention and whose nature was too inscrutable to copy
by any image. Act One was complete. Israel knew beyond
a shadow of doubt that there was one God, the Creator of
the whole world, who had disclosed himself in a special way to
their nation.

Act Two: on from Bethlehem

But this one who could not be named with impunity, who could
not be copied without distortion, still remained very much

beyond our ken. In Act Two God comes in person to make himself known. After years of scrutinising Jesus of Nazareth, of listening to his teaching, of watching his character, of observing his miracles, after witnessing that shameful death and experiencing that glorious resurrection, the men who had known him best were sure of it. This man had brought God into focus.

'God, who spoke of old in many and varied ways to our fathers through the prophets, has in these last days spoken to us in a Son. Him he has appointed the heir of all things. Through him he created the worlds. He reflects the glory of God, and bears the very stamp of his nature, upholding the universe by the word of his power.'

'In him dwells all the fulness of the Godhead in bodily form.'

'He is the image of the invisible God, the firstborn of all creation, for in him all things were created, in heaven and on earth . . . all things were created in him and for him. His is the priority over everything, and in him all things hold together.'

'No man has ever seen God; the only Son, himself God, who is in the bosom of the Father, he has made him known.'

In words like these Paul, John and the writer of the Epistle to the Hebrews struggle to express the unheard-of claim, that they themselves would have deemed blasphemous but for the irrefragable evidence of the life, death and resurrection of Jesus, that God had indeed visited and redeemed his people. The one it was unlawful to name had taken the name of 'Emmanuel' ('God with us') and 'Jesus' ('God saves'). He had done just that; lived with them, and saved them from a doom and a captivity worse than that which gripped their forefathers in Pharaoh's Egypt. They could no longer plead ignorance of God. He had become one of them, their contemporary. In Jesus all of God that could take on human expression had been expressed. God, they had come to see, was Christlike. Act Two was complete. The one true God was not only over them as their Creator. He had come alongside them, to reveal himself to them in human terms, and to rescue them from the self-induced estrangement into which they had fallen.

Act Three: on from Pentecost

Act Three began at Pentecost, and it has not ended. Nor will it end until the completion of God's purposes for this world at the return of Christ. God the Creator, the God who had come alongside men in Jesus, now made himself available to come within their very personalities. It is inconceivable that anyone sat down to think out any doctrine so intrinsically improbable as the Trinity. It was forced upon them by experience. Convinced as they were of the unity and uniqueness of God, the disciples became confident that he was present in Jesus. After Pentecost, they became assured that their experience of God's activity in their midst and in their mission was nothing less than the continued work and presence of Jesus among them. Accordingly, they did not shrink from speaking indifferently of 'the Spirit of God' and 'the Spirit of Jesus' or 'the Spirit of Christ'. Jesus of Nazareth was now the prism through which the various shafts of light in the Old Testament about the Spirit became luminous and in focus to them.

An analogy such as I have just drawn in this three act drama of salvation can be dangerously misleading. It could lead to what the theologians have called 'Modalism', as though God disclosed himself in these three successive modes or forms – forms which do not correspond to any differences in his own nature, but are merely adopted for our benefit. I do not think that this will do. The ministry of Jesus provides sufficient refutation. On the one hand he is conceived and baptised by the Holy Spirit, and promises the gift of that Spirit to his followers after his death. On the other hand, he clearly looks to God as his Father, and into this Father's hand he commits his spirit when he dies. There is, in other words, a double overlap in the ministry of Jesus, which prevents us from assuming that Father, Son and Spirit are three moulds into which the Deity pours himself at different periods in the history of salvation.

Despite the dangers, however, this three act drama can provide a useful provisional approach to our understanding of the person and work of the Holy Spirit, and is perhaps worth investigating in greater detail So in the next chapter I shall look at the main strands of teaching in the Old Testament about the Holy Spirit, in the light of fuller perspective brought about by Jesus, the supreme bearer of the Spirit.

2

The Spirit in the Old Testament

Spirit of God

The word used for the Spirit of God in both Hebrew and Greek is highly significant. *Ruach* in Hebrew and *pneuma* in Greek have the three main meanings of 'wind', 'breath' and 'spirit'. The Spirit of God is his life-giving breath without which man remains spiritually inert. It is his mysterious wind, which man cannot get under his own tidy control: as Nicodemus was reminded by Jesus, 'The wind (*pneuma*) blows where it will, and you hear its sound but you do not know where it comes from or where it is going. So it is with every one who is born of the Spirit (*pneuma*)' (John 3:8). As well as being mysterious, the wind is powerful: it was by a mighty wind that God assuaged the waters of the Flood (Gen. 8:1), and by a wind that he caused the waters to recede before Israel at the Exodus (Exod. 14:21). Those twin notions of power and mystery mark much of the teaching of Old and New Testaments alike when they treat of the Spirit of God.

Quality of man?

This brings us up short at the outset of our study. The Spirit of God in the Bible is no natural quality of man. It is no hidden recess within our bodies. For one thing, the Hebrews did not divide man up into spirit, mind and body as we tend to do: they thought of him as a single entity, an animated body, a living person. For another, they had a perfectly good word to describe our human vitality, the quality that marks off a living person from a dead one: and that was *nephesh*. Only comparatively rarely is this word brought into contact with *ruach*, though we cannot expect, and do not find, complete consistency. It is true that *ruach* is used of man's spirit in a number of ways. It is used in the story of the Flood, for instance, to denote 'the breath of life' (Gen. 6:17) which God gives – and takes back again. It is used to denote full vitality, real spirited living; contrast the deflation of the Queen of Sheba when she saw all Solomon's treasure – 'there was no more *ruach* left in her' (1 Kgs. 10:5). It comes to mean the seat of the emotions, intellect, and will – particularly often applied to the governing impulse in a man's life (e.g. Prov. 25:28, Ps. 32:2, Num. 14:24). Occasionally, therefore, a man's *ruach* 'spirit' seems to be equated with his *nephesh*, his 'life', but this is by no means the normal usage. *Ruach* and *nephesh* can be thought of as each having their own circle of meaning. Occasionally the circumferences of those circles intersect, but the main content of each is clear. *Nephesh* is natural; it belongs to man. *Ruach* is supernatural; it belongs to God. Though *ruach* may be found in man, it is always, so to speak, on loan, and not a possession; a resident alien, not a native.

Principle of life?

And just as the Spirit cannot be equated with any property in man; equally it cannot be regarded as the stuff of which the world is made, the comprehensive life principle which integrates the universe, as the Stoics maintained – a view which, through pagan philosophical influence, crept into the inter-testamental books of the Apocrypha. No, the Old Testament insists that this powerful, mysterious Spirit belongs to God, and to God alone. It is essentially the personal God, Yahweh, in action. It is therefore to the teaching of the Old Testament about the Spirit of the Lord, the *ruach adonai*, that we shall be looking in

order to get the background for the Christian doctrine of the
Holy Spirit.

Invading Spirit

Perhaps the first thing that strikes us as we come to the Old
Testament is the tremendous emphasis on the Spirit of God as
a violent, invading force. It is like the wind that hurtled across
the desert or whistled through the cedars or rushed down the
wadis. 'The grass withers, the flower fades when the *ruach
adonai* blows upon it. Surely the people is grass,' cried Isaiah
(40:7), and that is typical. There is a whole host of places where
we are told that God's action is like the wind, strong, boister-
ous, uncontrollable. He sends the wind. He controls it. He
causes it to cease.

In Scripture . . .

In speaking of the 'Spirit of the Lord' the Old Testament
writers significantly retain this emphasis on God's violent
invasion from outside our experience, disturbing and mysterious like the wind. It is their way of stressing that the Beyond
has come into our midst, and we can neither organise nor
domesticate him. This comes out very strongly in the Book of
Judges. The oppressed people of Israel cry to the Lord to send
them deliverance. His response is to 'raise up a deliverer for the
people, Othniel. The Spirit of the Lord came upon him; he
judged Israel; he went out to war; and his hand prevailed'
(Judg. 3:9,10). Again, Gideon was a very ordinary man until
'the Spirit of the Lord took possession of him' (Judg. 6:34).
Then he became instrumental in a signal deliverance for his
country. It was most noticeable in the case of that fabulous
strong man, Samson. It was when 'the Spirit of the Lord came
mightily upon him' that 'he tore a lion asunder as one tears a
kid' (Judg. 14:6). This strength which enabled him to do so
much for his country against the Philistine overlords was not

his own. He was sharply reminded of that when he disobeyed
God at Delilah's instigation, and woke up to find that 'the
Lord had left him' (Judg. 16:20). Sometimes the violent power
of the Spirit is seen in almost physical terms, as when the Spirit
of the Lord entered into Ezekiel and set him on his feet, or
lifted him up, or brought him out into the valley (Ezek. 2:2,
3:12, 37:1).

Today

I believe we have to take this aspect of the Spirit very seriously
today. We have grown used to expecting the Spirit of God to
speak in a gentle whisper, not a roaring wind. We have sought
him in the promptings of our hearts or the resolutions of our
committees. We are in danger of forgetting that it is God we
are talking about: the God who created us, the God who sustains us and has sovereign rights over us. This God can and
does break into human life, and sometimes he does it through
the violent, the unexpected, the alien. It was this same Spirit
that drove Jesus off into the desert to be tempted after his
baptism, that pioneered the mission of the early Church often
in the most bizarre, unexpected and 'unorthodox' ways; that
gripped a man like Philip, removed him from a flourishing
evangelistic campaign in Samaria and drove him into the
desert – because there was one man who needed his help.
When that help was given 'the Spirit of the Lord caught up
Philip', just like Ezekiel long before him, and 'Philip was
found at Azotus, and passing on he preached the gospel' (Acts
8:26,39,40).

I once met a girl who awoke to find herself gripped by the
Spirit of God at 2 a.m. She was a cripple, and at once her hip
was cured – a hip, incidentally, that had defied the efforts of the
country's best doctors – and she found herself praising God in
tongues. Now she is doing a remarkably useful piece of
Christian service.

I think of another man, devious, self-centred, arrogant, who went to criticise a charismatic meeting, but found himself seized with unaccountable trembling, tears, and a deep meeting with God, the God of the unexpected. The wind of God certainly blew on that man, Christian though he already was; he has not become a paragon of virtue overnight, but the manifest change in his disposition and attitudes cannot be denied. Perhaps this surrender to the invading power of God's Spirit, this willingness for him to take us and break us and use us, is one of the prime lessons which the charismatic movement throughout the churches is teaching us at the present time. Some years ago Bishop Joe Fison expressed it well in his book about the Spirit, *Fire upon the Earth* (p. 9):

> Of course, this uprush of the primitive, the elemental and the uncon-
> scious, this 'possession' by the Spirit, is not the be-all and end-all of
> the biblical evidence for the doctrine of the Holy Spirit. But it is the
> starting-point of this doctrine and only if we are prepared to start
> where the Bible starts are we likely to know in experience anything of
> the higher reaches of the Spirit's work. We cannot jump the queue.

Spirit of prophecy

Closely allied to this emphasis on the 'otherness' of the Spirit of God is the stress throughout the Old Testament on his inspiration of prophecy. It is one of the major themes of Scripture. This God who is beyond us and invades our world does not do so in order to terrify, but to communicate. The wind or Spirit of the Lord is indeed power, but it is morally defined power, designed to communicate the will of God and bring his creation into conformity with it. That is why, I think, there is a frequent link in the Bible between 'the Spirit of the Lord' and 'the Word of the Lord'. The breath of God and the message of God cannot be divorced. Time and again, therefore in the parallelism of Hebrew poetry *dabar* (word) and *ruach* (spirit) go hand in hand. Thus

By the word of the Lord were the heavens made and all the host of them
by the breath of his mouth. (Ps. 33:6)

or

The Spirit of the Lord speaks by me, his word is upon my tongue.
(2 Sam. 23:2)

Word and Spirit

When Saul disobeys God, and is rejected as king over Israel,
we read, 'You have rejected the word of the Lord,' and consequently, in judgment, 'the Spirit of the Lord departed from
Saul' (1 Sam. 15:26; 16:14). Bishop John Taylor, in his moving
and perceptive book *The Go-Between God*, has pointed out the
importance of this link between the Spirit, with all his
undifferentiated power, and the Word, with all its particularity
of meaning. By distinguishing too sharply between the divine
Word and the divine Spirit the Church has lost a most important biblical perspective. Certainly that link is strong and clear
in the Old Testament Scriptures. When the Spirit comes upon
a man, he communicates some message from God. This
message may take strange, mysterious forms. It may come
through dreams, as when Joseph was able to discern and interpret Pharaoh's dreams through the Spirit of God within him
(Gen. 41:38f). It may come through visions. Men like Abraham
(Gen. 15:1), Jacob (Gen. 46:1), Ezekiel (1:1) and Daniel (1:17,
4:5, 7:7) grasped something of the purposes of God in a vision.
It may come through ecstatic utterance, as when the Spirit of
the Lord came upon King Saul and he joined a band of wandering prophets. But even this medium was no mere excitement, as God broke in from the beyond and seized him: there
was communication. He not only prophesied, but he became
in some unspecified sense 'a different man' (1 Sam. 10:7–13).
The later prophets laid less emphasis on ecstasy. Amos protests
that he is no prophet in the ecstatic sense, such as were to be
found in attendance at the sanctuaries of his day. 'I am no
prophet, nor a prophet's son, I am a herdsman, and the Lord

took me from following the flock.' Nevertheless he is quite clear that God has inspired his message. 'The Lord said to me, "Go, prophesy to my people, Israel." Now, therefore, hear the word of the Lord . . .' (Amos 7:14–10). It is not ecstasy that marks prophecy, but meeting with God, so that God speaks through the prophet. Amos himself puts the matter with telling simplicity:

> The lion has roared: who will not fear?
> The Lord has spoken: who can but prophesy?
>
> (Amos 3:8)

An early prophet like David claims that when he delivers his oracles no less than 'the Spirit of the Lord speaks' (2 Sam. 23:2). In the eighth century B.C. Hosea describes the prophet as supremely 'the man of the Spirit' (9:7), and Micah spells it out more fully with his claim, over against the false prophets who get no word from God:

> But as for me, I am filled with power,
> with the Spirit of the Lord,
> and with justice and might,
> to declare to Jacob his transgression
> and to Israel his sin.
>
> (Mic. 3:8)

Isaiah of Babylon, in a later age, knows that his message is true, because 'The Lord God has sent me and his Spirit' (48:16). Zechariah, after the Return from Babylon, has no doubt that it is through the Spirit of the Lord that God has sent 'the law and the words' through the prophets (Zech. 7:12).

The point does not need labouring. When a man prophesies, it is because the Spirit of the Lord comes upon him and communicates a message through him. But there are several aspects of this prophetic Spirit that are especially important, and they are taken up in the New Testament.

Spirit and Servant

The Spirit of the Lord was promised to the Servant of Yahweh.

> Behold, my servant, whom I uphold,
> my chosen, in whom my soul delights;
> I have put my Spirit upon him,
> he will bring forth justice to the nations.

(Isa. 42:1)

Just as the will of God cannot be known without the revelation of the Spirit, so the service of God cannot be carried through without the equipment of that same Spirit. It is only through God's revelation that we can know him. It is only through his power that we can serve him. Isaiah 61:1 takes up this theme, and the prophet cries:

> The Spirit of the Lord God is upon me
> because the Lord has anointed me
> to bring good tidings to the afflicted;
> he has sent me to bind up the brokenhearted,
> to proclaim liberty to the captives,
> and the opening of the prison to those who are bound;
> to proclaim the year of the Lord's favour . . .

These prophetic visions of the Spirit coming upon the Servant of Yahweh and upon his anointed prophet were specifically claimed by Jesus. The first comes at his baptism, the second at the first sermon he preached (Mark 1:11, Luke 4:18). It is not easy to exaggerate their significance. As *the* prophet Jesus could say with authority, 'Amen, amen I say unto you,' and claim to speak final truth about God, 'We speak of what we know, and bear witness of what we have seen' (John 3:11). As *the* Servant of Yahweh, Jesus treads the path of suffering and obedience right the way to Calvary: so much so that Peter could describe his suffering and death in

terms culled from the famous prophecy of the Suffering
Servant in Isaiah:

> He committed no sin; no guile was found on his lips.
> When he was reviled, he did not revile in return;
> when he suffered, he did not threaten;
> but he trusted to him who judges justly.
> He himself bore our sins in his body on the tree,
> that we might die to sin and live to righteousness.
> By his wounds you have been healed.

> (1 Pet. 2:22ff)

Spirit and king

The ideals

There is another area in which Jesus strikingly fulfilled one of
the main strands of Old Testament teaching about the Spirit,
God had given his Spirit to his anointed king in order to equip
him for his leadership of the people. Saul is the classic example.
Samuel anoints him king: he is promised, and receives, the
power of the Spirit of God upon him (1 Sam. 10:1, 6).
Subsequently he disobeys God disastrously, and has to be set
aside as king in favour of David. Samuel anoints David, and we
read that 'the Spirit of the Lord came mightily (literally
'leaped') upon David from that day forward' (1 Sam. 16:13).
What happened to Saul, then? 'The Spirit of the Lord departed
from Saul,' and from now on we read that an evil or distressed
ruach elohim troubled him. The Spirit of the Lord, the *ruach
adonai* passes to David to equip him for his princely service. The
profane word *elohim* (which need not necessarily refer to
Yahweh) is now used to describe Saul's fits of mania and ecstasy.

The reality

Unfortunately the kings of Israel were a pretty disappointing
lot, and most of them showed little sign of the presence of the
Lord the Spirit in their lives and reigns. However the link was

not lost, and the hope grew in Israel that one day God would raise up a prince of the Davidic line for whom the Spirit would be no passing enduement, to be bestowed and withdrawn as he joined his predecessors in disobedience. Instead, the Spirit of the Lord would rest and remain on such a man, Hence the idyllic dream of Isaiah 11:1ff.

> There shall come forth a shoot from the stump of Jesse,
> and a branch shall grow out of his roots.
> And the Spirit of the Lord shall rest upon him,
> the Spirit of wisdom and understanding,
> the Spirit of counsel and might,
> the Spirit of knowledge and the fear of the Lord.

The hope

This hope lived on in Judaism. In the inter-testamental days we read of the Messiah, 'God will make him mighty in the Holy Spirit' (*Psalms of Solomon* 17:37), and in the Targum or Commentary on Isaiah 42:1, the Servant is seen as the Messiah, and God says of him, 'I will cause my Holy Spirit to rest on him.' It is therefore extremely significant that we read of Jesus in the New Testament that the Spirit descends and remains on him (John 1:32) and that God did not give his Spirit by measure or sparingly to him (John 3:34). In Jesus we have the final embodiment of God's ideal ruler, and he is fully equipped with an unwithdrawn endowment of the Holy Spirit.

Spirit and people

There was a further dimension to this prophetic hope. On the whole, you had to be someone rather special in Old Testament days to have the Spirit of God. A prophet, a national leader, a king, perhaps some specially wise man (Prov. 1:23) or artistic person (Exod. 31:3) – in which case you would be beautifying the Lord's Tent of Meeting, or enunciating the Lord's wisdom. But the Spirit of God was not for every Tom, Dick and Harry. To be sure, there were promises in a very general sense that 'My Spirit abides with you: fear not' (Hag. 2:5), but this was an assurance to the people as a whole, not a promise to the individual. The gift of God's Spirit was on the whole to special people for special tasks. It was not generally available, nor was it necessarily permanent.

Wanted: a new covenant

Many a godly Jew must have felt what a wonderful thing it would be if Moses' longing could be fulfilled, 'Would that all the Lord's people were prophets, that the Lord would put his Spirit upon them' (Num. 11:29): and that is just what the prophets were led by God to foretell for the last days.

> And it shall come to pass afterwards,
> that I will pour out my Spirit upon all flesh;
> your sons and your daughters shall prophesy,
> your old men shall dream dreams,
> and your young men shall see visions.
> Even upon the menservants and maidservants
> in those days, I will pour out my Spirit.
>
> (Joel 2:28ff)

He did precisely that, on the Day of Pentecost; and the gift has never been withdrawn. We shall be looking at this point more closely later, but for the moment it is sufficient to point out that the gift of the Spirit at Pentecost to all believers without distinction fulfilled one further hope of the prophets of old. Men like Jeremiah and Ezekiel looked for the day when God would forge a new covenant, or agreement, with men. The problem about the existing one was this. Although it all sprang from God's initiative, it was nevertheless very much a two-sided affair. 'If you will obey my voice,' said God to the Israelites after the Exodus, 'and keep my covenant, you shall be my own possession among all peoples' (Exod. 19:5). But there lay the rub. They could not and did not keep his covenant. They were con-

stantly breaking their side of it. And though God remained
faithful to his side of the agreement, and looked after his people
wonderfully down the centuries, it was not very satisfactory as
a covenant. It kept getting spoiled. Jeremiah longed for the day
when God would, so to speak, underwrite both sides of the covenant. He would not only keep his side of the bargain, but
enable Israel to keep hers, by putting his Spirit within her
people. Listen to his vision:

> The days are coming, says the Lord,
> when I will make a new covenant with the house of Israel . . .
> not like the covenant which I made with their fathers when I took them
>   by the hand
> to bring them out of the land of Egypt – my covenant which they broke,
> though I was a husband to them, says the Lord.
> But this is the covenant which I will make with the house of Israel
> after those days, says the Lord:
> I will put my law within them, and I will write it upon their hearts;
> and I will be their God, and they shall be my people.
> And no longer shall each man teach his neighbour and each his brother
> saying, 'Know the Lord,'
> for they shall all know me, from the least of them to the greatest, says
>   the Lord;
> for I will forgive their iniquity, and I will remember their sin no more.
>
> (Jer. 31:31ff)

A new covenant, involving a complete pardon, a personal
knowledge of the Lord, and the will of God no longer external
to them on tablets of stone, but written inwardly on their hearts.
A new covenant indeed! Ezekiel speaks in much the same strain,
and specifically attributes this change to the Spirit of God:

> I will sprinkle clean water upon you, and you shall be clean from all your
> uncleannesses, and from all your idols I will cleanse you. A new heart
> will I give you, and a new Spirit will I put within you; and I will take out
> of your flesh the heart of stone, and give you a heart of flesh. And I will
> put my Spirit within you, and cause you to walk in my statutes.
>
> (Ezek. 36:25ff)

That is what was wanted. A new Spirit, God's own Spirit within man, which would warm his heart to want to go God's way, and enable his will to keep it. Such was the hope for the last days, and this was the hope that the Christians had seen fulfilled since the resurrection and ascension of Jesus. Hebrews 8:7ff and 10:15ff work it out in detail.

Such was the prophetic hope, not only for the Suffering Servant or the Messiah of Israel but for the whole people of God. Of course, it could not come without national repentance and renewal on a grand scale. Ezekiel was bold enough to long for this too, and God gave him the marvellous vision of the valley of the dry bones (chapter 37) as an assurance that the longed-for day would indeed come. God's *ruach*, his breath, could infuse new life into dry bones; God's *ruach*, his Spirit, could bring the people of Israel out of their graves, and give them life.

Creator Spirit?

There are three further surprises for us as we look at the Old Testament teaching about the Spirit of God. In the first place, he is hardly ever connected with creation. This is all the more significant when one thinks of the nature mysticism that was so common in every variety of ancient paganism. There was no hint of it in the religion of Israel, which maintained such a clear emphasis on the otherness, the transcendence of the Creator God. Indeed, in the Old Testament, language about the Spirit is restricted almost exclusively to the area of relationship between God and *man*.

Despite this, whole theologies have been erected on the theme of the Creator Spirit. It is moving to think of the Spirit of God being involved in the continuous and on-going process of creation. It is fascinating to follow John Taylor's poetic imagination in attributing to the Spirit of God the 'inner awareness of the unattained', 'the stimulation of initiative and choice', and the 'principle of sacrifice' inherent in the creative development of our world (*The Go-Between God*, chapter 2). But the roots for all this in the Old Testament are rather shaky.

C. F. D. Moule seized on the fact that only in four places in the whole of the Old Testament does the Spirit seem to be associated with creation of the physical world – and even these four are patient of another interpretation. Genesis 1:2, 5, 'the Spirit of God was moving over the face of the waters' may indicate a creative function for the Spirit, but may equally describe the chaos referred to in the earlier part of that verse, 'the earth was without form and void, and darkness was upon the face of the water': and 'a r*uach adonai*, a mighty hurricane from God, was moving over the expanse of the unruly waters' may be a better translation. Psalm 104:30: 'When thou sendest forth thy Spirit they are created, and thou renewest the face of the ground' refers to the animal creation, and may mean not so much that the Spirit created them, but, as in Genesis 2:7, that God breathes his life into the already moulded form of animals and man. In other words Psalm 104:30 may speak of the energising rather than the creative work of the Spirit, and thus fall into line with the rest of the Old Testament teaching on *ruach* as 'breath'. Psalm 33:6 is no more certain. To be sure 'By the word of the Lord were the heavens made, and all their host by the breath (*ruach*) of his mouth' could mean that the *ruach*, the Spirit, created the heavens. But more probably, in the light of the parallel with 'word' in the first half of the verse, *ruach* means God's *fiat*. His word is creative. When he says 'Let there be light', light ensues. The last hint of a Creator Spirit in the Old Testament is in Job 33:4, but once again this is ambiguous. It may mean 'The Spirit of God has made me', but in view of the parallel 'and the breath of the Almighty gives me life' it is just as likely to mean that the Spirit is the animating principle of life.

Professor Moule may not be right in the interpretation he gave to these four verses. The Old Testament *may* give these few hints of a Creator Spirit, and certainly this thought is found in the inter-testamental period – where the parallelism between Wisdom, Word and Spirit is important – but the paucity of instances that can be adduced, and the plausibility of taking them in another sense, does make one very cautious of building up a great doctrine of co-operating with the Holy Spirit in his on-going work of creation. The Spirit of God breathes his life into man; he revives the dry bones; he infuses vitality into inert matter, but the evidence that he is involved in the work of creating the world is very slim indeed in the Old Testament and non-existent in the New. We would be wise not to build too high a building on such a flimsy foundation.

Nevertheless I find myself more willing now than when I wrote the first edition of this book to believe that these few allusions to the Creator Spirit should be given their full weight, and that they do point to the work of the Spirit in creation. For one thing, much recent theology has rediscovered a Trinitarian emphasis throughout the Bible, and Christ was clearly involved alongside the Father in the work of creation. How could the Spirit of this undivided true God not be involved? For another, the Spirit of God clearly has an absolutely crucial role in the *recreation* of individuals and of a community in the New Testament: why not in their *creation*? This is more likely to be a recapitulation than an innovation.

Holy Spirit?

The second surprise concerns the rarity of any mention in the Old Testament of the *Holy* Spirit. Pagan Greek literature does not have the phrase at all, and only twice do we find it in the Old Testament. In Isaiah 63:10, 11 we read that the people on whom God had set his love 'rebelled and grieved his Holy Spirit', although he had put his Holy Spirit in the midst of them when he rescued them from Egypt. In Psalm 51:11 the writer prays to God in penitence;

Create in me a clean heart O God,
and put a new and right spirit within me
Cast me not away from thy presence,
and take not thy Holy Spirit from me.

In both cases the writers are very conscious of the moral and
ethical aspect of God's *ruach*. The nation of Isaiah 63 had
grieved this Holy One to whom they were dedicated. The individual of Psalm 51 had done the same. The holiness of the Spirit
of the Lord stands in sharp contrast to the unholiness of his fal-
lible servants, and perhaps this is why the Spirit is here called
Holy. In the New Testament, of course, it is the normal name for
the Spirit. The reason for this may be because God was increasingly called 'the Holy One' (there was a slightly increasing tendency in inter-testamental writings and the Dead Sea Scrolls to
speak of 'the Holy Spirit') but might just be due to the character of Jesus. The one in whom the Spirit had a permanent dwelling amazed men by the sinlessness of his life. Such was the
character produced in human life by the Spirit of Yahweh once
he was given full control. Such, therefore, should be the character in the followers of Jesus, called as they were to be 'holy' or
'separated to God' as his special possession (1 Pet. 1:15f, 2:9). As
we have seen, Ezekiel and Jeremiah expected God to change men
in the days of the New Covenant by putting his Spirit within
them, so that they should walk in his ways and keep his commandments: after Pentecost the Holy Spirit begins to produce
holiness in God's people. This does not mean separation from
sinners, in a sense of isolation and self-satisfaction like the
monks of Qumran; instead, it means involvement with needy,
fallen, spoiled humanity, following the example and endued with
the Spirit of him who was a friend of tax gatherers and sinners.

Personalised Spirit?

The final surprise is that in the Old Testament the Spirit does
not appear as a divine being. He is rather seen as God's

personal presence and intervention. The point is well made in a
verse like Isaiah 31:3.

> The Egyptians are men, and not God;
> and their horses are flesh and not spirit.

In those words, Isaiah is not contrasting flesh and spirit in the
way we might, as the exterior and the interior of the same
being. No. He is grouping flesh and men together, and God and
Spirit together. The Spirit is on God's side of reality; quite
different from our side. And when the Spirit of the Lord is
present with men, it means the gracious and personal intervention of God himself. As we saw just now in that passage in
Isaiah 63, the Spirit is the personal expression of God himself,
and can be grieved: he is holy, not only the divine power but the
moral character of God: he is God in action for the benefit of
his people – notice how the Spirit is equated with the 'arm' of
Yahweh, that is to say his saving activity. The Spirit is no less
than the personal, moral, active power of the Lord God, and
for the further revelation of his nature we must await Act Two,
the coming of Jesus, to which we shall turn in the next chapter.

3

The Spirit of Jesus

Each in his own way, the four evangelists make it abundantly plain that a new era has dawned with the coming of Jesus of Nazareth. It is the long-awaited era of the messianic kingdom, the age characterised by the availability of the Spirit of God. And Jesus is the Messiah, by virtue of his unprecedented endowment with the Spirit of God. He is both the unique bearer of the Spirit, and the unique dispenser of that Spirit to the disciples; moreover, for ever afterwards the Spirit remains stamped with his character.

1. JESUS IS THE UNIQUE MAN OF THE SPIRIT

St. Mark on the baptism of Jesus

Mark was in all probability the earliest evangelist. He knew the power and the reality of the Holy Spirit in the Church of his day, when he wrote in the 60s of the first century. But he went to great pains to exclude from his Gospel all mention of the Spirit as available for believers, with one notable exception. Why was this? Surely because he wished to make it abundantly plain that it is Jesus, and Jesus only, who is the man of the Spirit. Not until his death and resurrection could that same Spirit become readily available for his followers.

37

The age of fulfilment

Accordingly, he begins his Gospel with the story of the baptism
of Jesus. The crowds who flocked to listen to John's preaching of
repentance were baptised by him in the Jordan in penitent expectation of the age of fulfilment which he proclaimed. But when
Jesus was baptised, Mark makes it plain that the age of fulfilment
has already dawned. A voice was heard from heaven. Now there
had been a great shortage of messages from heaven for a very
long time. The writings of the rabbis repeatedly maintain that the
Holy Spirit departed from Israel after the last of the prophets,
Haggai, Zechariah and Malachi (e.g. *T. Sota* 13:2). What is more,
the Spirit of God, and the *shekinah*, or glory of God, were not
to be found in the Second Temple (*b. Yoma* 21 b). Men cherished
a tremendous sense of nostalgia for the departed glories of the
previous temple, and for the Spirit of Yahweh which used in Old
Testament days to be displayed in mighty deliverers and inspired
prophets. Nostalgia, yes, and expectation, as men awaited the
promises of Ezekiel and Jeremiah, of Joel and Isaiah about
deliverance, an anointed king, and a renewal of the Spirit in the
days of fulfilment. Well, says Mark, in effect: those days of
fulfilment have arrived. In John the Baptist's ministry you find
the fulfilment of the prophecies made long ago that a messenger
would come to prepare the way of the Lord. That is precisely
what the Baptist was doing. And Mark immediately introduces
Jesus on to the scene: the messenger has indeed prepared the way
of the Lord. Daring words those, for in the prophet Malachi they
clearly referred to Yahweh himself. Mark is quietly claiming that
in Jesus we have to do with none other than Yahweh, who had
come to our world in the man Jesus. As if that is not enough, he
makes two other shattering claims.

The end of the silence

The first is that the age-long silence is ended. God has spoken
again. The heavens are no longer brazen and unyielding. The

rabbis believed that when the Holy Spirit was withdrawn
from Israel at the end of the prophetic era, God left them
with a substitute, the *bath qol*, which means literally 'daugh-
ter of the voice' or 'echo'. It is usually said that in the voice
from heaven at the baptism of Jesus we have an example of
the *bath qol*. But this is quite mistaken. The *bath qol* was an
inferior substitute for the Word of God formerly given by the
Spirit to a prophet. But this voice was no feeble substitute; it
was a direct address from the God who had been silent. It is
inconceivable that at this juncture when Mark is heralding in
the return of the Spirit in Jesus he should introduce it with
anything so banal and second-hand as an echo. And the
content of this voice is even more amazing than its occur-
rence. 'Thou art my beloved Son; in thee I am well pleased,'
seems to be a deliberate combination of two famous Old
Testament texts. 'Thou art my Son' comes from Psalm 2:7,
where the king of Israel is addressed as 'Son' of God. The
kings had been pretty poor specimens as 'sons': they showed
little enough of Yahweh's family likeness, and there was a
long-standing hope in Israel that one day God would bring
into the world a messianic Son, a worthy ruler to sit on
David's throne. We know people were treasuring this hope at
the time of Jesus, because in the caves of Qumran there has
turned up a messianic anthology which includes the prophecy given to David in 2 Samuel 7:14. There God undertakes
to give an everlasting kingdom to the boy 'and I will be his
Father and he shall be my Son'. The voice from heaven,
recorded by Mark, announced that the ultimate messianic
ruler had arrived in Jesus.

The role of the Messiah

But that was only half the message. The other half 'with thee I
am well pleased' comes from that picture of the Servant of
Yahweh in Isaiah 42:1 which we looked at in the last chapter.
At his baptism, then, Jesus publicly assumed a double role: the

role of the Messianic Son, and the role of the Suffering Servant. Such was the destiny he willingly undertook.

The availability of the Spirit

But the baptism of Jesus did not merely see the end of the long silence, and God's declaration that in Jesus the role of the Servant and the Son had converged: the age-long drought of the Holy Spirit was ended too. As we saw in the last chapter the anointed king of Israel was equipped with the Spirit to enable him to carry out his work; hence the expectation of Isaiah 11:1ff that the Messiah would also be equipped, in fuller measure, with that Spirit. It was just the same with the Servant. 'I have put my Spirit upon him; he will bring forth justice to the nations,' says God through the prophet. And now the Spirit had come, and Mark's account of the baptism makes it abundantly clear that he sees Jesus as the Messianic Son and the Suffering Servant, equipped for his stupendous task with the Spirit of God promised for the end-time. The last days are no longer entirely in the future; in the person of Jesus the end has dawned. No wonder Jesus' first recorded words in Mark's Gospel are 'The time is fulfilled: and God's kingly rule has drawn near' (Mark 1:15).

St. Mark on the battle with Satan

Mark has two ways of emphasising the fact that Jesus is fully and uniquely endowed with the Holy Spirit in his role as Son and Servant of Yahweh, who brings in the kingly rule of God in the end-time. First, he makes a great deal of the struggle with Satan in which Jesus is involved both in the temptation in the wilderness into which the Spirit thrusts him (Mark 1:12) immediately after his baptism; and also in the healings and exorcisms which follow during the ministry. He does so in a very subtle manner.

The temptation

In the Old Testament there was a use of *ruach* which I did not mention. It concerns evil spirits which are seen as rebellious creatures of Yahweh, bent on wrecking his purposes but ultimately subject to his control. In the earlier books of the Old Testament we read of these as evil spirits (1 Sam. 16:14, Judg. 9:23, 1 Kgs. 22:21); later they are personalised in Satan, whose name does not appear before the rather late books of 1 Chronicles (21:1ff), Job (1:6ff) and Zechariah (3:1ff). In the inter-testamental period there is a great deal about these evil spirits and their prince. It is important to bear in mind that there is no absolute dualism in the Hebrew religion. Even the devil is God's devil: he is on a chain held by God, even though the chain is a long one. The devil and his spirits are seen as a distortion of the original good creation of God, and though they are allowed to tempt and hurt men because of men's wickedness (see, e.g. *Jubilees* 10:7–11) in the last-time they will be bound and punished. Now against that background of thought we must set Mark's emphasis on the binding of Satan by Jesus. Jesus, filled with the Spirit, goes off into the wilderness, the place where Israel had been tested for forty years after the Exodus, and wrestles with the tempter for forty days. He wins, where Israel's forebears failed. In him the days of fulfilment, the days of Satan's defeat, have dawned.

The exorcisms

And so it continues throughout his ministry. Time and again we find him casting out unclean spirits from afflicted people: it is one of the well-known characteristics of Mark's Gospel, which on the whole contains little teaching, but a great deal of action by Jesus. That action includes many miracles of healing, the most important being the curing of people who were possessed. The meaning is clear. Jesus is the conqueror of demonic forces through the power of the Spirit. He is the victor over Satan, and he tells a gem of a story to drive the point home. 'No one can enter a strong man's house and plunder his goods unless he first binds the strong man; then indeed he may plunder his house.' The context in Mark 3:20–30 makes it abundantly clear that by his cures and exorcisms Jesus is driving out the demons. The man endued with the Holy Spirit is more than a match for the unclean spirits which are such a feature in Mark's account. Jesus is the conqueror. And people are amazed. They see in the presence and power of Jesus a cameo of the final victor over the forces of evil. 'With authority he commands even the unclean spirits and they obey him' (1:27).

The controversies

But it is not only through his healings and exorcisms that Jesus shows himself as the bearer of the Spirit: he claims it explicitly in the controversy with the scribes about Beelzebul (apparently another name for Satan, conceived of as 'lord of the house'). In response to their charge (Mark 3:22) that it is through demonic power that he casts out demons, he replies that no divided house can stand: if Satan casts out Satan, his empire is doomed. And he makes that terrifying statement about the sin against the Holy Spirit, over which many people have needlessly tortured themselves.

'All sins will be forgiven the sons of men, and whatever blasphemies they utter; but whoever blasphemes against the Holy Spirit never has forgiveness . . . for they said, "He has an unclean spirit."' More light is shed on this verse by the form in which it occurs in the 'Q' material (sayings of Jesus preserved in Matthew and Luke independently of Mark). Whoever says a word against the Son of Man, it shall be forgiven him. But the man who blasphemes against the Holy Spirit will not be forgiven' (Luke 12:10). It is one thing to mistake and misrepresent Jesus, clothed in all his humility as Son of Man; it is one thing to misread his parabolic teaching, coming as it does in riddles. But it is quite another thing to see the truth clearly and wilfully

to reject it; quite another thing to ascribe the power of the Holy
Spirit to the devil – which is what the scribes were doing. If
people firmly reject the saving work of God in Jesus, they forfeit
the very possibility of rescue, not because God will not have
them, but because they say, like Satan in *Paradise Lost*,
'Darkness, be thou my light.'

Jesus, then, is the bearer of the Spirit: he, and he alone during
the period of the ministry. It is a mark of the extraordinary
faithfulness of St. Mark to the historical situation of the life of
Jesus that he does not read back into those days the experience
of the Spirit to which he and his friends were used in the post-
resurrection era. There is one place only where he lifts the
curtain. In the 'apocalyptic discourse' of Mark 13, Jesus promises the disciples that in the coming days when they are out
preaching the gospel, they will be put on the spot time and
again when arrested and unjustly accused. And then the Holy
Spirit will give them words to say. He will equip them for
witness-bearing. The promise refers to the post-resurrection
days; it does not provide an exception to Mark's sharp portrait
of Jesus alone as the man uniquely possessed by the Holy
Spirit.

The teaching of Matthew

Matthew is equally convinced that Jesus is the focus of the
Spirit's activity. He brings it out in a number of ways, in addition to those we have noticed in Mark.

The birth of Jesus

For one thing he carries the story of Jesus back far beyond the
baptism to his very conception. This too was specially brought
about by the Holy Spirit (Matt. 1:18,20). Just as the Spirit was
active in breathing life into the first man (Gen. 2:7), so here he
is associated with the birth of the last Adam. But Matthew is
claiming more than this. He knows that the Messiah is uniquely

endued with the Spirit, and he stresses that from the outset of Jesus' life this was the case.

The role of the Servant

Matthew makes quite explicit the way in which Jesus fulfils the role of the Servant. He quotes Isaiah 42:1–4 in full, and says that Jesus' works of healing are the fulfilment of that prophecy. In other words, the power of the Spirit is specifically set out as the energising principle in Jesus' healing ministry.

The equipment for mission

Finally, this evangelist is as well aware as Mark that the Spirit was during the ministry concentrated, as it were, in Jesus, and will only be available to the disciples when they, too, are engaged in the mission. Then they will baptise those they evangelise in the name of the Father, the Son, and the Holy Spirit (Matt. 28:19), but in the meantime they are given one trial run, if we may so call it, when they are sent out on a missionary journey (10:20). Mark's promise that the Holy Spirit will look after their words when arraigned before councils for the sake of the gospel is brought into the Mission Charge by Matthew: it seems clear that he is looking forward from an isolated incident in the ministry of Jesus to the continuing mission of the post-resurrection church of which he was a member.

The teaching of Luke

Luke has a lot to say about the Holy Spirit, both in the Gospel and the Acts. At present it is sufficient to notice his agreement with the other evangelists that Jesus is the unique messianic bearer of the Spirit.

New dawn

He makes a very special point of emphasising the presence and activity of the Spirit in the birth stories of John and Jesus, and in underlining the new outbreak of prophecy, which had been silent so long, but as we have seen, was confidently expected afresh in the Age to Come. Right at the start of the gospel story we find the Spirit active in full vigour. The new age had dawned, and the signs of its presence were experienced. It is a weakness in James Dunn's useful book *Baptism in the Holy Spirit* that he sweeps aside these dozen or so references to the Spirit in the first three chapters of Luke and insists that the kingdom did not come until the baptism of Jesus. In fact, Luke could hardly go to greater lengths in stressing that the Age to Come dawned with Jesus' birth. The Spirit, active in an upsurge of prophecy, active in the birth of John and Jesus, rests upon Jesus and in its power he carries out his mighty works and after the resurrection imparts that same Spirit to his disciples. From Bethlehem at the beginning of his Gospel to Rome at the end of Acts it is the one Spirit active throughout: first showing us the nature of that messianic salvation brought by Jesus, and then showing us how it was spread.

Luke lays even more stress on the Spirit activating the whole life and ministry of Jesus than any other evangelist. By the Spirit he went into the wilderness, by the Spirit he was led there, and in the power of the Spirit he returned to Galilee to begin his ministry (Luke 4:1,14).

Messiah and Spirit

Luke persistently links the coming of the messianic age with the gift of the Spirit in various subtle ways. There is an ancient variant in the Lucan version of the Lord's Prayer, which is attested as early as Marcion in the second century and reads, 'May thy Holy Spirit come upon us and cleanse us,' instead of, 'Thy kingdom come.' This, if it is original, would suggest that Luke saw the Holy Spirit as the supremely desirable object of prayer (as in his version of the saying of Jesus, recorded in 11:13, 'If you, being evil, know how to give good gifts to your children, how much more shall the heavenly Father give the Holy Spirit to those who ask him' – compared with Matthew who reads 'good gifts' for 'the Holy Spirit'). It also suggests that he saw the gift of the Spirit as the supreme characteristic of the kingdom. But the experience of this Spirit must wait for the disciples until after the death and resurrection of the man filled with the Spirit. As in Matthew, the isolated promise of the Spirit in the Mission Charge points beyond the resurrection to the days when they really are engaged in the mission. Meanwhile, it is Jesus alone on whom the Spirit rests in his fulness. And the prophecy of Isaiah 61:1, 'The Spirit of the Lord is upon me, for he has anointed me to preach the good news to the poor . . .' stands in Luke's Gospel (4:18), as a beacon shedding light over the whole of his ministry. It is the passage he reads in the synagogue of his home town at the outset of his work. It contains all the great themes of the Gospel. It identifies the Spirit with the anointed one. And he calmly tells them that 'Today this scripture has been fulfilled in your hearing.' Could anything stress more strongly the concentration of the Spirit in the person of the Messiah for his mission? It is exactly the same point as John makes by his assertion that 'the Spirit was not given by measure' to Jesus, but rested upon him and remained – in fulfilment of the promises of the Old Testament (3:34, 1:32, 33).

There is a striking passage in the early second-century *Gospel according to the Hebrews* which may serve as a summary of this point. The *Gospel* itself has perished, though it was very popular in the early Jewish Christian community. This fragment of it survives, however, because it is quoted by Jerome – significantly in his Commentary on the messianic prophecy of Isaiah 11:1. It runs as follows:

> It came to pass that when the Lord had ascended from the water, the whole fountain of the Holy Spirit descended and rested upon him, and said to him, 'My Son, in all the prophets I looked for thee, that thou mightest come and I might rest in thee; for thou art my rest, thou art my Son, my first-born, who art king for evermore.'

2. JESUS IS THE UNIQUE DISPENSER OF THE SPIRIT

If, then, all the evangelists agree that Jesus is the unique *bearer* of the Spirit, in whose power he ushers in the Messianic Age, they are no less agreed on a second vital point. And here the *Gospel according to the Hebrews* is silent. The whole fountain of the Spirit is indeed his, but not for himself alone; rather that he should shower it upon his followers. And this the canonical evangelists stress, each in his own way. The point is that Jesus is the unique *dispenser* of the Holy Spirit. You cannot get him except through Jesus, or get to Jesus except through him.

John's baptism: mercy

All four evangelists record the promise of John the Baptist that whereas he baptises in water, the One who comes after him will baptise with the Holy Spirit (and, according to Matthew and Luke, 'with fire'). Precisely what John expected, it is difficult to know. But it is evident that John's work was preparatory: to get men ready for the forgiveness of sins which his baptism foreshadowed but did not profess to provide, and to warn men of judgment, the wrath to come. His baptism exemplified these two themes of his teaching. The prophet Ezekiel had given this oracle from God, looking ahead to the age of fulfilment:

> I will sprinkle clean water upon you, and you shall be clean from all your uncleannesses, and from all your idols I will cleanse you. I will give you a new heart, and a new spirit will I put within you.
>
> (Ezek. 36:25f)

John saw his baptism as the preparation for this new era. He was under no illusions that water could convey forgiveness. In common with the men of Qumran, with whom he seems to have had some links, John saw washing with water as merely a preparatory rite, while the great cleansing and the gift of the Spirit lay in the future (1QS 9:10f and 4:21).

John's baptism: judgment

But judgment as well as mercy was presaged in John's baptism. The Old Testament had a lot to say about God administering fire. And it always means either destruction or cleansing. Daniel 7:10 had spoken of the stream of fire issuing from the throne of God, and this too is picked up in one of the Qumran hymns which describe the molten river of judgment that will befall the world in the last day (1QH 3:28ff). Probably this idea was in John's mind. In the very book of Malachi from which he derived the understanding of his own mission to prepare the way of the Lord, he would have read of fire both burning up evil-doers and also refining and purifying the faithful like a refiner's fire (Mal. 4:1f, 3:1–4). Perhaps those who came in repentance and were prepared for the running waters of Jordan to flow over their heads in judgment were thought of as undergoing the judgment of God in symbol so that they would not have to undergo it in its awful reality on the Day of Judgment.

John's baptism: preparatory

At all events, John knows that his baptism is merely preparatory. The coming Messiah will baptise with the Holy Spirit and fire. T. E. Yates has tried to maintain in *The Spirit and the Kingdom* that this prophecy was fulfilled in the ministry of Jesus, for he was not only filled with the Holy Spirit but constituted the fire of judgment to his hearers by means of his teaching and miracles. It is of course true that the coming of Jesus did bring a fire upon the earth, a fire of judgment; men judged themselves by their response to him. But he did not baptise with the Holy Spirit until after his death and resurrection. We do not have to rely on the verse which embarrasses Yates ('the Spirit had not yet been given, because Jesus was not yet glorified,' John 7:39) for this, though that is unambiguous enough. It is the concerted teaching of the whole New Testament that the

Christian experience of the Holy Spirit is possible only after the
death and resurrection of Jesus.

We have seen the evidence for this clearly enough in the preceding pages. Mark emphasises it by only allowing one reference in his Gospel to Christians having the Holy Spirit, and that
in a prophecy about what would be their lot in the days after the
passion (13:11). Matthew and Luke in their Gospels speak of
the Holy Spirit for Christians only in the Mission Charge which
anticipates their future role as ambassadors of Christ.
Furthermore, Matthew stresses that the task of telling men the
good news and baptising them into the possession of the Holy
Spirit will only be theirs after the cross and resurrection have
given them a gospel to proclaim and a Spirit to receive (28:19).
Luke, as we have seen, makes the prayer for the Holy Spirit the
supreme blessing of the Messianic Age, and shows how wonderfully it is shed upon the thirsty disciples of Jesus from the
day of Pentecost onwards – but not before.

John, whose Gospel scheme does not include, except by
implication, the story of what the Church, equipped with the
Holy Spirit, achieved, and therefore could not make room for
Pentecost (as Luke does at the outset of his second volume),
nevertheless makes the same point with considerable clarity. In
the first chapter of his Gospel he stresses that the Spirit rests
exclusively upon Jesus, the fulfilment of the messianic hopes of
the Old Testament for the bearer of the Spirit. In the twentieth
chapter, significantly after the cross and resurrection, he shows
how Jesus fulfils the second part of Old Testament expectation
for the Messianic Age by breathing upon his disciples, charging
them with his mission, bidding them continue his role of proclaiming remission of sins to the penitent and judgment to
those who refused to hear, and saying to them 'Receive the
Holy Spirit' (20:22f). The Spirit which rested upon him is now
made over to them, along with the mission on which he was
engaged; this too is theirs. As we shall see, the mission and
the Spirit belong together. The important point is not to try to

harmonise this account with that of Luke in the Acts – after all, John in all probability never read Luke's work, and presents the material in a very different manner and with different aims. I do not think we get much further by supposing that Jesus gave two insufflations of his Holy Spirit, one in John's upper room, and one at Luke's Pentecost. No, the point they both make is that Jesus was equipped for his messianic mission by the Spirit promised for the last days; that this Spirit was not available to others in the days of his flesh; and that after his death and res- urrection the last days were extended, so to speak, by the fol- lowers of Jesus inheriting his mission, his authority and his Spirit. On this point the evangelists are agreed.

3. JESUS STAMPS A NEW CHARACTER ON THE SPIRIT

This leads us on to a third important point about the relation of the Holy Spirit to Jesus. We have seen that the Spirit of God which appeared fitfully, in a variety of forms, and prophetically in the Old Testament days shone steadily, personally, and fully in the Man of Nazareth. No longer is the Holy Spirit encoun- tered as naked power; he is clothed with the personality and character of Jesus. If you like, Jesus is the funnel through whom the Spirit becomes available to men. Jesus transposes the Spirit into a fully personal key. Jesus is the prism through whom the diffused and fitful light of the Spirit is concentrated. Jesus is *the* prophet (Luke 7:16, Acts 3:22, 7:37) the long- awaited prophet of the end-time, through whom the prophetic Spirit, so active in the Old Testament, gave full and final reve- lation. We have seen that Jesus gave this Spirit to his disciples in virtue of, and subsequent to, his death and resurrection. What follows is that the Spirit is for ever afterwards marked with the character of Jesus. Indeed, he can be called 'the Spirit of Jesus' (Acts 16:7).

This is the common teaching of the New Testament, but no writer brings it into sharper focus than St. John. In the fourth

Gospel Jesus tells his followers, heart-broken because he is going to leave them, that it is better for them that he should do so:

> I tell you the truth: it is to your advantage that I go away; for if I do not go away, the Paraclete will not come to you; but if I go I will send him to you.
>
> (John 16:7)

In a word, it is the task of the Paraclete to universalise the presence of Jesus. In the days of his flesh Jesus was limited by space and time. His physical departure made possible the coming of the Spirit as Paraclete and there would be no barriers of space and time to prevent disciples being in intimate contact with him. Indeed, they would find the relationship even closer than companionship with Jesus in the days of his flesh. They have known Jesus as their Paraclete (we will examine the meaning of the word in a moment) during his ministry. He has dwelt *with* them, but the one whom he promises as another Paraclete will dwell *in* them (John 14:17). There it is in a nutshell. The Spirit universalises the presence of Jesus in the hearts of disciples.

The Spirit as Paraclete

The teaching of John

It is well worth taking a careful look at the teaching of St. John's Gospel about the Spirit as Paraclete. There are five references to him in the farewell discourses. They are 14:15–18, 14:25–27, 15:26–27, 16:7–11, 16:13–15. Once only in the rest of the New Testament do we meet this title, in 1 John 2:1. And this, I think, is very significant. In the Epistle of St. John we find that Jesus is the Paraclete. He is the one who represents us before his heavenly Father. The righteous Lord Jesus having dealt with the defilement of our sins, represents us – stands in for us if you

like, before his Father. As such he is the guarantor of our acceptance. In the Gospel, too, Jesus alludes to himself as Paraclete:
for when promising 'another paraclete' or 'another as paraclete' in 14:16 (it makes no difference which way you take the
Greek) Jesus is clearly insisting that he is their Paraclete
already, just as the Epistle says he is. The identity between Jesus
and the Spirit could scarcely be more strongly stressed, particularly as he goes on to say, 'I will not leave you orphans: *I* will
come to you' (14:18). Nothing of the personality of the Spirit
as embodied in Jesus will be lost when the disciples come to
experience him as Paraclete. Indeed, John breaks all the rules of
Greek by referring to the Spirit (a neuter word in Greek) by the
masculine pronoun. The Spirit is as personal as the Jesus at
whose behest he comes.

A tandem relationship . . .

A great deal of discussion has centred around the meaning of
this word Paraclete. It has been understood as 'Comforter',
'Intercessor', 'Interpreter', 'Preacher' and either 'Prosecutor'
or 'Defence Counsel'. The basic meaning of the word is 'One
called alongside to help'. Jesus is the one called to the Father's
side to help us, according to the Epistle. The Spirit is the one
called from the Father's side to help us, according to the
Gospel. The way in which he helps will be best discovered by
looking at the text, not by speculating about the meaning of
the term. But before we do so, it is worth mentioning the
shrewd suggestion of Professor Raymond Brown that foremost in the complex imagery behind this word is the idea of
what he calls a 'tandem relationship'. Sometimes in Old
Testament days God granted a man signally endued with his
Spirit to pass it on to his successor. Thus Moses passes on the
Spirit of the Lord to Joshua (Deut. 34:9) and Elijah does the
same to Elisha (2 Kgs. 2:9, 10, 15). So Jesus passes on to his
disciples the Spirit which has 'rested' upon him throughout his
ministry.

. . . among disciples

What do we find when we look at the detailed promises about
the Paraclete? Precisely what this tandem relationship and the
reiterated link with the historical Jesus would lead us to expect.
Namely, that the Spirit acts for, and in, and against men in precisely the same way as Jesus had done when on earth. Just as
Jesus had come forth from the Father into the world as the
Father's gift to mankind, so it is with the Paraclete (5:43, 16:28,
3:16f). Just as the Father sent the Son into the world as his representative, so the Paraclete will be sent in Jesus' name (5:43,
14:26). Just as Jesus remained with and guided the disciples, so
will the Paraclete (14:16–18). Just as Jesus taught them the
truth because he was Truth, so the Spirit of Truth would lead
them into all the truth about Jesus (14:6,17, 15:26, 16:13). Just
as Jesus did not draw attention to himself but set out to glorify
his Father by passing on the Father's message to men (8:28,
12:28, 17:4), so the Paraclete 'will not speak on his own authority . . . but will take what is mine and declare it to you' (16:14).
Jesus bore witness to the Father (8:14) and the Spirit would bear
witness to Jesus (15:26, 27). For Jesus had still much to teach
the disciples which they could not understand before his
passion; so he assured them that the Spirit would continue his
teaching function among them when he had left them (16:13).

. . . in the world

Not only was the Spirit to universalise the person of Jesus to
future believers, he was to do the same to the unbelieving world.
One of the prime purposes of his coming was to nerve the disciples themselves to witness to Jesus in the face of hostile or
apathetic society. Look at 15:26, 27: 'He will bear witness to me
. . . and you also will bear witness.' Through the witness of the
disciples which he will apply to the hearts of the hearers, the
Spirit will convict men of being in the wrong. Three of the great
themes of the apostolic preaching are then mentioned; sin,

righteousness and judgment. Through the witness of the apostles and the witness of the Spirit (now seen as Accuser), people are shown that they are wrong with their moralistic ideas of sin: sin is essentially the refusal to commit themselves to Jesus, God's saviour. They are wrong in their views of righteousness, supposing Jesus to be a sinner like themselves – and worse, because he ended up in the place of cursing on a cross (cf. Deut. 21:23): his sinlessness had been vindicated by the resurrection ('I go to the Father'). And they are wrong in thinking that the judgment lay entirely in the future: the decisive battle which dethroned Satan had been won on the cross, and from now on he was a defeated foe, and believers were ransacking his empire. But is this triple message, taken home by the Paraclete in the apostolic mission, not precisely what the Johannine Christ proclaims throughout the Gospel, and particularly in a passage like 9:35–41?

In a word, the Paraclete takes over the role of Jesus. Just as the world refused to accept Jesus, so it will refuse to accept the Paraclete (1:10, 11 and 14:17). Just as Jesus had to bear his witness against a background of hate because he told people the unwelcome truth (7:7) so will the Spirit (16:8). Whether we look at the Paraclete's role in the world or among the disciples the answer is the same. The Holy Spirit is 'another Jesus'.

Another Jesus

He is sent to replace Jesus among the disciples and to do for them what Jesus had done on earth. More, he is to equip them for their mission just as he had equipped Jesus for his. Yet there is no complete autonomy for the Spirit, just as there had been none for Jesus. He had lived his life in dependence on his heavenly Father: if he was to give a true representation in human terms of the nature of Yahweh, then he needed to live, as man, in constant obedience to Yahweh both as his anointed Ruler and as his obedient Servant. And if the Spirit was truly to represent Jesus, he had to remain bound to the person and character of Jesus. Jesus was God's Last Word to man; and the function of the Spirit was not to give some new revelation of his own, but to bear witness to Jesus, to draw out the implications of God's Last Word. We shall look at some of them in the next chapter, but before closing this one it might be pertinent to speculate why it was in St. John's Gospel, of all places, that we get such stress laid on the Spirit as Paraclete. The reason is probably two-fold.

The Spirit replaces the apostles

There is good reason to suppose that St. John's is the latest of the Gospels to be written. Chapter 21, which seems to have been composed as an afterthought to the main body of the Gospel with its climax in 20:31, indicates that there was a tradition doing the rounds in Christian circles to the effect that John would not die: he would be there until the Second Coming of Christ. Imagine the feelings of the Christians when the old man died!

On the one hand the last of the apostles had passed on; the last of those authorised interpreters of the person and work of Jesus had left them bereft. On the other hand the promised Advent had not materialised. What would help them most in such a situation? Well, the record must first be set straight. Jesus did not actually say that John would survive until the Second Coming, but, 'If it is my will that he remain until I come, what is that to you?' (21:23). After doing that, the problem must be faced head on, in both its aspects.

The Holy Spirit, the Paraclete, provides the answer to both problems. Christians were distressed because the age of revelation was over (and they were acutely conscious of this with the passing of the apostolic generation, as is made clear not only by the speedy recognition in the second century that their writings were determinative for the Christian faith, but also by the deep sense of nostalgia to be found in the earliest of the sub-apostolic writers like Polycarp and Ignatius). Yet to them comes the promise that they are not worse off, but if anything better. They may have lost their apostles, but they have the Spirit of the Lord himself remaining with them to teach and to inspire. The risen Christ carries on his teaching work through the Spirit whom he has given to the Church. Sometimes people today bewail the fact that they were not contemporaries of the historical Jesus, and imply that it would be much easier to believe and much more advantageous generally if they had been. To them the words of Jesus still apply. 'It is to your advantage that I go away, for if I do not go away the Paraclete will not come to you. But if I go, I will send him to you.' And that is what he has done. The Spirit is his parting gift to the Church to make his presence as real to them as if they were listening to him teaching beside the Sea of Galilee: and the Spirit can do more for us than ever Jesus could have done had we been his contemporaries. He can come within us, and take up residence within our very beings. He can not only bring to our remembrance what Jesus taught, but can reveal to us the deeper significance of his person, his death and resurrection which we could never have grasped by historical contemporaneity. We are indeed not worse off but better.

The Spirit anticipates the end-time

The second problem that would have troubled the faithful at the death of the last apostle was this. Why had the promised Advent not happened? It was a problem as early as 1 Thessalonians which was partly written in order to meet it. It was a more acute problem by the time of 2 Peter: chapter 3 of that Letter is specifically directed towards those who have given up hope in the Return of Christ. But when the last apostle died, and Jesus, who had uttered the mysterious words, 'There are some of those standing here who will not taste death before they see the kingdom of God come with power' (Mark 9:1), had not returned – what were they to think? Had they been misled?

No, they had not. In a very real sense, though not the sense they were expecting, the kingdom *had* come in power. It came in the power of the Holy Spirit on the Day of Pentecost, and that power had never been withdrawn, and never would be. The previous chapter in St. John had drawn attention to it. Jesus had breathed his Spirit upon his disciples. This was the gift through which the Messiah had accomplished his work. This was the endowment of the end-time which he had lived and died with – and yet the last page of the last chapter of human history had not been written. Were the disciples to be any different from their Lord? No. To be sure, the last page of the last chapter had not been written at the death of the last apostle any more than it had at the death of the Messiah; but, like him, the disciples enjoyed the characteristic gift of the end, the Holy Spirit whom the prophets knew would be poured out in the last days. Let them not therefore bewail the delay of the Parousia. Jesus had not left them orphans: he had come to them in the person of the Spirit, who was not only the special gift of the Messiah to the messianic people in order to enable them to know his continued presence with them, but was the first instalment of the Age to Come, the pledge that the last days which had dawned with Jesus of Nazareth would, one day, come to God's perfect conclusion.

4

The Spirit and Jesus

You may well be wondering why I have taken such pains to show that the Spirit of God, his active intervention on the human scene which took such varied forms in the Old Testament, became concentrated in the person of Jesus the Messiah, and then was poured out by him upon the messianic community. Why does it matter?

It matters a great deal, and I want in this chapter to sketch out some of the implications of this inviolable link which the New Testament writers make between Jesus and the Spirit.

The Spirit in the Gospels?

For one thing, it gives an answer to an otherwise very puzzling problem. Why is it that there is so little about the Holy Spirit in the Gospels? We know that the early Church was intoxicated with the experience of the Spirit, and the comparative silence of the Gospels about him is a great credit to their historical trustworthiness in not reading back the conditions of their post-resurrection situation into the days of Jesus' life. This in itself is highly significant, particularly since many New Testament scholars seem to believe that the early Christians had no sense of historical propriety and would be perfectly happy to dream up some saying and attribute it to Jesus, or to listen to a message from one of the Christian prophets in the congregation, and then put that into the mouth of the historical Jesus. It is a staggering compliment to their historical reliability that we find almost nothing of the major concerns which engaged the primitive Church written back into the Gospels. How easily they could have tried to solve their problems about law keeping, Spirit possession, circumcision, law and grace by inventing 'words of Jesus' to settle the matters in question.

But granted the credit for historical reliability which accrues to the evangelists through their reserve about the Spirit, that still does not help us with the problem of why there is practically nothing in the Gospels about men and women being filled with the Holy Spirit now that he was clearly in business again. If he was active in Jesus, why not in the disciples? The answer is clear. Because the Spirit was tied up with the person of Jesus. He was the funnel through whom all subsequent experience of the Spirit of God would be mediated. That is why other men do not receive the Spirit between his baptism and Pentecost. The gift of the messianic Spirit, promised to the people of God in the end-time, depends upon the Messiah accomplishing his mission. Until he had died for man's forgiveness, until God had raised him from the dead by way of vindication, the Spirit which rested upon him was not available to be passed on to others.

The Spirit in other faiths?

A second problem is this. Why is there nothing said in the New Testament about the Holy Spirit disclosing himself in other faiths, in the struggles of men to find God, and in the ethical endeavours of decent people? In our day, as mentioned in chapter one, we are sometimes told that the efforts of our statesmen, the voting procedures of our councils, the ethical advances of our humanitarians, are being directed by the Holy Spirit. We go further, and it is often said that God has revealed his Spirit as much in Buddhism and Hinduism as in Christianity; indeed, as much in atheism as in theism.

The scandal of particularity

In these days when inter-faith dialogue can easily slip into syn-
cretism, and when man's search for God can easily supplant all
idea of God's self-disclosure to man, it is most important to
remember the emphatic union which the New Testament
asserts between the Holy Spirit and Jesus. If God really has disclosed himself in a Son; and if that Son was characterised by
his possession of the Holy Spirit which he has passed on to his
followers, then we cannot without denying Christ maintain that
God has revealed himself as much in Buddhism as in
Christianity; we cannot make an amalgam of religions as if we
were all honest seekers after a God who hides himself. I think
it is of the utmost significance that the New Testament writers
do not assign to the inspiration of the Holy Spirit the noble elements in pagan ethics or in other religions. For the task of the
Spirit is to bear witness to Jesus. He is the Spirit of Christ.

The light in other faiths

This does not mean that there is little truth in the tenets of other
faiths. Of course there is much that is true, alongside much that
is not. It does not mean that God has failed to give any indication of his person through 'the moral law within and the starry
heaven above'. It does not mean that the Holy Spirit cannot
work on men of other faiths and draw their inner longings to
Christ. John Taylor, in *The Go-Between God* says rightly, 'The
eternal Spirit has been at work in all ages and all cultures
making men aware and evoking their response, and always the
one to whom he was pointing and bearing witness was the
Logos, the Lamb slain before the foundation of the world.
Every religion has been a tradition of response to him, however
darkly it groped towards him, however anxiously it shied away
from him.' He goes on to give a splendid example of the thing
he has in mind, when an old Muslim tribesman went on urging
a drug-addicted English hippy to 'pray to Jesus the Messiah',

until he was converted and delivered. The old man explained his views on the matter afterwards to a Christian friend, 'For an ordinary man in normal circumstances it is enough that he believe faithfully in God. But when anyone is beset by such evil power as this, nothing can save him but Jesus Christ: this I firmly believe.'

Dr. Taylor gives another example of the Spirit of God drawing a man to Jesus in circumstances that were very unpropitious and through a medium that was to say the least opaque. The first missionaries to preach in the Muslim north of Nigeria were greeted by a handful of people who were already believers in Jesus and claimed to follow him. They were the disciples of one Malam Ibrahim, a teacher of the Koran whose studies had slowly convinced him that the Jesus of whom he read in its pages was the mediator through whom the prayers of the faithful are offered up to the All-Merciful. So he gathered around him a group who began to pray regularly in the name of Isa Masih, Jesus the Messiah. When the Islamic authorities discovered this, he was charged with heresy, refused to recant, and was crucified in Kano market-place thirty years before a Christian preacher arrived in the country.

The importance of biblical language

Under such circumstances it is thoroughly in line with the teaching of the New Testament to ascribe such leanings among non-Christians to the agency of the Holy Spirit. Is it not his task to convince the world of sin, righteousness and judgment? Is it not through his agency that anyone makes the Christian confession 'Jesus is Lord' (1 Cor. 12:3) and is born again (John 3:5)? After all, it is the role of the Paraclete to bear witness to Jesus, and he does it with and without our testimony, to men of any faith or none.

But that is a very different matter from the exegetically unjustified expedient adopted by some modern students of mission, of divorcing the Spirit from Jesus, evading the

scandal of his particularity, and attributing to the Spirit's
agency whatever seems to them to be admirable in the beliefs
and practice of other faiths. If we wish to claim the leading of
the Spirit of God with any assurance, we shall find that the
leading is always towards Jesus. As Professor Moule has
written in an unpublished paper, 'to generalise the Holy Spirit
and use the term to denote God's activity anywhere and everywhere, is to miss the biblical theme of election for service, and
to ignore God's strange way of particularising in order to
universalise.'

Bishop Stephen Neill, in an article in *The Church Quarterly*
for April 1971, made the same point. The Spirit in the New
Testament is 'not found anywhere outside the realm of direct
and personal encounter with the risen Christ . . . It would be an
advantage if Christian writers would take as their example the
actual usage of the Christian Scriptures.'

The Spirit in person?

There is a third problem to which this link between Jesus and
the Spirit provides the key. In the Old Testament, as we have
seen, the Spirit of God was manifested in a variety of ways –
strength, wisdom, ecstasy, even frenzy being attributed to the
wind or Spirit of Yahweh. By the time of the New Testament
Epistles, on the other hand, the Spirit is the fully personal
embodiment of the Godhead. How comes this change?

It is simply due to the fact that the diffused, little-defined,
fitfully manifested and sometimes sub-personal presence of
God as Spirit which we found in the Old Testament, becomes
clearly focused for the first time in Jesus of Nazareth. No longer
is this presence diffused; it is sharply localised in Jesus. No
longer is it ill-defined: it is marked with the lineaments of his
character. No longer fitfully manifested, the Spirit rests upon
him with unwithdrawn steadiness. No longer subpersonal, the
Spirit is stamped with the personality of Jesus. From now on

the Spirit is seen as a person within the Trinity, though the New Testament is not interested in doctrinal formulations of this type. The sheer facts of experience, however, drive the Christians to acknowledge the deity of Yahweh, Jesus, and the Spirit, while distinguishing between them. Thus, Jesus is divine, but he is not all of God that there is: he lived his earthly life in dependence on Yahweh. The Spirit is divine, marked with the very stamp of Jesus, and yet distinct: for Jesus was anointed by the Spirit, lived in the Spirit and passed his Spirit on to the Church. A growing and almost unreflective recognition of the diversity and unity within the Godhead led the New Testament writers to make the assertions which became the raw material for later Trinitarian orthodoxy. Thus in 1 Corinthians 12:4–6 Paul correlates the work of the Spirit, the Lord (i.e. the Lord Jesus) and God. He does it again in Ephesians 4:4–6, 2 Thessalonians 2:13,14, Galatians 4:4–7, Romans 8:9–11 and in the well known 'grace' of 2 Corinthians 13:14. We have already mentioned the baptism into the name of 'the Father, the Son and the Holy Spirit' which is enjoined upon the disciples by the risen Christ in Matthew 28:19. In various other places and strands of the New Testament we find similar unselfconscious allusions to the three persons in the deity. One of the most interesting is attributed to the sermon of Peter on the day of Pentecost, where he maintains that 'This Jesus God raised up, and of that we are all witnesses. Being therefore exalted at the right hand of God, and having received from the Father the promise of the Holy Spirit, he has poured out what you now see and hear' (Acts 2:32ff). You find the same thing brought out in 1 Peter 1:2 and Revelation 1:4, 5.

If, then, the Spirit is fully personal, and the personality he wears is the personality of Jesus, two very important conse- quences follow. We cannot rightly attribute to the Spirit any teaching which does not shed light on Jesus, or any religious experience which is not congruous with the life of Jesus. There is a danger of falling into both these traps in the present

spate of Christian enthusiasm for the Spirit. Let me enlarge
on this a little.

A criterion for doctrine

In contrast to a few decades ago when one would rarely hear
any teaching on the Holy Spirit, it seems that some people can
speak of nothing else these days. There is a cult of the Holy
Spirit, and often it has precious little to say about Jesus or God
the Father. It was very apt of Tom Smail to write a book entitled *The Forgotten Father*. Now in view of the past neglect, this
is understandable enough. But it is none the less dangerous. The
Holy Spirit does not draw attention to himself. He is sent by the
Father to glorify Jesus, to show Jesus' attractiveness, and not to
take the centre of the stage. One of the wisest criteria we can
apply to any of the claims made for the Holy Spirit and any of
the teaching about the Spirit which is being advanced from all
sides today is this: does it glorify Christ? It is the characteristic
of the Paraclete to bear witness to Jesus, to glorify Jesus, to take
the things of Jesus and declare them to us (John 15:26, 16:13f).
In contrast to this emphasis of the New Testament writers,
much of the stress on the Spirit today dishonours Jesus, tends
to squeeze him out of the picture, and infers that allegiance to
Jesus is only the lower reaches of the Christian life, the heights
of which belong to the Holy Spirit. Imbalance of this sort is
only to be expected; for we are very human and our understanding is limited and our perspectives often determined by
what has particularly struck us. But it is a salutary reminder
that nothing less than a fully Trinitarian Christianity can stand.

Catholic danger

Some strands in Christendom, particularly the Catholic, have
laid stress on God the Father almost to the exclusion of the Son
and the Spirit. They need to remember that the Father said,
'This is my Son, my beloved, in whom I am well pleased. Listen

to him,' and to reflect on St. John's assertion, 'No man has ever seen God. The only begotten one, himself God, has made him known' (John 1:18).

Evangelical danger

Other strands, particularly the Evangelical, have so concentrated on 'the Lord Jesus' in their teaching and worship that they have virtually made an idol of the flesh of Christ instead of coming to the Father through him. They need to remember that even Jesus did not primarily draw attention to himself, but taught men that they could find the Father through the way he showed, the truth he revealed, and the life he lived.

Pentecostal danger

Other strands, particularly the Pentecostal, make the mistake of concentrating on the Spirit to the prejudice of the Father and Jesus. At the end of the second century, Montanism was a Spirit-centred movement which had great strengths but fell into terrible error because it lost sight of Jesus as the controlling factor in spirituality. If I may quote Professor Moule's wise words again, 'Authentic Christianity finds itself uttering, in the power of the Spirit of God, the address of Jesus Christ the Son of God to God the Father, and thus bearing witness about Jesus to the world. It is this balance that keeps it authentic.'

A criterion for experience

If remembering that the Spirit is the Spirit of Jesus keeps doctrinal formulation authentic, the same may be said for experience. There is real danger in prizing, let us say, speaking in tongues (which I believe can be a real gift of the Holy Spirit) so highly that those who lack it are regarded as second-class Christians, if Christians at all. So far as we know, Jesus never spoke in tongues. And the Spirit is the Spirit of Jesus. It cannot, therefore, be a *Christian* insight to urge that speaking in tongues

is an indispensable mark of life in the Spirit of Christ; whereas
it is an undeniably Christian insight to insist that love and holiness, so manifest in the life of the incarnate One, should mark
those who claim to have his Spirit. The Spirit of Jesus points us
back to Jesus. If we want to understand and possess the Spirit
in his fulness, we need to keep our eyes firmly on Christ himself,
for it is to him that all the Spirit's authentic witness is directed.
If we do this we shall not claim as the teaching of the Spirit
what does not relate to Jesus. And we shall not claim as experience of the Spirit what cannot be shown to flow from Jesus.

There is a further sense in which the very strong link between
the Spirit and Jesus will determine our experience of the Spirit.
The Spirit of Jesus is the Spirit which marked him out as Son
of God, as Servant of Yahweh, and sent him on his mission to
Israel and the world. If the Spirit of Jesus is the gift bestowed
on his followers, we shall expect to find the same characteristics
marking authentic Christian life in the Spirit. And that is very
much what we do find in the pages of the New Testament.

The Spirit of sonship

Take first the question of sonship. Now there is a very obvious
difference between us and Jesus. He was born by the express
agency of the Holy Spirit: we are not. He was Son of God by
right: we are sons and daughters only by adoption. Nevertheless
it was the possession of the Spirit that set Jesus apart as the messianic Son of God, and brought the voice from heaven at his
baptism 'Thou art my Son'. As Son, Jesus coined a new word for
God. He called him 'Abba' (Mark 14:36). Jeremias has shown in
The Central Message of the New Testament that nowhere in pre-
Christian literature does anyone dare to call God by this intimate, family word which could better be translated as 'Daddy'
or 'Dear Father'. It was a word for the intimacies of the family,
not for the worship of God. Jesus, the one set apart by the Spirit
as *the* Son of God, dares to call God by this name. He alone has

the right to, for he alone enjoys the intimate relation of sonship with God the Father.

Adoption

It is into this sonship that he installs us. He enables us to pray the Lord's Prayer, which, in the form known to Luke, begins simply 'Abba', 'Father'. It is the Spirit who adopts us alongside Christ into this sonship with God, and who enables us to cry the 'Abba' of little children in the family of God. 'You have received the Spirit which makes you sons,' exults the apostle Paul. 'When we cry "Abba! Father", it is the Spirit himself bearing witness with our Spirit that we are children of God, and if children then heirs, heirs of God and fellow-heirs with Christ, provided we suffer with him in order that we may also be glorified with him' (Rom. 8:15ff). That is the incredible privilege and status of the Christian. He possesses the Spirit of God's Son, which makes him a son of God, and enables him to utter the family cry to God as 'Abba'. Well may Jeremias conclude that the whole of the good news is concentrated in that single word, Abba.

The Spirit of servanthood

For Jesus

But even in that word of highest privilege and relationship there lie hints of another aspect of the Spirit-filled life of Christ that devolves upon his followers. 'Provided that we suffer with him,' says Paul, reminding us, perhaps, that the agonising context in which Jesus is actually recorded as calling God 'Abba' is in the Garden of Gethsemane. Unlike the kings of Israel who had aspired to the title of 'Son' of Yahweh, Jesus displayed utter trust in his heavenly Father though the outlook was black as night; utter obedience to his Father, even though it would take him to a cross; and utter readiness to suffer – in bloody sweat there and then, and the blood, sweat and hell of crucifixion thereafter. Sonship could not be divorced from servanthood. The Messianic Son was appointed by the Spirit at his baptism to be also the Suffering Servant.

For Christians

In this respect, too, authentic Christian experience is stamped with the mark of the Servant. In the enthusiasm of the renewed emphasis on the Spirit these days he is sometimes presented as the pathway to power in the Christian life, the secret of success in personal living and in service. There is truth in this, but it is only a half truth. The other side of the coin is the agonising trust in the dark, the utter obedience when all our inclinations go the other way, and the willingness to suffer which marked our Lord. It is when they first suffer for Christ that the earliest apostles return to their friends, pray (not for safety but for boldness), and find the place shaken by the Holy Spirit (Acts 4:29–31). It is the Spirit who not only convinces Paul that 'imprisonment and afflictions' await him if he goes to Jerusalem, but constrains him to accept that destiny (Acts 20:22, 23). Peter, too, stresses that the Spirit calls us into the experience of suffering which Christ underwent. He calls on his persecuted readers to rejoice when they suffer as Christians and so share Christ's sufferings, for 'the Spirit of glory and of God rests upon you' (1 Pet. 4:13–16).

Crowns with thorns

But perhaps the most striking example of the sombre side of suffering in obedience to God which the Spirit of Jesus calls us to is provided by Paul in the Corinthian correspondence. Käsemann has perceptively observed, in *Jesus Means Freedom*, that this church at Corinth was infatuated with a theology of the Spirit while allergic to a theology of the cross. They revelled in charismatic experiences of the Spirit, so richly was their community endowed with tongues, miraculous healings and prophecy. They reckoned that they had already entered into their reign with Christ: they were already rich, already filled with the powers of the Age to Come (1 Cor. 4:8). Paul comes down immediately like a ton of bricks on this attitude which regards the Spirit as a medium of religious experience or an embodiment of supernatural power, rather than as the vocation to and equipment for the role of the Servant. He contrasts their position of self-satisfaction with his own. 'God has exhibited us apostles as last of all (like gladiators in the arena), as men sentenced to death. For we have become a spectacle to the world, to angels, and to men (like the dying gladiators).' He goes on to speak of the hardships he endured, the thirst, the hard work, the opposition, the homelessness, the abuse, and concludes, 'we have become, and still are, the refuse of the world, the off-scourings of everything' (1 Cor. 4:8–13). He could scarcely put more vividly the truth that the Spirit who has come upon Christians is the Spirit of Jesus, and that our destiny will involve the suffering and the hardship of the Servant of the Lord. That is why he is determined to know nothing among these Corinthian enthusiasts but 'Jesus Christ, and him crucified' (1 Cor. 2:2). For the power of Christ's resurrection, as he puts it elsewhere, is available only to those who are willing 'to share his sufferings and become like him in his death' (Phil. 3:10). The era of the Spirit in which Christians may exult (2 Cor. 3 throughout) leads inescapably to the rejection, the hardship, perplexity and physical sufferings of which the apostle speaks in chapter four, for he carries about in his body the death of Jesus, so that the life of Jesus may shine through his personality (2 Cor. 4:10). In short, no crown without thorns. No exultant, joyous experience of the Spirit of Christ without a corresponding taste of Christ's suffering.

The Spirit of witness

Son, Servant, and Witness. This was the third notable characteristic of the Spirit in Christ, and this too is everywhere to be noted in the early Church's experience of the Spirit. It was in

the power of the Spirit that Jesus carried out his work of proclaiming the good news of God's kingly rule (Luke 4:18): and
it was in the power of the same Spirit that the disciples got to
work after the resurrection. They were told by Jesus not to
speculate about the time when God would bring in the kingdom
in all its fulness, but, once they had received the Holy Spirit,
they were to witness to Jesus in Jerusalem, Judea, Samaria, and
throughout the world (Acts 1:8). That is precisely what they
did, and we shall be examining it more closely later. It is
sufficient here to notice the pronounced link between the Spirit
and power to witness which can be seen both in the life of Jesus
and that of the post-ascension Church.

Conclusion

In drawing these three threads together, it is fair to say that if,
as I have shown, the Spirit is the Spirit of Jesus, we shall expect
similar marks in the Church of our age and every age as the
Spirit displayed in the life of our Lord. We shall expect the
Spirit to bring us assurance that we are indeed the children of
God, and conversely we shall be careful not to deny that any
Christian people, any children of the heavenly Father, possess
the Spirit of adoption. Secondly, we shall be very suspicious of
any claim to spiritual blessings which does not render the one
who claims it willing to tread the path of the Servant, and
endure suffering joyfully. And thirdly, we shall be unimpressed
with any claims to the Holy Spirit's presence where men are
unwilling, in the power and joy of that same Spirit, to go and
bear witness to Jesus. To crown it all, we shall realise that this
strong link between the Spirit and Jesus leads us to think of him
in personal terms, as the one who makes Jesus real to us and
works out in the common clay of our lives the priceless treasure of Christ's character.

5

The Spirit in Mission

Why did God send us his Holy Spirit? It is a fair question, and allows of more than one answer. The Spirit of God came upon Christian individuals in order to create in them a quality of life that would otherwise be beyond their powers. The Spirit of God came upon the Christian community in order to unite them in a fellowship which could not be paralleled in any other group. We shall be looking at both these important functions of the Holy Spirit in the next two chapters. But there can be no doubt from a candid examination of the New Testament accounts that the prime purpose of the coming of the Spirit of God upon the disciples was to equip them for mission. The Comforter comes not in order to allow men to be comfortable, but to make them missionaries.

This is so contrary to our general assumptions (namely that the Holy Spirit, however vaguely we conceive of him, is an internal gift for the faithful, appropriate only to be mentioned in church) that it is important for us to see the crucial link between the Spirit and mission which is presented to us in the pages of the New Testament. The evangelists make the point in their own characteristic ways.

The age of the Spirit and the mission

Mark's perspective

Mark's only mention of the Holy Spirit for Christians is, as we have seen, placed in the Apocalyptic Discourse in chapter 13,

71

where Jesus is looking ahead to the tribulations which will face
his followers in the years running up to the fall of Jerusalem,
and, interwoven with that theme, up to the end of the world.
They will be hard times, with opposition, persecution, famines,
wars and distress. Yet against this sombre background (so
matching the experience of the hard pressed Christians in
Rome of the 60s A.D., for whom Mark wrote his Gospel) two
clear and closely linked rays of light shine out. The coming age
will be the age of the gospel being preached among the nations:
equally, it will be marked by the presence of the Holy Spirit enabling the Christians to bear faithful witness to Jesus, despite the
costly consequences (Mark 13:9–13). Only the one reference, it
is true: Mark is recording the story of Jesus, not of the Church.
But that one reference speaks volumes. The age of the Church
to which Jesus looked forward is to be marked by evangelism
and the Spirit. He is the power for mission.

Matthew's outlook

Matthew's way of expressing the same point is this. He makes
a great deal, as we have seen, of the gift of the Holy Spirit to
Jesus: but only once in the ministry does he speak of the disciples having the Spirit. In 10:1ff he solemnly names the
twelve disciples, and tells how Jesus sent them out on a
mission. He then makes two very significant points. First, for
the only time in his Gospel, he calls them apostles. Second, he
says that Jesus gave them power over unclean spirits, and that
when they were under pressure the Spirit of their Father
would speak within them (11:20). Whatever the meaning for
those twelve disciples on that short mission (and the Spirit
may well have come upon them temporarily as he did upon
the Old Testament prophets of God to equip them for a
special purpose), it is hard to mistake the shadow this event
casts towards the time of the Church, when those sent out by
Jesus ('sent one' is the root meaning of the word 'apostle')
would be equipped by the Spirit given them by Jesus, for car-

rying out Jesus' own mission in the world. The Holy Spirit is for mission. As if to emphasise the point, Matthew ends the Gospel by Jesus' mission charge to the disciples, 'Go therefore, and make disciples of all nations.' How is this to be done? Why, it is in the power of Jesus to whom all authority in heaven and earth is entrusted; this Jesus is with them always in their mission, to the end of the age; and naturally, therefore, they baptise people not only into the possession, the 'name', of God the Father and the Lord Jesus, but into the sphere of that Holy Spirit who makes real to them the presence of the risen Christ, and empowers them for their work of making him known (Matt. 28:18–20).

John's vision

If we turn to St. John, it is precisely the same picture that meets us, although painted in very different colours. The Paraclete will come upon the disciples when Jesus is taken from them. He will bear witness against the world, as Jesus did, and he will bring conviction (John 16:8). But he will not do it on his own. 'The Spirit will bear witness to me . . . and you will bear witness' (15:27). So when Jesus breathes his Spirit upon them after the resurrection, it is to enable them to enter into his own mission received from the Father and proclaim forgiveness of sins to believers, and doom to the impenitent (20:20–23). John is saying, loud and clear, that the coming of the Spirit upon the Church is to equip it for evangelism.

Paul's emphasis

If we turn to Paul, we find him characterising his missionary work at Christ's behest among the Gentiles as a sort of priestly offering, sanctified by the Holy Spirit (Rom. 15:16). Unusual and striking imagery, but the same linking of the Holy Spirit with evangelism at Christ's command. If we turn to 1 Peter 1:11, 12, we find that the Spirit, once active in the prophets, led towards the suffering Christ, at whose instigation and in

whose Spirit evangelists have brought the readers of the
Epistle to faith.

Luke's vista

But the man who gives us the clearest picture of the link
between the Spirit and evangelism is St. Luke in his two-volume
work. In volume one he showed how Jesus was the bearer of the
Spirit: he was conceived and born in an atmosphere where the
Spirit had been poured out afresh, in the days of messianic salvation. He was baptised and, as Peter put it later, 'God anointed
Jesus of Nazareth with the Holy Spirit and with power' (Acts
10:38). The word 'anointed' (*echrisen*) is the one from which
Messiah (Greek *christos*) is derived. Jesus was designated as
Messiah or 'Christed' by the coming of the Spirit to rest upon
him, and he could claim that the prophecy of Isaiah 61:1 had
been fulfilled – 'He has anointed me (*echrisen*) to preach the
good news' (Luke 4:18). In Jesus the Spirit destined for the messianic days, the days of salvation *had come to stay*. That is why
there is so much stress in Luke's account of the life of Jesus that
his deeds and words were at the inspiration of the Spirit (Luke
4:1,14, 10:21, 23:46, etc.). Accordingly, as he leads up to the day
of Pentecost, Luke is at greatest pains to maintain that the
Spirit, who equipped Jesus for his mission, equips the disciples
to carry it on.

Beginning at Jerusalem

The end of the beginning

Notice, first, how Luke links the ascension of Jesus with the
Spirit and evangelism. In the Gospel we have been told that
Jesus will bring about a new *exodus* (9:31) by his death and resurrection at Jerusalem: a release from a worse bondage and a
more terrible death than that which befell the Israelites in
Egypt. Three times Luke tells us that Jerusalem was Jesus' goal
(9:51, 13:22, 17:11). It is to Jerusalem that the Spirit of the

Suffering Servant leads Jesus. At the end of the Gospel, therefore, we find the resurrection appearances that Luke records are
confined to the city where these climactic events have taken
place. No mention of the Holy Spirit, you notice: merely a foreshadowing of the role of the disciples in being witnesses to the
Messiah who had to suffer and rise from the dead so that repentance and forgiveness could be preached to the nations, *beginning from Jerusalem* (Luke 24:46f). And with that the curtain
comes down on the Gospel. The volume telling us of the
coming of salvation to Israel is complete with the death and resurrection of Jesus. His ascension to the place of power at God's
right hand is the fitting conclusion.

The beginning of the end

But at the beginning of Acts, volume two in the drama, we find
the story of the ascension related again, and from a very
different point of view. This time the ascension does not bring
down the curtain on the life of Jesus; instead, the curtain goes
up on the life of the Church. The exaltation of Jesus to the
Father's right hand is not only God's vindication of his person
and his achievement; it is the precondition of the coming of his
Spirit upon the witnesses who are to carry on his mission (Acts
2:32f). Volume one tells of what Jesus began to do and to teach
until his ascension to the right hand of God; volume two tells
of what Jesus continued to do and to teach through the apostolic Church after his ascension, through the gift of the Holy
Spirit which he shed upon it. That, surely, is the implication of
Acts 1:1ff, with its studied throw-back to the beginning of the
Gospel. Just as there was a great outpouring of the Spirit at the
coming of the Messiah – prophecy, divine begetting, voice from
heaven, baptism and so forth; so at the beginning of the age of
the Church's witness-bearing to Jesus we find a similar intensive manifestation of the Spirit. As the Spirit equipped Jesus for
his ministry, so it is with the people of Jesus.

Luke makes part of his point through the misunderstanding

of the disciples. They were still thinking of the kingdom in materialistic terms. When was Jesus going to fulfil his promise and bring it in? They had to learn that the final day of God's victory might be long delayed, and they could not tell its date (a point to which successive generations of enthusiastic date-guessers have remained remarkably blind). However, the first instalment of the kingdom would soon be sent them by the ascended King himself. Until God's final day when he will bring in the kingdom, two characteristics would mark the age of the Church: the Holy Spirit, and witness to Jesus. The Spirit, who had inspired Jesus to teach and heal and proclaim the good news of God's kingly rule among men, would come upon them, marked with all Jesus' character. The mission on which Jesus had been engaged would devolve on to their shoulders. 'You shall receive power when the Holy Spirit comes upon you, and you shall be my witnesses' (Acts 1:8). Precisely as in Mark, we find the Spirit and mission being the two notable marks of the Church in the age stretching between the advents. The Spirit, mediated in evangelism, is the mode of the kingdom's presence among men until the return of the King.

Spreading from Jerusalem

And just as the Gospel had concentrated on Jerusalem, the location of God's great exodus for humanity, so the Acts shows the mission spreading out from that centre in ever-widening circles. As Jesus insisted in Luke 24:47, it was all to *begin* in Jerusalem: hence the emphasis on Jerusalem as the place where the Pentecostal gift arrived. It was *never to lose touch with Jerusalem*: hence the repeated journeys of Paul back to the metropolis (e.g. Acts 18:22, 19:21) and the supervisory visits of Jerusalem leaders to various parts of the expanding Christian arena (e.g. Acts 8:14, 11:22). But *it was to move out from Jerusalem*. The Acts is the story of that moving out.

New initiatives

First within Jerusalem, where three thousand are converted on the day of Pentecost itself; it would be hard to stress more emphatically the link between the Spirit and mission than by showing such effective evangelism as the result of the reception of the Holy Spirit on that notable day! Then the good news spreads out in the pattern outlined in Acts 1:8. At every point in the advance, it is the Holy Spirit of God who takes the initiative.

It is the Spirit who inspires Peter to withstand the rulers of Israel (4:8ff) and proclaim to them the Messiahship of Jesus. The Spirit marks out Stephen as a special vehicle of God when he refuses to remain restricted to the static categories of the temple and moves into broader pastures (6:3,5,10, 7:55).

It is the Holy Spirit who so signally lays his mark of blessing upon the preaching of the good news to those untouchables (from the traditional Jewish viewpoint) the Samaritans in the first half of Acts chapter 8, and the eunuch in the second part of that chapter. For it was the Spirit who called Philip from his successful mission in Samaria to reach the Ethiopian eunuch with the gospel (8:29 and probably 26), and led him on his further preaching tour as far as the very Hellenised city of Caesarea.

It was here in Caesarea that Peter had his memorable lesson not to call any man 'unclean' – which, as a Jew, he would instinctively have done to all Gentiles. In order to drive home the point that the messianic Spirit, the Spirit of the days of salvation, was really available to all believers, the Spirit had first of all to inspire Peter with his vision of the unclean animals in the sheet which were intended for him to eat, and then to apply that vision to a Gentile officer whose men were at that very moment waiting in the courtyard for Peter to accompany them to Cornelius so that he might receive the good news of Jesus. Even then, such is Peter's Jewish prejudice, the Holy Spirit has to take the initiative in falling upon Cornelius and his company before ever Peter had got round to making any appeal to repentance, faith and baptism (10:44f)

The Spirit has shown that he validates the Christian mission among Jews, proselytes, 'Godfearers' (as Gentile adherents on the fringe of the synagogue were called), and even outsiders like eunuchs and Samaritans. But more was to come.

Gentile mission

The second part of Acts is dominated by the mission to the Gentiles, under the leadership of Paul. It is the Spirit who leads the Antioch church to send out Saul and Barnabas on the first missionary journey (13:2,4) which enabled them to return and report that, 'The Lord has opened the door of faith to the Gentiles' (14:27). This is the keystone in the expanding arch of mission in Acts. The Holy Spirit has broken through all the man-made obstacles, and has incorporated all types and backgrounds of people in the messianic community. 'The greatness of Luke's view,' wrote Professor Eduard Schweizer in *Church Order in the New Testament* (p. 75), 'lies in his showing more impressively than anyone else that the Church can live only by evangelising, and by following whatever new paths the Spirit indicates.' Those paths lead ever wider and wider afield in the cause of Christ. The evangelist who tells us three times that Jesus contracted his perspective to concentrate on Jerusalem and that at Jerusalem the disciples had to await the coming of the Spirit that would equip them for mission, ends his second volume with a triple reminder that this good news, beginning from Jerusalem (Luke 24:47) reaches Rome (19:21, 23:11, 27:24). The butterfly of the gospel has broken out of its chrysalis at Jerusalem and has flown to the centre of the civilised world. The Spirit that dwelt in the Messiah of Israel is available to the citizens of Rome. The faith of Israel is good news for the world.

Perfect balance

It is one of the remarkable indications of the balance of St. Luke that he manages to stress the initiative of the Spirit in ever-expanding circles of evangelism with the reminder that there is only one mission. The Paul who receives his mission to the Gentiles does so in a trance in the temple at Jerusalem (Acts 22:17ff). The apostle who brings the Acts to an end by preaching unhindered in the capital of the pagan world is also shown as arguing all day with the leaders of the Jews 'declaring to them the kingdom of God' and 'persuading them about Jesus' by appeal to the law and the prophets (28:16–31). To the Jew first and also to the Greek, the Spirit of the Messiah is available through the preaching of the good news of what the Messiah has done. There is neither Jewish nor Gentile bias in this chronicler of the Holy Spirit's initiative in mission throughout the world, though his application of the famous 'blinding' passage of Isaiah 6 to Jewish leaders who refused to receive their Messiah, and his assertion, 'Be it known to you that this salvation of God has been sent to the Gentiles: *they will listen*' (28:25–28), is suggestive of the direction in which the Christian mission would, for the most part, go.

The Spirit initiates mission

The initiations of the Spirit

Now all this emphasis on the Spirit as the author, the controller and the energiser of the Church's mission is highly significant. It reminds us that mission did not originate, in the earliest days, in the leadership of the Church. It was not a matter of Peter and subsequently Paul saying 'What about a bit of evangelism?' Luke does not teach us that the apostles initiated mission. They sat quietly in Jerusalem until the Spirit came upon them at Pentecost; then they could not keep quiet about the mighty deeds of God. It was not the Twelve who fulfilled their Lord's command to go and teach all nations the good news. It was rather an ex-Pharisee opponent of the gospel, converted through the direct agency of God and thrust out on the mission at the direct leading of the Lord the Spirit. It was not the apostles at Jerusalem who ever dreamed of reaching eunuchs or Samaritans with the good news: the Holy Spirit led the way. It was not the Jerusalem leaders who agreed to the first widespread dissemination of the Word. That came through their being cooped up at Jerusalem in the persecution which followed on the death of Stephen: as a result of the ordinary followers of Jesus being scattered by that persecution, they were able to preach the good news along the Phoenician seaboard until they came to Antioch, later to become the home of the Gentile mission. And so one could go on. The initiatives in evangelism were always those of the Holy Spirit. So much so that the crucial coming of the Holy Spirit on Cornelius is recorded three times in Acts, so that no one might miss the message. The Holy Spirit was not to be confined to the narrow straits of Jewish respectability, nor was he the perquisite of the Church leadership. He was sovereign, and he was the leader of the whole Christian outreach as well as its energising power. The Church was only effective when it broke through its old taboos and shibboleths and followed the Spirit who could come upon Samaritans and Gentiles as well as Jews. So far from the Church being the possessor and dispenser of the Spirit, as Käsemann would have it with his astonishing reading of primitive Catholicism into Acts (see *Essays on New Testament Themes* p. 89ff), it is the Spirit who energises the evangelism of the Church and drives its often unwilling members into the task for which God laid his hand on them: mission.

The sovereignty of the Spirit

This sovereignty of the Spirit is worth dwelling on. It humbles us, as God intended it to do, to find that there is no tidy doctrine of the Spirit to be found in Acts or, for that matter, in the whole of the New Testament. He always retains that unpredictable, mysterious otherness of the *ruach adonai*. Utterly unmediated in his coming on the day of Pentecost, and on what has been called 'the Gentile Pentecost' to Cornelius and his entourage, the Spirit works in many varied ways. He leads through a committee at the Council of Jerusalem (15:28), through a prophet in 11:2 8, through a trance in 10:19. In 13:2 he reveals his will to the community gathered at worship. Sometimes it is through a mysterious inner constraint that he makes his presence felt, as when he guided Paul's evangelistic direction away from the province of Asia in 16:6,7 and towards the hardships and opposition he realised he would have to face if he went up for that last journey to Jerusalem (Acts 20:22,23). It is impossible to get the Holy Spirit taped, and to fit his movements in the Acts into any tidy ecclesiastical or doctrinal pattern. He remains the sovereign Spirit, but always the Spirit who is bent on leading the people of Jesus out into mission.

The Spirit universalises mission

We have already seen some of the emphasis on this in the account Luke gives of Pentecost. But there are more subtle nuances in that story. Luke clearly interprets Pentecost as the fulfilment of the prophecy of John the Baptist, which he quotes in Acts 1:5. It is the fiery baptism of Holy Spirit which John looked forward to. Hence the emphasis Luke gives on the physical manifestation to the disciples of tongues of fire and rushing wind, which equipped them for their mission, just as the physical coming of the Spirit upon Jesus 'in bodily form, as of a dove' (Luke 3:22) equipped him for his ministry. Once baptised in the fiery power of the Spirit which had been in Jesus, the disciples at once interpret it as the fulfilment of Joel's prophecy about the availability of the Spirit in the last days, and proclaim the good news to the representative crowd from 'every nation under heaven' which had gathered in Jerusalem for the feast of Pentecost (2:16ff).

Aspects of Pentecost

Pentecost did not only mean the offering of the firstfruits to God (and what remarkable firstfruits of the Spirit were offered to the Lord that day as three thousand people believed, were baptised, and joined the company of the disciples praising God in the temple): first-century Jews would also have recalled the giving of the law on Mount Sinai (see *Jubilees* 1:1, 6:17). According to one rabbinic tradition (preserved in *Tanchuma* 26) when the law was given on Sinai, 'the ten commandments were promulgated with a single sound,' yet the Jewish Midrash says, 'All the people perceived the voices' (Exod. 20:18). This means that when the voice went forth it 'went into seventy tongues, and every people received the law in their own language'. The nations of the world were reckoned to number seventy, after the indication in Genesis 10. It may be that Luke is referring to this tradition, and if so, he will mean us to understand that on the day of Pentecost, the gathered representatives 'from every nation under heaven' heard the mighty deeds of God being proclaimed, 'every man . . . in his own language'. The Christian Pentecost would thus not only reverse the Curse of Babel (Gen. 11:9) but be the antitype of the covenant inaugurated on Sinai through the giving of the law. What was there external to men has now, in the new covenant, become interiorised through the Spirit.

Good news for all

Such an interpretation is attractive but speculative. It would fit the teaching of Paul, who makes just this contrast between the law and the Spirit in 2 Corinthians 3; it would fit Hebrews chapters 8 and 10. But Luke nowhere speaks of the new covenant unless Luke 22:19b and 20 are original (against the main weight of manuscript attestation). He prefers to see believers as the heirs to the one Abrahamic covenant which inaugurated the Old Testament people of God (Acts 3:25). At all events we shall not go wrong in assuming that it is not without good reason that he tells us of so impressive a roll call of nationalities on the day of Pentecost (2:5–11). At the very least he is showing us that the Christian good news is for the whole world.

The Spirit uses testimony

The unsung missionaries

The agents in this mission inaugurated by the Spirit are, of course, the disciples of Jesus. But this role is by no means confined to the Twelve. 'The great mission of Christianity was in reality accomplished by means of informal missionaries,' wrote Harnack long ago (*The Mission and Expansion of Christianity* p. 368). He was right. As early as Acts 6 we find the apostles seeking deputies to manage the administration of the church, while they give themselves to prayer and the ministry of the Word. The Seven, sometimes improperly called deacons, are accordingly appointed. But the next thing we find is one of these administrators, Stephen, preaching his heart out! As soon as he has been executed, another of the Seven, Philip, takes over. And he has four daughters with the gift of prophecy: doubtless they engaged in the mission too. That same eighth chapter of Acts records the spread of the gospel by informal missionaries, men and women evicted from Jerusalem by the persecution which followed Stephen's death. The message is clear. All disciples are expected to bear their testimony to Jesus. That is what the Holy Spirit is given them for.

The meaning of 'witness'

The word 'witness' is significant. Its root figures over thirty times in the Acts, in one form or another. The apostles, the folk who had known Jesus in the old days in Galilee, Stephen, Paul, all are 'witnesses of these things, and so is the Holy Spirit whom God had given to those who obey him' (Acts 5:32). The witness attests his own experience: he does not necessarily preach. The Acts gives us many examples of Christian people bearing witness to Jesus, in particular his death and resurrection, to soldiers and governors, princelings and mediums, crowds and individuals. Witness in the New Testament is neither the silent churchgoing that passes for witness among many Christians, nor the sickening self-advertisement that often results when a believer 'gives his testimony'; but simple factual reference to the historical Jesus, his death and resurrection, his gift of the Spirit, and his present availability and power.

The power of testimony

This emphasis on testimony is one of the great strengths of the present Pentecostal revival in South America. You are scarcely accounted a Christian in Chile until you have got up in the street and given testimony to Jesus. This is not necessarily the best way of passing on the good news, but it does stir the passers-by to find not the paid priest but the cobbler, the miner, the man who sells meat fritters telling them about Jesus. In his book, *Haven of the Masses* (p. 47), C. L. d'Epinay describes the impact of such witness. It offends the élite, of course. 'These men,' said a teacher, 'do not even speak in Castilian, but in slang; sometimes they don't even know how to write, and can hardly read. And they quote epistles of St. Paul so difficult that the theologians, who have been working on them for two thousand years, have not got to the bottom of them. By what authority do they teach?' That is just the reaction provoked by Jesus and by the informal missionaries in the Acts (Mark 1:27, Acts 4:13). The élite were offended, but the common people loved it. If the language is slang, what does it matter so long as the preachers are radiant with the experience they speak of, and live in the midst of the same social situation, with all its problems and difficulties, as the listeners? When ordinary men and women are fired by the Spirit to bear witness to 'a Lord who pardons and loves, a Lord who is just as powerful as the landowners, the mine-managers or the trade union secretaries, because he is God, a God who desires to be called Father, and who treats the most wretched of men as his son' (d'Epinay) then people will sit up and take notice. They did in the first century, and they do still when the Christians come out of their ghettos and chatter the good news in the streets.

The Spirit enlivens the Word

The power of the Word

It is not only this informal witness to Jesus which is promised
the aid of the Holy Spirit. So is the more formal proclaiming of
the Word. 'The Word' is as common in the Acts as 'The Spirit',
and they belong very closely together. One of the great merits
of C. K. Barrett's book, *Luke the Historian in Recent Study* is
the weight he gives to the Word as the prime agency through
which the Spirit extends the good news of Christ. It is expressed
in a number of ways: 'the Word of God', 'the Word of salvation', 'the Word of the gospel' or quite simply 'the Word'. It
means the message about Jesus. Wherever the early Christians
went, it was the Word they carried (Acts 8:4). When Paul was
encouraged at Corinth by the fellowship of Priscilla and Aquila
we read that he became gripped by the Word (18:5). During the
two years and more of his mission in Ephesus 'all the residents
of Asia heard the word of the Lord' (19:10). When Luke wants
to indicate the success of evangelistic work, he can say that 'the
word of the Lord grew and prevailed'. So it was in Judea (6:7),
Samaria (8:4–7,14), on the first missionary journey (13:49) and
in Asia (19:10). The Word makes its own impact on Theophilus
(Luke 1:1, Acts 1:1), Cornelius (10:44), the proconsul of
Cyprus (13:7), and on the citizens of Antioch (13:44). No
wonder the Twelve made it their priority, and the nameless missionaries of 8:4 took it as their great weapon. For if a man
believes, it is because the Word brings faith (4:4). If a man
receives the Spirit, it is because he has responded to the Word
(10:44). It is no exaggeration to say that the Word is the prime
tool used by the Spirit of God in advancing the Christian
mission.

The content of the apostolic message

It would take us too far afield to examine the content of this
apostolic 'Word'. Essentially it was concerned with Jesus. Many

people have tried to summarise it, and perhaps the most celebrated attempt is that of C. H. Dodd in *The Apostolic Preaching and its Development*. He maintained that the good news about Jesus had a clearly defined form. This form is discernible in Mark's Gospel, the Acts sermons, the Pauline Letters and in certain other parts of the New Testament. The kerygma of the early Church, contained in that outline, amounted to something like this:

'The age of fulfilment has dawned. This has taken place through the ministry, death and resurrection of Jesus of Nazareth. By virtue of the resurrection Jesus has been raised to the right hand of God, as messianic head of the Israel of God. The Holy Spirit in the Church is the sign of Christ's present power and glory. The Messianic Age will shortly reach its culmination in the return of Christ. Hence the importance of repentance, faith, baptism into the messianic community, and the reception of God's offer of forgiveness and the Holy Spirit.'

Footnotes in plenty have been added to Dodd, but his pattern remains a fair summary of the early preaching so far as we can reconstruct it. But such summaries will inevitably remain speculative since we have only one source in the New Testament for determining the content of the early preaching to people who were not Christians, and that is the sermons in Acts. And it remains a matter of debate to what extent Luke is exercising editorial privilege in his accounts of the apostolic preaching. Furthermore, as I have tried to show in my book *Evangelism in the Early Church*, there was considerable flexibility in the way the gospel was preached to different audiences in different circumstances, coupled with great unity in presenting men with the person of Jesus, the offer of forgiveness through his death on the cross, the promise of the Holy Spirit, and the challenge to repent and believe and be baptised. Such, in essence, was the Word that the Holy Spirit could confidently be expected to take home to the hearts of the hearers. He still does.

The mystery of preaching

Preaching is a very humbling thing. You feel such a fool. Paul catches the feeling precisely in 2 Corinthians 4:1–6. The preacher is involved in a titanic confrontation, in which he is a tiny Lilliputian. He becomes aware that 'the god of this age (i.e. the devil) has blinded the minds of those who do not believe, lest the light of the glorious gospel of Christ, who is the image of God, should shine on them'. Every effective preacher knows that proclamation involves not mere communication, but confrontation. 'For we are not contending against flesh and blood, but against principalities and powers, against the world rulers of this present darkness' (Eph. 6:12). We don't get anywhere by what Paul calls 'preaching ourselves': gimmicks do not help. It is by being prepared to be people's servants for Jesus' sake so that the light may shine through to them. For light is not lacking: 'the God who commanded light to shine out of (primeval) darkness has shone in our hearts to give the light of the knowledge of the glory of God in the face of Jesus Christ' (2 Cor. 4:6). But how is this glory to shine through to others? Only as the Holy Spirit takes the 'foolish' message of the gospel home to people's hearts, and convinces them of its truth; that it is indeed 'the wisdom of God to every one who believes' (1 Cor. 1:18ff). We come back to this theme of the double witness, by the Holy Spirit and ourselves, which the New Testament continually brings before us. A preacher can talk till he is blue in the face, but he can never bring anyone to faith in Christ. Yet the Holy Spirit can take his words home to the conscience of the hearer and bring that person low in repentance and faith before the crucified and risen Christ. Anyone who has been instrumental in this transformation of another person's life through the impact of the Word of God and the Spirit of God will know that it is not his own doing. I have on occasion preached the same sermon in two different churches. In one, between twenty and thirty people professed conversion. In the other, nobody did. The Spirit and the message and the messenger all combine to carry out this strange alchemy of new birth. But only the Spirit is indispensable.

The Spirit and the Word

I once heard a remarkable story from a leading Indian Christian, the Revd. Samuel Kamelesan. A friend of his, who was engaged in Christian colportage work, decided to go to the heart of Brahmin country in Kumbbakoman in Southern India. He wanted to bear witness to Jesus in this tough spot, and invited some of the nearby Christians to accompany him. They declined. 'We have to live here,' they replied! So he went alone.

This brave man entered the courtyards of the main temple, and began to preach Jesus. He expected to be killed. Instead he had hardly begun before he was embraced by a Brahmin woman and was asked, 'Why did you not come sooner?' Her story was a fascinating one. This rich, high-caste woman had had terminal cancer. She was given a very short expectation of life by the doctors. So she went to Madras, in whose pleasant climate she would live out the few remaining weeks of her life. Then, apparently, she died. She was laid out in the mortuary. But she was not dead, only deeply unconscious. In this state she had a vision of Jesus, about whom she knew nothing. In the vision the Lord looked on her with love. 'If you will let me live again, Lord, I will give my life for you,' she promised.

While the woman was lying there in the mortuary unconscious, a crossing sweeper happened to notice a faint movement in this supposed corpse. She went immediately to the doctor who had signed the death certificate. The doctor examined her, found a faint pulse, and immediately swung into action to resuscitate the patient. A blood transfusion was necessary. It so happened that the crossing sweeper had blood of the same group as this rich Brahmin lady. And she happened to be a Christian. She gladly gave her blood for a substantial blood transfusion, and the patient was told afterwards by the doctor, 'You owe the fact that you are alive today to the crossing sweeper who first detected a movement in you when you were in the mortuary and then gave her blood for you.' The Brahmin lady was as good as her word. From that day onward she worshipped Jesus only, and renounced her Hinduism. This provoked intense opposition, not least from her own family, in a militantly Hindu city like Kumbbakoman. The woman began to bear witness to the Jesus of whom she knew almost nothing, and was physically beaten up for her pains. Indeed, her own brothers knocked two of her teeth out. Yet her simple witness led three of her five brothers to Christ. And when the colporteur started to preach Jesus in that temple courtyard the lady ran out and embraced him, delighted to find a fellow believer in that unexpected place. He taught her much more about the Lord in whom she believed, rather as Paul, Aquila and Priscilla did to Apollos.

Now in that story only one of the normal evangelising agencies was present, the Holy Spirit. There was no proclamation of the Word to bring the Brahmin woman to belief. And there was no human messenger to tell her about Jesus, though the part played by the Christian outcaste crossing sweeper was of the utmost importance. The Spirit of life not only revived the woman, and caused a spontaneous remission of the cancer, but brought her to trust in Christ – which from that background was quite as great a miracle. In more senses than one we can say with the Creed, 'I believe in the Holy Spirit, the Lord, the Lifegiver.'

The Spirit convicts and attracts

Conviction

At every point the Holy Spirit is involved in the process of someone becoming a Christian. As we saw in discussing John 16:8, it is the Holy Spirit who acts as prosecuting counsel, and

NB|

convicts a person of sin. No one can do that to anyone else. If this conviction arises through my preaching, it is frequently through some phrase or thrust that I had not intended. I well recall one tough Yorkshire girl who was on drugs at the time, coming to a service where I was preaching, and being pierced to the heart by a throwaway line I had never intended saying, about God hardening Pharaoh's heart. I knew nothing about this convicting work of the Spirit in her, until a week later when she rang me from Halifax and asked, 'Does God really harden people's hearts?' It was through this most improbable passage of Scripture, taken home to her by the Spirit, that she in due course became a Christian. I think of another man, to whom I had said something about Jesus Christ while marching down alongside him to an army parade! He had seemed very uninterested, and I had not pursued the conversation. In any case, the conditions were scarcely suitable. To this day I cannot recall what it was I said to him. Nevertheless, the Spirit took it home with unerring aim. A day later he came to see me, unable to sleep and distraught. He had begun to see what he looked like to God, and now he was not in the least uninterested to hear what Jesus Christ had done about it. Before that night was out he had surrendered himself to Christ.

Attraction

NB|

Not only is the Spirit the one who convicts a person of sin: it is he, and only he, who can make Jesus attractive. As we have already seen, it is the Spirit who bears witness to Jesus and glorifies him (John 15:26, 16:14). Sometimes this happens over a long period, as a person finds himself constrained to attend a Christian place of worship, or drawn to read the Christian Scriptures. Time and again I have met folk who have been warmed by the Spirit to perceive the beauty of Christ in the life of a group of believers or in the story of the New Testament, and have come to faith that way. Sometimes this attraction to Jesus happens instantaneously. The penny suddenly drops, and he is revealed as the one who makes sense of life. I remember an English don once coming to me at the end of a meeting, and saying that she had suddenly seen that evening in Jesus Christ the answer to the rather negative existentialist framework into which her life had been cast. That was the work of the Spirit, revealing Christ to her.

The Spirit brings repentance and faith

Repentance

The Spirit is probably meant by passages of the New Testament which speak of repentance as a gift of God. Acts 11:15–18 is a case in point. Peter is recounting the Cornelius episode. He tells how the Holy Spirit fell on Cornelius, and points out that God had given Cornelius the same gift as the Jewish believers. Their response is, 'Then God has given the Gentiles also the gift of repentance leading to life.' The plain inference is that it is through the operation of the Spirit that these Gentiles have come to repentance. The same is probably intended by Acts 5:31 and 2 Timothy 2:25.

Faith

When it comes to faith, we are left in no doubt that this is a gift of God brought about by the Holy Spirit. No man can make the Christian confession 'Jesus is Lord' without the Holy Spirit enabling him to do so (1 Cor. 12:3). Seen in its context, that is a most significant verse. For the Corinthians were fascinated with the charismatic and ecstatic aspects of the work of the Spirit. St. Paul tells them at the outset of his three-chapter discussion on spiritual gifts, that ecstasy is no sure mark of inspiration by the Spirit. So-called spiritual men could, and did, call Jesus accursed in ecstatic cries in the Corinthian assembly (12:3). The true mark of the Spirit's operation is when someone can say from the heart, 'Jesus is my Lord.' Once again we see the Spirit is related securely to the person of Jesus, and it is when the Spirit enables a man or woman to see who Jesus is and respond to him in allegiance that faith is born. It is the Spirit who takes the things of God and reveals them to us (1 Cor. 2:12), and Paul can rightly say that the very capacity to respond in faith is a gift of God and no man-made attribute of which we can boast (Eph. 2:8). The Spirit can therefore be called 'the Spirit of faith' (2 Cor. 4:13). And to possess the pledge of the Spirit is interpreted as living the life of faith (2 Cor. 5:5,7)

Adoption

In other words, it is due to the work of the Holy Spirit that we become Christians at all. He is the Spirit who adopts us into the family of God alongside Jesus (Rom. 8:15, Gal. 4:6). Though by nature we Gentiles are 'without Christ, aliens from the commonwealth of Israel, strangers from the covenant of promise, having no hope and without God in the world', the Holy Spirit has given us access, through Christ's self-sacrifice for us (Eph. 2:12–18). 'Now you are no longer strangers and foreigners,' Paul exultantly reminds his readers, 'but fellow citizens with the Old Testament believers, and in the very household of God.' The New Testament writers use a variety of terms to speak of the Holy Spirit's work in making us Christians. 'You received the Spirit,' says Paul to the Galatians. 'You began in the Spirit.' You accepted 'the gracious provision of the Spirit', or 'the promise of the Spirit' (Gal. 3:2, 3, 5, 14). Sometimes this initial encounter with the Spirit is seen as a great washing (1 Cor. 6:11). Sometimes it is a new birth (Titus 3:5, John 3:3, 5) brought about by the entry of the Spirit into our lives. Whatever the imagery, one thing remains constant. It is only through the agency of the Holy Spirit, enabling us to repent and believe, convicting us of sin and making Jesus attractive to us, that we ever become Christians. It is the Spirit of Christ that unites us with Christ: so much so that Paul can say 'If any man does not have the Spirit of Christ, he does not belong to Christ' (Rom. 8:9).

We shall be looking further at this vexed question of
Christian initiation and the relation of the Holy Spirit to
baptism in a later chapter. But we have seen enough to be able
to frame a clear answer to the question formulated at the outset
of this chapter. God sent the Spirit of Jesus to his followers in
order to equip them to carry on the mission of his Son in the
world. Empowered by that Spirit, and bearing witness to the
crucified and risen Jesus, the early Christians and succeeding
generations alike have found hard hearts softened, strong men
brought to repentance, sceptics coming to faith, and people of
all ages, backgrounds and classes coming to taste the salvation
of the messianic community, and being born into the very
family of God.

6

The Spirit in the Individual

If God's overall strategy in sending us his Spirit is to equip the Church for mission, and bring people into the messianic kingdom, the sphere of salvation – we may well ask what he does when he has got them there? Why does he give his Holy Spirit to the individual?

1. THE SPIRIT IN CHRISTIAN INITIATION

The Spirit initiates us

Christian incorporation

As we have seen, it is the Spirit who brings people to repentance, faith and incorporation into Christ. To believe the gospel, respond to Jesus or receive the Spirit are three ways of looking at the same thing (2 Cor. 11:4). The whole Godhead is involved in the rescue and restoration of mankind, and so we read of Paul giving thanks over Christians, for 'God chose you from the beginning to be saved'. How was that achieved? When 'the Spirit set you apart' – that was God's side; and 'when you believed the truth' – that was your side. 'To this he called you through our gospel, so that you may obtain the glory of our Lord Jesus Christ' (2 Thess. 2:14). Christians are people who have tasted the 'grace of our Lord Jesus Christ, and the love of God, and the fellowship of (better "joint participation in") the Holy Spirit' (2 Cor. 13:14). The three experiences cannot be

94

divorced. As Peter puts it, 'you are chosen by God the Father, and set apart as his own by the Spirit for obedience to Jesus Christ and sprinkling with his blood' (1 Pet. 1:2). In other words, any experience of Christ is also an experience of the Holy Spirit who mediates Christ to us. In that fascinating passage in Romans 8:9–11 Paul recognises 'the Spirit of God' from Old Testament days to be none other than 'the Spirit of Christ', the Spirit who indwelt Christ and who is given us from Christ. Thus to have the Spirit is to have Christ, and vice versa. The Spirit is the one who makes Christ real to us. So 'if any man have not the Spirit of Christ he is no Christian'. It is right to say, 'If Christ is in you,' and in the next verse to say, 'If the Spirit of him who raised Jesus from the dead dwells in you,' for it is by means of the Spirit, the Spirit of God, the Spirit of Christ, that Jesus makes his home in the believer. The Spirit is the mode of the divine indwelling. That is why Jesus in St. John's Gospel can promise that through the arrival of the Paraclete not only he himself will come back and indwell the disciples, but so will the Father (John 14:17,18,21,23). We are back to the three act drama with which we began. Act Three reveals the deity actually resident within believers; and it is through the Spirit that this takes place.

Mutual indwelling

The New Testament writers sometimes speak of Christ living within Christians, sometimes of the Spirit doing so (Gal. 2:20, Col. 1:27, Rom. 8:10, 11, 1 Cor. 3:16). They sometimes speak of Christians being in Christ, and sometimes of being in the Spirit (Phil. 1:1, 1 Cor. 3:1, Rom. 8:1, 8:9, Col. 1:8, Eph. 2:22). It does not seem to matter very much which way we look at it. If you intertwine your fingers together, it is equally true to say that your right hand is in your left, or that your left hand is in your right. The point is that they are firmly connected. And that is what the New Testament wants to say about our relationship to Christ and his Spirit. On the whole there is a tendency to speak of us being in Christ, and of the Spirit being in us. That is the predominant emphasis, and it is a helpful one. Christ is the new man, the last Adam (1 Cor. 15:45), and Christians are members of his body (1 Cor. 12:12ff). The Spirit comes and takes up residence in our bodies, which he wants to use as his temple (1 Cor. 6:19).

Very well then. The Spirit comes and takes up residence in a person once he is invited in. What does he want to do?

The Spirit assures us – through sacraments

Assurance . . .

The first requirement, when someone passes 'out of darkness into light, from the power of Satan to God' (Acts 26:18) would seem to be that they need assurance. He needs to know he belongs to the new family, that he is 'accepted in the beloved one' (Eph. 1:6). And that is just what the Spirit does. St. John tells us that this is one of his main functions. 'This is how we know that he remains in us, by means of the Spirit whom he has given us' (1 John 3:24). He repeats it in 4:13, 'This is how we know that we remain in him, and he in us, because he has given us a portion of his Spirit.' And in chapter 5 he expands his meaning.

. . . through baptism

There are three grounds for Christian assurance, he tells us: 'the Spirit, the water and the blood'. This passage should be seen against its background. The Gnostic teacher, Cerinthus, was active in Asia Minor at the time when John wrote, and he taught that the heavenly Christ came upon the human Jesus only at his baptism, and left him before his passion: the union between them only *seemed* to be real – actually it was merely temporary. Had this been the case, there would have been no Christian gospel to preach: no incarnation of the Son of God, no real solidarity between him and us, no expiatory death upon the cross. John therefore opposes it strongly. Jesus, the Christ, is the one who has come through the water of his baptism, through the blood of his cross, and is mediated to us through the Holy Spirit. The coming through water, the cross, and the gift of the Spirit are all thoroughly historical events: and yet they are more than that. They are continuing factors in the life of the Church through the experience Christians have of the Spirit, and through the sacraments of water (baptism) and blood (the eucharist) which seem to be alluded to here. Baptism is a mark of belonging, a ground of assurance, which the Spirit can take home to our hearts. It was so to Martin Luther when he was tempted to despair of his spiritual state: '*Baptizatus sum*' he recalled with joy. Joy, because it did not rest upon his own faith, strongly through he valued that: but when in the morass of doubt, one has no confidence in subjective attitudes such as faith. But his baptism, administered to him by another, sealing physically upon him the objectiveness of what Christ did for him on the cross, that was indeed a ground of assurance. It was the sacrament of justification by grace; the physical, palpable reminder that God acted for him without his aid and prior to his response.

. . . and eucharist

The eucharist, too, is one of the ways in which the Spirit gives us assurance. This is strongly implied in John chapter 6 where the Spirit is brought closely into relation with 'eating his body and drinking his blood' and so being confident of dwelling in Christ, being fed by him, and being raised up by him at the last day (6:54,56,63); just as he is in chapter 3:3–8 in connection with the new birth. Of course the sacraments can be completely empty, like the marriage ceremony. But just as it is proper for me to look back to my wedding day as assurance that I am really married, so it is proper to look back to my baptism as a mark given me by the Holy Spirit that I am really born again in Christ, and to the eucharist as a pledge that I do partake of his life, feed on him, and shall in the last day share his resurrection.

The Spirit assures us – through signs

Signs of life

But it is not only through the sacraments that the Spirit assures us we belong to Christ. 1 John gives several other ways which enable us to be confident of our new status. The Spirit means us to know where we stand (1 John 3:24, 5:13) and the Epistle is at pains to point out various signs which give confidence to true believers, while breaking down false assurance.

Changed behaviour

Christians should expect the indwelling Spirit to make a difference. If there is no difference, there is good reason to suppose that the Spirit has not been received into someone's life. Thus a believer begins to 'keep God's word' or 'walk as Christ walked' (2:5,6): 'he does not go on sinning, because God's seed remains in him, and he cannot go on sinning, because he is born of God' (3:9). Of course John does not mean that the Christian becomes sinless overnight. He knows full well that Christians can and do sin, and if we pretend otherwise we are lying (1:8,10). But he is insisting, in black and white terms, that the divine sonship, mediated by the Spirit, must show itself in changed behaviour. We cannot go on untouched in the old self-centred ways if the Holy Spirit has made his residence within us.

Fellowship

Another of the marks of belonging is a willingness to face the opposition of 'the world' (a technical term in the Johannine literature to indicate society which has left God out), and to get involved in the loving fellowship of the family of Christ. 'Do not be surprised, my brothers, if the world hates you. We know that we have passed from death to life because we love brother Christians' (3:13f).

Love, joy, and power

What is more, the Spirit who has become resident in the followers of Jesus mediates to them the victory over the world which Jesus had (4:4) as they trust him for the power to overcome temptation (5:3,4). Joyous fellowship, too, is a mark of the new life which the Spirit initiates in us (1:3,4), and so is the experience of answered prayer (5:14). Most of all, perhaps, the love for God and for our fellows which the Holy Spirit produces in our hearts, a quality which we do not possess independently of him (4:18ff).

Inner confidence

Over and above all this, John tells us of the internal testimony of the Holy Spirit with the spirit of the believer, assuring him that God's testimony to his Son is reliable, assuring him that the Christian experience is real. Christians are meant not only to *believe* in Jesus, but to *know* that we have eternal life (5:13) and it is the task of the Spirit to bring this quiet confidence home to us.

Assurance not presumption

After all, we need to know we belong. No one can erect a building of any serious dimensions on a rickety foundation. It would not be possible to live a Christian life on the shifting sand of doubt as to our relationship with our Lord. Accordingly, it is not modesty to say, 'I hope I am a Christian, but I cannot say more.' That might indeed be the proper thing to say if being a Christian were the result of my own efforts, goodness or achievements. But the New Testament writers insist with one voice that it is nothing of the kind. I am saved by God's gracious intervention on my behalf, not by 'works' of whatever type. So I have nothing to boast of. 'It is all of God that you are in Christ Jesus', says Paul to the Corinthians (1 Cor. 1:30), 'and God makes Christ to be our wisdom, righteousness, sanctification and redemption, so that, as the Scripture says, "He that boasts must boast in the Lord."' It is not, therefore, presumptuous to say with quiet confidence, 'I know that I belong to Christ. I have not done anything to earn it, but God has given me the Spirit and accepted me into his family; and he means me to know that I belong.'

Five aspects of belonging to the Spirit

There are five words in particular which the New Testament writers use to describe different aspects of this work of assurance which the Holy Spirit does for the believer.

Adoption

The first is the metaphor of 'adoption'. Paul alludes to a pagan custom, rare indeed in the Jewish world, whereby a man might adopt the children of another family into his own. It was quite common for the Emperor to adopt his putative successor in this way. And this, says the apostle, is what God has done for us. Jesus died to redeem us, and adopt us into the Father's family; and because we are sons God has sent the Spirit of his Son into our hearts, enabling us to call 'Abba Father' (Gal. 4:5,6, Eph. 1:5, Rom. 8:15). The Spirit of Jesus, entering our lives, comes to us as God's adoption present, so to speak, and enables us to call God by the intimate family name which Jesus used and which we have already considered. The Holy Spirit accomplishes and applies to us our sonship, and all the privileges that flow from it: 'for if children, then we are heirs, heirs of God and joint heirs with Christ' (Rom. 8:17).

Seal

The second word is 'seal'. Paul tells the Ephesians that having heard the word of truth and having believed the good news of salvation, they are 'in Christ' and have been sealed with the Holy Spirit who was promised long ago (1:13, cf. 2 Cor. 2:21).

'Seal' is a property word. It speaks of belonging. The Holy
Spirit is given us to identify us as belonging to Jesus, just as the
seal on a letter or the brand on a sheep identifies it as mine.
There may even be a double nuance in the assurance of ownership that is mentioned here. The seal of the Spirit is meant to
assure us that we belong to Christ, and to let others also know
the fact. It is perhaps an anachronism to read back into New
Testament times the usage of second-century Christians
whereby this word 'seal' was explicitly used of baptism, or
sometimes confirmation. Paul uses it of the Spirit, without any
indication of any outward sign. But in view of passages in
Revelation like 7:3 which speak of 'sealing the servants of God
in their foreheads', and Romans 4:11 which speaks of circumcision as 'the sign and seal of being in the right with God
through faith', it is not impossible that baptism may have been
in the apostle's mind when he spoke of this sealing with the
Spirit. What circumcision was to men of faith under the old
covenant, assuring them that they belonged to Yahweh, so
baptism is to the Christian; and Colossians 2:11,12 brings the
two ordinances together round the cross of Christ which alone
gives them meaning.

First instalment

Another word which Paul uses of the Spirit who assures
Christians of their position is 'guarantee' or pledge. Two of its
three occurrences go with the 'sealing' work of the Spirit (2 Cor.
1:22, Eph. 1:14. The other one is 2 Corinthians 5:5). If 'seal' is
the property word, 'pledge' is the prophetic word. It looks
forward to a greater gift in the future while stressing a real gift
in the present. Often used in commerce for a 'down-payment',
or 'first instalment', it is a highly appropriate word for the Holy
Spirit. He is God's first instalment of the future salvation that
awaits us; the part of the future we have now in the present; the
pledge of the fuller life that is to come. Indeed, the modern
Greeks use that word for an engagement ring, and that gives not

a bad idea of the Holy Spirit's work as 'pledge' in Paul's thought. He is the heavenly Lover's engagement ring given to us. We shall carry that engagement ring with us into God's future, when we have the full wedding ring of final union with Christ. At present, the Spirit is the pledge of blessing to come. He is a real part of the age to come that is available to us here and now: he will never be supplanted. But there is more to come, in the fulness of God's time. Such is the nuance of the Spirit as 'earnest of our inheritance'.

Firstfruits

The fourth word is 'firstfruits'. This is a word from farming. If the firstfruits are good, so will the main crop be. The metaphor is used in the New Testament in a variety of ways. Epaenetus was the firstfruit of the harvest of converts in the province of Asia (Rom. 16:5). Christ's resurrection is seen as a firstfruit from the grave, and pledge of the great harvest to come when those who are in Christ will share his risen life in heaven (1 Cor. 15:20,23). Paul takes comfort from the firstfruits of Jewish believers that the whole nation will, in God's time, turn back to the Lord (Rom. 11:16). And the Holy Spirit is given as a firstfruit of the harvest God has in store for us (Rom. 8:23).

Assurance

A fifth word to describe this witness of the Spirit with our spirit that we are indeed sons of God (Rom. 8:16) is 'assurance'. In 1 Thessalonians 1:5 Paul reminds his readers how the gospel was first preached to them: 'it came not in word only, but in power and in the Holy Spirit and in full assurance'. The literal meaning seems to be that a man is so full of the Holy Spirit that he carries conviction when he speaks about Christ. Christian assurance is no merely intellectual persuasion, but an overwhelmingly convincing experience of the indwelling Spirit welling up within us and

flowing out to others. Such is the confidence that the Spirit
means to give believers.

Already . . . and not yet

But a final word is needed before we leave this side of the
Spirit's work. There is an 'already' and a 'not yet' about the
Spirit's witness of assurance. This reminder of the 'not yet' is
clear in the 'pledge'. God has not yet come back to buy up his
possessions (the Christians), for whom he has given the
down-payment of the Spirit (Eph. 1:14); and it is in the
context of our future inheritance beyond death that Paul
speaks of the Spirit as our 'guarantee' in 2 Corinthians 5:5.
Similarly 'seal' has a future look to it. Ephesians 4:30 tells us
that the Spirit seals us in preparation for the day of redemption: the 'already' and the 'not yet' are united in that phrase.
To speak of a 'firstfruits' inevitably takes one's eyes to the 'not
yet' (and this is made explicit in Romans 8:23). Even our
sonship, mediated to us by the Spirit, has this ambiguity
about it. On the one hand we can be sure that the Spirit makes
us sons (Rom. 8:15). On the other, we have still to wait for our
final adoption at the Second Coming (Rom. 8:23). And to
match our assurance, our being so full of the Spirit that he
bubbles over from us, there is the other side of the picture: we
also groan in the Spirit, and he groans with us (Rom. 8:26).
For the Spirit's work in assurance is to give us a firm foundation to build on, not to make us arrogant; the 'already' and
the 'not yet' of the Spirit's internal witness enable us to be sure
without being cocksure.

2. THE SPIRIT IN CHRISTIAN CHARACTER

After assuring us of our sonship the Spirit sets out to reproduce
in us the character and graces of the family into which we have
been adopted. First and foremost he brings us into an entirely
new dimension of freedom.

The Spirit of freedom

Christian freedom – not trying hard

Paul in particular found that when he preached the forgiveness
and gift of the Spirit which Christ made possible he ran up
against a deeply entrenched problem. The Jews of his day had
come to see the Old Testament law not as a pointer to the life
of trusting obedience in God which it was meant to be, but
rather a code to be scrupulously followed in every detail. If you
managed to do this, you would earn, indeed almost compel
from God, a favourable verdict at the Last Day. It all depended
on human effort. Justification would come from law-keeping.
This belief, though not taught in the Old Testament, was widely
held in the Jewish constituency among whom Paul worked: it is
widely believed today that if only you try hard and do your
best, God will accept you at the last. The apostle attacks this
belief with a battery of arguments. Galatians 3:10–14 is a good
example.

Trying hard will not do . . .

First, he shows scathingly that it cannot be done, this perfect
law-keeping. If you do not keep *all* the things written in the
book of the law, you remain under its curse as a lawbreaker. As
James put it in his Epistle, 'whoever keeps the whole law but
fails in one point has become guilty of all of it' (2:10). If legal
contract is what you are after, one slip in the contract is
sufficient to invalidate it. And which of us has not broken the
law of God not just once but thousands of times? So getting in
the right with God is impossible for human beings to achieve
by their own efforts. As guilty failures we all come beneath that
'curse' imposed on lawbreakers. 'All the world is guilty before
God,' Jew and Gentile, virtuous and wicked alike (Rom. 3:19).
All have come short of the divine standard for human life; none
can lay claim to earning the verdict of acquittal by keeping the
law in its entirety: 'for there is no distinction, since all have

sinned and come short of the glory of God' (Rom. 3:23). It is not only overt actions which are reprehensible, but rather the thoughts of the heart and that attitude of rebellion against God which characterise us all (Rom. 3:9–20).

. . . and is unacceptable

Secondly, even if we could achieve the impossible and live a perfect life, fulfilling the divine requirements in all particulars, a doctrine of merit would remain unacceptable to the God of the Bible. For, according to the prophets, 'he who by faith is righteous shall live'; and the law does not rest on faith, for 'he who does them shall live by them' (Gal. 3:12). The whole principle of merit militates against the personal God whom Scripture depicts as wanting to have personal relations with his creatures. The father in a family can never be satisfied if his children clean his shoes and lay the table, but never talk to him, and never hug him. How could the heavenly Father be satisfied with mechanical obedience devoid of love and trust?

. . . and is not God's way

And thirdly, Paul argues that the way of self-commendation to God by merit is not the way of God's heroes in the Old Testament. The Jews of Paul's day could draw no credit for being sons of Abraham unless their attitude was like that of Abraham. God gave his inheritance to Abraham by promise, not as a reward for law-keeping (Gal. 3:18). He graciously appeared to Abraham, who had no claim on him, and offered to give him a posterity like the stars of heaven: Abraham responded to this grace by an act of faith which issued in a life of obedience. The whole thrust of Paul's argument at this point, and again in Romans, is that the true Jew follows the example of Abraham, and responds in faith and obedience to the God who meets him in grace: and that is precisely the terms of the gospel which Paul preaches. The only difference is this. Abraham was accepted by God in virtue of what Christ *would do* upon the cross by bearing the curse of the broken law upon his representative shoulders: men living after the cross could be accepted by God as they put their trust in what God *had done* for them through Jesus. That is the only difference. 'Christ redeemed us from the curse of the law, having become a curse for us – for it is written "Cursed be every one who hangs upon a tree" – so that in Christ Jesus the blessing accorded to Abraham might come upon the Gentiles, that we might receive the promised Spirit through faith' (Gal. 3:14). The mysterious irony of salvation lay in this paradox: Jesus, the only one who kept the law in its entirety, paid the penalty of lawbreakers, by being exposed upon that accursed cross and subject to the judgment of God. He acted as the substitute and the representative for the whole human race. As a result believers under the old covenant and under the new are accepted before God as if they were sinless, for they are incorporated in the sinless Messiah who stood in their place of sin and judgment (2 Cor. 5:21). They are 'justified' by the grace of God that gives them what they do not deserve, and by the 'faith' which grasps that proffered gift and responds in obedient dedication to that proffered love. God's way of salvation is shown to be the same throughout the ages: men respond in faith to his initiative in grace. Through the crucial action of Abraham's offspring, 'which is Christ' (Gal. 3:16) even the despised Gentiles can become children of that archetypal believer, Abraham, and receive the promised Spirit.

The deadness of legalism

Away, then, with all attempts at self-justification before God. They are impossible, immoral, and out of step with the whole history of salvation. The Messiah has done for us what we could never do by putting us in the right with God; and the gift of his Spirit releases us from the need to try to justify ourselves. 'Did you receive the Spirit: by works of the law, or by hearing with faith?' asks Paul of the Galatians who were being tempted to go back to legalism (Gal. 3:2). The Spirit brings new life, new freedom from those old legalistic attitudes. 'We serve not under the old written code, but in the new life of the Spirit' (Rom. 7:6). 'The written code kills, but the Spirit gives life' (2 Cor. 3:6); new life, and liberation from this whole depressing attempt to justify ourselves. 'Where the Spirit of the Lord is, there is liberty' (2 Cor. 3:17).

The Spirit of power

Liberty not licence

But liberty does not mean licence. If Jesus died in order to make the unjust justified, he also endowed them with his Spirit in order to make them just. God has done for us what law-keeping, weakened by the frailties of our own fallen nature, could never do. He sent his own Son in human flesh, identical with us except for sin, and he condemned man's sinfulness in Christ's person, hanging upon the cross, as a sin-offering for us. He did so in order that the just requirement set out in God's law might be fulfilled in us who live our lives not after the principle of self-effort but in the power of the Spirit. That is a rough paraphrase of Romans 8:3,4. It shows that Christ's work of sin-bearing did not abrogate the moral claims of the law, but was the precondition to men being able to face up to them. In other words, we are not forgiven because we keep the law: but once we are forgiven we are called to keep it. The claim of a holy God that those who have fellowship with him should not only be acquitted and accounted righteous, but actually and progressively be made righteous in an ethical sense is strongly brought out in the Pauline letters. He will not for a moment allow that the doctrine of justification through free grace, received by faith, can lead to antinomianism (Rom. 6:1ff). Far from it. For justification, and the baptism which is its outward symbol, means dying with Christ and rising again; dying to the old sinful ways, and being prepared to see them as characteristics of the unregenerate nature that was dealt with on the cross by Jesus and must be kept there. And it means rising with Christ too; rising to share in the new life which he makes possible, and which in the fullest detail Paul, in Romans chapter eight, ascribes to the Spirit of Jesus, resident within us.

The power to fulfil God's law

The law of God had demanded holiness, but could not enable it. The law remained an external authority expressing God's requirements, but providing no power to keep them. The demand and the requirements still stand. But through the Spirit, God has given us the ability to fulfil those requirements. Not only is there 'no condemnation for those who are in Christ Jesus', but 'the law of the Spirit of life in Christ Jesus has set me free from the law of sin and death' (Rom. 8:1, 2). Paul finds himself not only with a new pardon now he is united with Christ: but also with a new power. The Spirit of Jesus has come within him, and provides a higher law than the law of sin and death. By this he means that the principle he had known as dominant in his life was the principle of sin and the death to which it inevitably led. Now in Christ, he has a new principle active within him, a higher law, the life-giving power of the Spirit. Just as the higher law of life stops an apple held in my hand from obeying the law of gravity to which it would otherwise be subject, so the law (as he daringly calls it) of the Spirit overcomes the sin-death principle to which the Christian would otherwise be subject.

The battle

There is nothing automatic about this. Paul knows, not only from pre-conversion experience but, as a careful reading of Romans 7 will show, from painful experience of struggle and failure *as a Christian*, that when he relies on himself and his own resources (such seems to be the nuance of 'I of myself' in Romans 7:25), he remains subject to the law of sin. But, thanks to what God has made available through Jesus Christ our Lord, Paul knows that we need not remain defeated. Though the sinful propensities remain in us till our dying day, they need not be dominant. Through the Spirit we can put to death the deeds of the 'flesh' (by which he means unredeemed human nature, alienated from God, Rom. 8:13). And at the end of our human course, the Spirit who can overcome sin, will also prove his ability to transcend death. 'If the Spirit of him who raised Jesus from the dead dwells in you, he who raised up Christ Jesus from the dead will also give life to your mortal bodies through his Spirit which dwells in you' (8:11).

In other words, it is the Spirit of Jesus who reproduces in us the crucifixion and the resurrection of our Lord. The old unregenerate 'I' is nailed to the cross with Christ (Gal. 2:20): we 'live in the Spirit' or 'walk in the Spirit' precisely in so far as we allow the Spirit to 'crucify the flesh with its affections and lusts' (Gal. 5:24). And equally it is the Spirit who liberates Christ's risen power in us and enables us to share in his triumph. So 'walk in the Spirit, and you shall not fulfil the lusts of the flesh' (Gal. 5:16). In Romans 8 and Galatians 5 Paul makes it very clear that a battle royal rages in the lives of believers; a far greater battle than before their union with Christ. This is because the Spirit is opposed to the fallen human nature I am born with (and do not lose after my incorporation into Christ). The two principles are opposed to one another. And the ensuing battle, of which all Christians are aware in their experience, means either that they cannot achieve the good intentions they have or, if the Greek is taken in another sense, that the presence of the mighty Spirit prevents them doing what, if they followed the dictates of mere self-will, they otherwise would (Gal. 5:17). In any case, we are reminded of the spiritual battle. Power over the inclinations of the fallen 'flesh' is possible only when the Spirit is given control by our act of deliberate choice. He has the power to overcome my fallen appetites, but he will not use it in me unless I ask him.

The transformation

Mercifully, the Spirit works deeply within my subconscious self.
When I am so self-centred that I would not dream of asking the
Spirit for his strength, preferring to go my own way, I am
encouraged to recall that 'God is at work in you both to will and
to work for his good pleasure' (Phil. 2:13). We shall not be mistaken in seeing that as a reference to God the Holy Spirit. He it
is who not only empowers us to do right, but works in us the
desire to want to do right, without which we would never dream
of turning to ask him for his strength.

But that strength is available to all who are in Christ. It is
none other than the superhuman power which raised Christ
from the dead which is let loose within our human bodies (Eph.
1:18f). Paul is evidently referring to the Spirit when talking of
this power, since he not only prays that the Spirit will reveal it
to his readers, but he, in common with other New Testament
writers, associates the Spirit with the resurrection of Christ
from the dead (1 Tim. 3:16, cf. 1 Pet. 3:18). In Ephesians 3:16
Paul makes it quite explicit. He prays that 'according to the
riches of his glory, the Father may grant you to be strengthened
with might through his Spirit in the inner man'.

The Spirit of Christlikeness

The seed of the Spirit

This power given to individuals by the Spirit is not the naked
ruach that we sometimes met with in the Old Testament days in
men like Saul and Samson. It is the powerful application to
believers of the character of Christ. Thus when Paul is talking
about the spiritual battle in Galatians 5, the content of the
Christian freedom he advocates is defined by the character of
Jesus. This powerful, victorious Spirit which indwells believers,
and can keep their sinful natures nailed upon the cross, is like a
seed planted in the soil of the believer's life. If cultivated and

THE SPIRIT IN THE INDIVIDUAL

nourished, this seed will grow into a lovely fruitful tree; and this is what the fruit is like:

> love, joy, peace, patience, kindness, goodness, faithfulness, gentleness, self-control (Gal. 5:22).

And what is that, but a description of the character of Jesus? A holy God requires his people to be holy. But the God who 'has called us for holiness . . . gives us his Holy Spirit' (1 Thess. 4:7,8) to enable us to fulfil his requirement. This holiness is not merely a devotion to the deity (there was plenty of such attachment in the ancient world that was far from holy – for instance the cult prostitution that was so common in the temples), nor a mere adherence to ethical rules (there were plenty of those current in antiquity, too, and they possessed all the disadvantages, while lacking the advantages, of the Jewish law). Christian holiness involves both devotion and ethics; it springs from allegiance to Jesus, who embodies in himself the ideal of human conduct.

The qualities of Jesus

Consequently we find the characteristics of Jesus being stressed time and again throughout the New Testament as the qualities which the Holy Spirit seeks to produce in Christ's people. The kingly rule of God which Jesus proclaimed and so signally embodied is not a matter of mere externals, what you eat or drink; but righteousness, peace and joy in the Holy Spirit (Rom. 14:17), and all three were pre-eminently to be found in Jesus. Power marked the apostolic preaching in the Holy Spirit at Thessalonica, and joy marked its reception by the new believers (1 Thess. 1:5f). The Spirit that rested upon the suffering Messiah rests upon suffering Christians (1 Pet. 4:14). Just as Jesus' life was the embodiment of God's love, so we find that the Holy Spirit is particularly given to believers to live out God's own love in their loveless lives. 'God's own love has been poured into our hearts by the Holy Spirit who has been given us,' says

Paul in Romans 5:5, and he rejoices to hear of that 'love in the Spirit', which is to be found in the church at Colossae (1:8). So cardinal a quality is this, so clear a mark of a man being filled with the Spirit of Christ, that in the middle of his three chapters on spiritual gifts (1 Cor. 12–14), Paul sets the crowning gift of love. One has only to substitute the name of Jesus for 'love' in that chapter to see that the whole thing is a pen picture of Christ's way of life. The first and foremost fruit of the Spirit is that outgoing love for others, irrespective of their deserts, which marked the Giver of the Spirit in his earthly life.

The way to holiness

True holiness, into which the Spirit calls us, is nothing other than Christlikeness. And in one marvellous passage, in which he contrasts the old dispensation with the new, Paul reaches this point as the climax of his theme. The Lord who had revealed himself fitfully and alternately under the old covenant, when Moses commuted between the Lord on Sinai and the people on the plain (with the glory reflected from his communing with God waxing and waning correspondingly), has now revealed himself steadily and with unwithdrawn accessibility. Under the new covenant Yahweh makes himself present to his people as Spirit (which seems to be the meaning of the much discussed 'Now the Lord is the Spirit', 2 Cor. 3:17); and as such his presence is constant, unwithdrawn and steady. The divine presence, concentrated in Christ, and universalised through his death and resurrection, becomes available to transform his people. As we fix our gaze upon the Lord Jesus, worship him, and reflect on his character brought before us in the Gospels, our faces will shine, as Moses' did when he went in to seek the presence of the Lord. But the glory will not fade from the Christian as it did from Moses. It will increase. God's purpose is to change us by his Spirit within us (the word 'change' is used in the Gospels to denote Jesus' transfiguration!); and to change us from one degree of glory to another. 'Glory' indicates the person and character of God, under the imagery of light. If we want to see the glory of God (which no-one can do in all its unmediated radiance, and live, Exod. 33:20) then we must seek it in the person of Jesus. In him the glory of God shines out in human form (John 1:14, 2 Cor. 4:4). Well, the work of the Spirit in the believer is supremely to transform us from one degree of glory to another: that is to say, to make us more and more like Christ.

Daily reward

In Titus 3:5 the Holy Spirit is said to be the one who not only regenerates us, but who renews us; and this work of renewal of our natures from within is stressed in Romans 12:2 (as we present our bodies a living sacrifice to God) and in Colossians 3:10. There Paul explains that the new kind of life they live through union with the crucified and risen Christ involves having done with 'anger, wrath, malice, blasphemy, filthy talk' which characterised 'the old man' (i.e. their fallen human nature). Instead they are to put on, as if it were a suit of new clothes, the new humanity that is brought to them in Christ and is constantly renewed by a deepening knowledge of Christ, into the Creator's original image in man, a likeness to God himself: hence the 'compassion, kindness, lowliness, meekness, patience, forbearance', love, peace and gratitude of which he goes on to speak (Col. 3:1, 5–16). It is the work of the Spirit, then, to make us progressively reflect the character of Christ, himself the Last Man who demonstrates the image of God which God intended for humankind when he originally created us.

Progressive sanctification

The process of Christlikeness is a progressive one: let nobody think he has attained it. Paul himself after decades of knowing Christ could still say that he had not attained the purpose for which Christ laid hold of him; he was still following on (Phil. 3:8–15). But as he grew older, and felt the signs of decay in his mortal body, he rejoiced to think that his inner man was being renewed every day, until he should attain that 'being at home with the Lord' to which his whole Christian life was directed and of which he had been given the Holy Spirit as a guarantee (2 Cor. 4:16f, 5:1ff,5,8).

So in our sanctification as in our assurance, there is always an 'already' and a 'not yet' about the work of the Spirit. He is indeed given us to actualise in us the character of Christ: but that process will not be complete until we see him as he is, either at death or the Parousia. Let St. John have the last word on the subject. 'Beloved, we are God's children now; it does not yet appear what we shall be, but we know that when he appears we shall be like him, for we shall see him as he is. And everyone who thus hopes in him purifies himself' (1 John 3:2f).

3. THE SPIRIT IN CHRISTIAN GROWTH

The Holy Spirit, who is both one with God and resident in us, has a further role in the life of the believer. He is indeed, as John Taylor has aptly called him, 'the go-between God', for he both takes the things of God and makes them real to us on the one hand, and takes our faint longings and prayers and brings them to the Father on the other.

The Spirit illuminates God

Paul develops an interesting and original line of argument in 1 Corinthians 2. He is explaining that the Christian message is no earthly wisdom, such as the travelling philosophers of the day peddled, and with which some of the Corinthians were confusing it. No, it is nothing less than God's truth mediated to them by God's Spirit (2:9). And just as human wisdom is only perceived and passed on by the human spirit inside us, so it is with the truth of God. Nobody can comprehend the things of God: if there is to be any comprehension on our part, then the onus is on God to reveal himself. That he has done. The Spirit has been given us to enable us to understand not the future, but the gracious gifts God has already made over to us (2:12).

Jesus, the focus of all illumination

But did we not read in St. John that it is Jesus who makes the Father known and discloses to us his nature (John 1:18, 3:13 etc.)? Certainly. But the same Gospel makes it plain that the Spirit will interpret Jesus as the focal point of all God's revelation. That is why 'the Spirit of truth, who proceeds from the Father' is shown in his role of bearing witness to Jesus who is the truth of God incarnate (John 15:16, 16:14,15,14:6). Paul sees it in precisely the same way as John. In 1 Corinthians 2 he can say almost in the same breath that it is the Spirit who shows believers the deep things of God, and that we have the mind of Christ. Once again we come up against the indissoluble link between the Spirit and Jesus. He does indeed reveal to us God's gracious provision for us. But the name of that provision is Jesus. In many other places in the New Testament the Spirit who was active in the prophets is promised to the Christians to guide them, but always that guidance centres upon Jesus in whom the truth of God took personal form. Thus in Romans 8:14 we are promised the guidance of the Spirit, but it is along the pathway of sonship wherein we follow Jesus in addressing God as 'Abba', and share his mortification and risen life.

A prayer for Ephesus

In Ephesians 1:17f Paul prays that the readers may have the spiritual illumination afforded by the Spirit. But this illumination is granted by the God of our Lord Jesus Christ and is possible only 'in knowing him'. The Spirit enables us to know the Master, to sense his will, to grasp his mind and to see things his way. In particular it is Paul's prayer that the Spirit would reveal to them three things.

First, 'the hope of his calling'. In that phrase the Spirit

characteristically mediates between the 'already' and the 'not yet'. The calling is past. The hope is future. The first instalment of heaven, the Spirit himself, enables us to see the reality of our calling and its future consummation.

Second, 'the wealth of the glory of his inheritance in the saints', a deliberately ambiguous phrase which could mean that the saints have God as their inheritance – and what inexhaustible riches lie there! But it could also mean the even more staggering truth that the saints are God's inheritance, and pose the question to what extent he is allowed the freehold of that inheritance which is our lives.

Third, Paul prays that they may perceive 'the extreme greatness of his power to aid believers, the very power that raised Christ from the dead of God's right hand'. And so we are brought by the Spirit's revelations back to Christ again. No further light has broken, nor will break, from God than Christ: the Spirit's task is to illuminate him to us. And to make this centrality of Christ even more emphatic the apostle ends his paragraph by reminding the readers that this mighty, risen, ascended Christ is the head of the body constituted by the Church, and his fulness fills their lives (or, perhaps, their lives are the complement of his fulness, Eph. 1:23).

A prayer for Colossae

When in Colossians 1:9ff Paul prays for Christians he has never met, his first request is that the Spirit would give them understanding of the Lord's will for their lives; then, that they should live their lives in accordance with that will by pleasing the Lord in everything; then, that they should increase in their knowledge of God; and finally, that they should be strengthened with all might according to the measure of his glorious power which should result for them as it did for Christ, not in arrogance but in patience and long-suffering. Such was the Christian path of *imitatio Christi* on which the Spirit could be relied to shed the light of his illumination. The

Christocentric nature of his revelation is once more to the fore; so is the characteristic Hebrew emphasis on knowledge leading to obedience.

Illumination in 1 John

In the Gnostic situation to which 1 John was addressed, 'knowledge' was the 'in' word, and false teachers were laying exclusive claims to it. John's response is to say that they did not need false teachers, or any other teachers for that matter: 'you have been anointed (lit. "Christed") by the Holy One, and you all know' (2:20). There is no doubt about the content of this divinely imparted illumination: 'who is a liar but he who denies that Jesus is the Christ?' (2:22) They are warned not to believe every spiritual manifestation, because the authentic disclosures of the Spirit always bear witness to the incarnate Jesus. 'By this you know the Spirit of God: every spirit that confesses that Jesus has come in the flesh is of God, and every spirit that does not confess Jesus is not of God' (4:2). Confident that the anointing they have all received is the person of the Spirit of the Anointed One, who remains with them (2:27), John knows he can safely leave their instruction to that same Spirit who is true and who shows them how to abide in Christ, the Christ who will one day return (2:28f). It is thoroughly in line with this that the author of Revelation can say, 'Witness to Jesus is the Spirit of prophecy' (19:10). For Jesus is God's final word to men; and the Spirit illuminates and interprets but does not add to that word.

The Spirit will teach

This means that if a man is truly brought to faith in Christ, he is not dependent on human teachers to lead him on, helpful though these may be. He has the heavenly Spirit to be his teacher. And he can safely set down to the Spirit's guidance anything which brings Jesus into sharper focus. I learnt this lesson some years ago when the soldier to whom I referred earlier came to Christ. I was at the time very concerned, because he was posted almost immediately to North Africa, and there was no chance of helping him forward in the early days of his Christian life. I heard some months later that he was organising a Bible study in his quarters in North Africa to which not only fellow subalterns were coming but even such exalted members of the Army hierarchy as majors! He had no human teacher, but he had the Spirit of Christ and the Scriptures, and through them he grew in knowledge and in spiritual stature.

The Spirit guides believers

Two common mistakes

The problem of how the Spirit of God guides us is one which confronts every humble Christian. There is no easy answer, for the Spirit blows where he wills, and man can neither prescribe to him nor control him. In practice, two tendencies are discernible in the Church. The first is to suppose that God always guides by the majority vote, by the reasonable thing, by sanctified common sense. This can easily deteriorate into prudential judgment, worldly planning and manipulation of voting procedures. The second is to suppose that the guidance of God is always extraordinary, individualistic and sudden.

Four strands in guidance

David Watson has some wise words to say on the matter in his *One in the Spirit* (p. 54ff). He draws together from the Bible four strands in divine guidance which, taken together, provide a confident basis for action, and avoid excessive recourse to that overworked claim, 'The Lord told me to do such and such.'

First, God guides through circumstances (Acts 16:10). God closes some doors and opens others; our responsibility is to be sensitive to his leading, and to follow through the doors when they open.

Second, God guides through other Christians, as he did in
Acts 6 when the whole multitude chose the Seven, or in Acts
13 when the Spirit spoke to the church at Antioch about the
need for Paul and Barnabas to go abroad. Personal convictions
should be open to testing by the guidance of other Christians.
If our conviction really comes from God, others, who are in
touch with God, will confirm it. 'The Christian who will not
listen to reason is a fool,' says Watson forthrightly. To be sure,
this is not the only criterion: the voices of other Christians may
be very confused. But at least we must be willing in principle
to receive guidance through other members of the Body of
Christ.

Third, God guides us through the Scriptures. The Spirit who
inspired their writing is perfectly well capable of taking some
part of them and writing it on our hearts so that it becomes an
inescapable pointer to a particular course of action. This
method, also, taken by itself, is liable to abuse. To pick verses at
random from the Bible proves nothing at all, except that we are
gullible and are not using the Scriptures as we are intended to.
Paul's advice is very different: 'Let the word of Christ dwell in
you richly, as you teach and admonish one another in all
wisdom' (Col. 3:16). An increasingly broad appreciation of the
Scriptures will give us a developing ability to scent the will of
God in any given situation.

Fourth, God guides us in prayer. Watson points to
Colossians 3:15, 'Let the peace of Christ rule (i.e. be the arbiter)
in your hearts.' There is such a thing as praying a situation
through until one is virtually sure of the will of God on the
matter. One has a deep inner peace about it; not absolute intellectual certainty, but practical confidence, which allows one to
proceed to action with joyful assurance. These are some of the
ways in which we may expect the Spirit of God to illuminate not
only the person of God but his will for us. He is the supreme
Teacher for Christians who are growing in grace and in knowledge of their Lord.

The Spirit empowers prayer

The Spirit – object of prayer

As go-between, the Spirit not only teaches us the truth of God,
he opens our eyes to the one in whom that truth became incarnate, and guides us in our lives. He also enables us to approach
God in prayer. We have already seen that it is through the
uniting Spirit that Jew and Gentile alike have access to the
Father (Eph. 2:18). We have noticed that it is the Spirit who
enables the adopted sons to call God 'Father', 'Abba', that intimate form of address first found on the lips of Jesus. Bearing in
mind that 'Abba' is the opening word of the Lord's Prayer in
Aramaic, we could rightly say that only through the Spirit can
we pray and live out that prayer. Indeed, in the immediate
context of the Lucan Lord's Prayer, Jesus promises that the
Father will give the Holy Spirit to those who ask him. The Spirit
is thus the supreme object of prayer. And it is interesting to see
how Luke works this theme out in his two-volume work. He
tells us that as Jesus was praying before his baptism the Spirit
came upon him. As the disciples were at prayer in Jerusalem
awaiting Pentecost, the Spirit came upon them. Saul of Tarsus
after his Damascus road experience spent three days in fasting
and prayer; that showed he was in the receptive mood which
invited the Spirit to come. It was the same with Cornelius,
another great landmark in the spread of the gospel in Acts. It
was as Cornelius waited humbly and receptively in prayer, that
God's supreme gift, the Holy Spirit, was poured out upon him
before ever Peter who was preaching the good news to him,
reached the climax of his sermon! Luke could scarcely under-
line more strongly that the supreme object of prayer is the Holy
Spirit of God.

The Spirit – inspirer of prayer

But that is not all. The Spirit who is the supreme object of
prayer is also the prime inspirer of prayer. Not only does he

enable us to cry 'Abba' with the joyous obedience and trust of newly adopted members of the family; not only does he enable us to pray and articulate words of the prayer that Jesus taught us. He initiates prayer within us on at least three other levels.

In the first place, we read of Christians 'praying in the Holy Spirit' (Jude 20, Eph. 6:18). This seems to indicate a deep, free, and intensive time of prayer, when the Spirit takes over and controls and leads the prayers, and one can go on praying for several hours without being aware of the passage of time. Those who have taken part in nights of prayer can, no doubt, all recall such times when the Holy Spirit has led people to pray in harmony, with intensity, with breadth, with perseverance and assurance. 'Pray at all times in the Spirit,' writes Paul, 'with all prayer and supplication. To that end keep alert with all perseverance, making supplication for all saints, and also for me . . . that I may declare the gospel boldly, as I ought to' (Eph. 6:18f). It is fascinating in this context concerning the spiritual warfare in which we are engaged to notice how he ascribes the work of the Spirit to two juxtaposed concepts: prayer, and the Word of God which he calls the sword of the Spirit. The go-between God addresses us primarily through the Word or message enshrined in the Scriptures; and he enables us to address God with freedom and confidence in prayer.

A second way in which the Spirit inspires prayer is by giving to the person in question the gift of tongues. We shall be examining this in another chapter. It is sufficient to notice here that speaking in tongues is one of the gifts of the Spirit to his people (1 Cor. 12:10), and that the primary purpose is to enable the recipient to pray to God from the depths of his being and not merely from the conscious levels of his mind. Indeed, the conscious mind is not employed when the Christian prays in tongues to the Lord (1 Cor. 14:14). But perhaps we have grown over-concerned about the conscious levels of rationality and suppressed for too long the reservoirs of subconscious feeling which the Spirit seems to touch and use when a person prays in tongues, with the result that he is built up, even though he cannot understand what he is saying (1 Cor. 14:4). There is no doubt among those who have been given the gift of tongues that their prayer life and their ability to praise God in all circumstances has grown dramatically. It is one of the ways in which the Spirit evokes prayer in the people of the Messiah.

The third level at which the Spirit undertakes for us in our weakness is brought movingly before us in Romans 8:26f. 'The Spirit helps us in our weakness. For we do not know what to pray for as we ought, but the Spirit itself intercedes for us with sighs too deep for words. And he who searches the hearts of men knows what is the mind of the Spirit, because he intercedes for the saints according to the will of God. And we know that in all respects he co-operates with those who love God.' There are some profound depths here for the Christian to ponder. For many of us, prayer in the Holy Spirit is something about which we know very little. Our prayers tend to be mechanical or at best self-centred, and prayer in the Holy Spirit means allowing the Spirit of Christ to pray in us, to pour into our souls his overflowing life of intercession.

'Praying Hyde'

I came across a striking example of this recently in the story of John Hyde – nicknamed 'Praying Hyde', a missionary to India early in the last century. A man once asked him to pray for him. 'He came to my room, turned the key in the door, dropped on his knees, waited five minutes without a single syllable coming from his lips. I could hear my own heart thumping and beating. I felt the hot tears running down my face. I knew I was with God. Then with upturned face, down which the tears were streaming, he said "O God". Then, for five minutes at least, he was still again, and then, when he knew he was talking with God, his arm went around my shoulder and there came up from the depth of his heart such petitions for men as I had never heard before. I rose from my knees to know what real prayer was.' Prayer in the Spirit need not, I think, always have that emotional intensity. It does need to have that direct meeting with God.

The Spirit's aid in prayer

This is where the Spirit's aid is so crucial in our prayers. For the Holy Spirit understands not only the mind of the Lord, as we saw in 1 Corinthians 2, but the mind of struggling Christians. He knows we find it hard to pray. He knows there are times when we feel so deeply and yet so confusedly that we cannot frame petitions, but simply come in silent pleading to the Lord. He knows that we are often very unsure what is the will of God, and therefore cannot pray with clarity and confidence about it. He knows the varied and perplexing circumstances in which we are placed. And he helps – the very word in Greek is highly suggestive. It means he grasps the situation *for* us and *with* us. He frames the petitions in our lips; and he prays within us to the Father, with sighs too deep for words. As for the variety of circumstances to which we are exposed, the Spirit works with us in them all, and his aim is to promote our good.

What a tremendously encouraging thing this is. We have in the Spirit a divine intercessor, resident within us, to teach us to pray and to pray alongside us. Perhaps this is the reason why we rarely if ever find a prayer in the New Testament addressed to the Spirit. The Holy Spirit is that part of the deity given us to enable us to pray. Christian prayer is normally offered *to* the Father *through* the Son, or 'in his name', and '*in*' or at the instigation of the Spirit.

Jesus' aid in prayer

There is a fascinating passage in Hebrews 7:25, where the Lord Jesus is said to be able to 'save to the uttermost those who come to God by him, because he is always alive to make intercession for them'. The word for 'make intercession' is the same in Hebrews 7:25 as in Romans 8:26; except that in Romans it has a prefix which indicates intensity, or, perhaps, stresses that it is done *for* us. But the basic thought is the same in both cases. It does not say that the Spirit or the Son begs the Father to give us what he otherwise might not. The usual word for 'ask' is not used; instead, we have this strange, rare word which literally means 'to be around'. Is that, perhaps, significant? What higher confidence could a Christian have than to reflect that in heaven the risen Christ in his ascended manhood 'is around' on our behalf? His presence at the Father's side is the silent guarantee that we are accepted. There is in the Godhead in heaven one who fully understands us and is there as our representative and our head. Equally, what an encouragement it is to know that there is, in struggling Christians on earth, one of the Godhead who 'is around' on our behalf; and that when we are agonising in prayer, we do not approach the Almighty on our own, in all our poverty. We have the Spirit as the divine representative in our hearts who enables us to pray acceptably.

The sum of the matter

This has been a long chapter on the work of the Spirit in the individual Christian. But it is no use making out an extensive list of the treasures in our inheritance if we do not make use of them. The Holy Spirit is God's gift to us, and he means us not just to read about him but to make use of him. God means us to know that we are in Christ, and has given us the Spirit to assure us. God means us to grow in Christlikeness, and has given us the Spirit to change us. God means to free us from the bondage to the self-centredness and self-vindication which marked us in the old days, and has equipped us with the Spirit of the Messiah to set us free to serve him unselfconsciously, effectively and joyfully. God has set the seed of his Spirit in our hearts and intends to produce in us a crop of lovely qualities of character if we do not grieve the Spirit (Eph. 4:30) by wilful dis-obedience or neglect. God undertakes to teach us through the Spirit if we will allow him to lead us into a closer understanding of and obedience to Jesus Christ. And God will not only listen to our insignificant prayers, but has given us his Spirit to enable us to pray and to share with us in that most demanding task. Nor is that the full extent of God's generosity. The Spirit groans (Rom. 8:26): we, who have the firstfruit of the Spirit, groan as we await the redemption of our body (8:23); indeed, the whole created order groans (8:22), as on tip-toe it awaits the day when it will be redeemed from all its anguish and frustration and share in the glorious liberty of the sons of God. The Spirit, then, is fully involved in the anguish of our world-in-the-making, and of us Christians-in-the-making; and he points towards the day when the pains of travail will give way to the joys of birth. His very presence in our world and in our lives is guarantee of that future day: he is the one part of God's future present here and now. That is why time and again in the New Testament he is linked with hope. We can only 'abound in hope through the power of the Holy Spirit' (Rom. 15:13). For the Holy Spirit and hope are two sides of the same coin; respectively the objective and the subjective modes in which the future is made real to us in the present. No wonder that in that same verse Paul bids us be filled with all joy and peace in believing. With so powerful and so complete an equipment as the Holy Spirit, the Christian has every reason for peace and joy in believing.

7

The Spirit in the Church

What is the function of the Holy Spirit within the Christian Church? Historically speaking there have been two main tendencies. Sometimes the Church has tried to exercise proprietary rights over the Holy Spirit, confining him to its basis of faith, its ministerial orders, its sacraments. Sometimes the 'spiritual people' have reacted against the institutional church of their day, and broken off to form a 'pure church' consisting of themselves and likeminded friends – and before long this new church has usually become as encrusted with barnacles as the one from which they broke away.

In the New Testament era the Christians had to face similar problems, and yet they managed to live with them and surmount them. This chapter will, therefore, examine the ways in which the early Christians were conscious of the Spirit's presence in their community; the next four chapters will glance at some of our contemporary problems concerning the Spirit in the Church, when set against this background.

But there are two basic convictions about the Spirit in the community that we must glance at first.

The Spirit is the renewed presence of God

In Old Testament days, the presence of God was normally experienced in Israel through the tabernacle in the wilderness and later the temple in Jerusalem. The tabernacle was marked

126

by God's glorious presence: 'if your presence does not go with us, do not send us up from here. How will anyone know you are pleased with me and your people unless you go with us? What else will distinguish me and your people from all other people on the face of the earth?' (Exod. 33:15,16). It was the presence of God that marked out Israel as special.

The same was true of the temple, once Solomon had built it. God's glory descended and 'filled the temple' (1 Kings 8:11). And so Jerusalem and the temple are regularly described as the place where God chooses to dwell (Ps. 68:15, 84:1 etc.). But Israel failed badly, was taken into captivity, and they were no longer characterised as the people where God made his home. The glory of the Lord had departed from the ruined temple in Jerusalem (Ezek. 10).

But there was hope that God would renew his presence among his people. And that hope was still associated with a (future) temple. 'My dwelling place will be with them: I will be their God and they will be my people' (Ezek. 37:27). And Malachi prophesies, 'The Lord you are seeking will suddenly come to his temple' (3:1). Unfortunately the second temple did not live up to these hopes. Haggai complains, 'Who of you is left who saw this house in its former glory? How does it look to you now? Does it not seem to you like nothing?' (2:3). There was no *shekinah*, no manifest divine glory in the second temple.

With the coming of Jesus that hope was fulfilled. All four Gospels show his claim to embody the new temple in his own person (see particularly John 2:13–22). The glory of the Lord was manifested once again, no longer in a building subject to decay but in the perfect embodiment of God's presence among men, Jesus himself. 'The Word became flesh, and dwelt among us, full of grace and truth; we have beheld his glory, as of the only Son from the Father' (John 1:14). The Greek word used for 'dwelt' literally means 'pitched his tent' and its consonants, *skn*, are the same as the Hebrew consonants for the word *shekinah*, glory. The allusion is obvious. John's profound claim is that the glory of God's presence, temporarily displayed in the tabernacle and then the temple, was now for ever embodied in Jesus. Here was the New Temple.

But it did not end there. The New Testament writers were awestruck to realise that the presence of God, equated with his Spirit (see Isa. 63:9–14) was, since Pentecost, permanently dwelling in their midst. They, poor uneducated individuals of different nations and backgrounds, constituted the temple of God as they met for worship. They were the place where his Spirit was to be encountered (1 Cor. 3:16, Eph. 2:22). And they were called to a distinctive lifestyle precisely because God dwelt in their midst. To be sure, that is true of the individual also (1 Cor. 6:19). But the corporate aspect is primary. The Church, gathered for worship and then dispersed in mission and service, is the people God had chosen for his own possession, to manifest something of his glory as the Spirit makes his presence known among them, and through them to others.

The Spirit is the presence of God's future

The Jews, particularly in the two centuries before Christ when they were constantly harried and overrun by hostile powers, contrasted the present 'evil age', dominated by sin and death, with the glorious 'age to come' when God would vindicate his people, bring about universal righteousness, pour out his Spirit and raise the dead. It would be the culmination of all history. This age and the age to come were set in sharp counterpoint.

But this simple pattern was shattered by the coming of Jesus, who vigorously proclaimed that he was launching the invasion of God's kingdom into human society. From now on the kingdom was inaugurated, but it was not yet consummated. And the first Christians caught on to this understanding with enthusiasm. The End had dawned with the coming of Jesus, his death, resurrection and gift of the Spirit. They lived now between the times. This present age, the age of the flesh, lay behind them. The coming age, the age of the Spirit, lay ahead of them. But not entirely ahead. Even now they experienced the Spirit, the gift of the end-time. Even now they knew God's salvation, even though that salvation was still to be experienced in all its fulness at the final coming of Christ. Even now they could anticipate the final verdict of 'acquitted', though they had to struggle to show forth that righteous character in their lives. Even now they knew Jesus had been raised from the dead, the firstfruit of a glorious crop to come, although they still had to face their own death. There was no doubt about it: the Beyond had invaded their midst. The 'age to come' was no longer exclusively future. It had begun, and they were the people of the future living in the land of the present. 'We are those on whom the ends of the ages have come' (1 Cor. 10:11). The Church is the community of the end-time, God's counter culture. And the proof of all this is the manifest presence of the Spirit in their midst. From the very first, on the day of Pentecost, they realised that Joel's prophecy had been fulfilled: 'Afterwards, I will pour out my Spirit on all people' (2:28f). The gift of the Holy Spirit, poured out without distinction on believing Jews and Gentiles alike, was proof positive that the messianic age, the age of salvation, had begun. The Holy Spirit is the certain evidence that the future has dawned, and is also the reliable guarantee of its final consummation.

And that is what the images of the Spirit which we have already glanced at, 'first instalment' and 'firstfruits', denote (see pp. 101–102). The Spirit is a 'first instalment, a down payment' (2 Cor. 1:21, 5:5, Eph. 1:14) – a gift which we enjoy now but which will be completed in heaven. The Spirit is, if you like, the only bit of God's future which we have now, and is, at the same time, the pledge of all the future holds in store. The metaphor of the Spirit as 'firstfruits' in Rom. 8:23 makes the point well. The Spirit is like the first plum on the tree in our garden: to be enjoyed now, but equally the sure evidence of the main crop to come. In a word, the Spirit is the supreme sign that the future has invaded the present, that the new age has begun.

Moreover, the Spirit of the crucified and risen Jesus in our lives is the guarantee of future resurrection for those who trust him. Through the Holy Spirit believers have tasted something of the age to come and are oriented towards its fulfilment. Life in the Spirit is meant to be the distinguishing mark of the Christian Church. No wonder Paul is so insistent that 'Anyone who does not have the Spirit of Christ does not belong to him' (Rom. 8:9). The Church is the community where this mighty Spirit of God, who brings the future into the present, is active.

And now, if we are clear on these two fundamental perspectives about the Church and the Spirit, we can look at some of the transforming work he does among the people where he discloses his presence.

The Spirit creates unity

The Spirit makes unity

One of the notable ways in which the Spirit expressed himself in the Christian community was through creating unity. When in Ephesians 4:3,4 Paul is sketching some of the things all Christians have in common, he has this to say: 'Endeavour to keep the unity of the Spirit in the bond of peace. There is one body, and one Spirit, as you are called in one hope of your calling; one Lord, one faith, one baptism, one God and Father of us all, who is above all, and through all, and in all. But grace was given to each of us according to the measure of Christ's gift.' He then goes on to outline some of the gifts of the ascended Christ. 'His gifts were that some should be apostles, some prophets, some evangelists, some pastors and teachers.' While therefore making full allowance for the diversity of gifts God has given to his Church in the varying capacities he has accorded to different members, Paul insists that the Spirit creates unity, and that it is the job of the Christians to keep that unity and not spoil it. Paradoxically, like so much in the Christian life, unity is a gift of God, and yet we have to work at it.

The Church must preserve unity

This given unity is not surprising. As we have seen, the first Christians were aware that the Spirit of the Messiah had come to indwell them. Hardly surprising, then, that with this Spirit of their Master making them into sons of God, they should be conscious of the closest ties with other members of the family. In this family, seen as one Body indwelt by one Spirit, there was no place for distinctions of wealth or station, sex or nationality; no room for pride in education or religious privilege (Col. 3:11, Jas. 2:1f). After all, not one of them had anything to boast about. All had been rescued by their Lord when they could never have earned their salvation. As for their differing gifts, well, they were God's gifts to them, and no reason for pride. 'Who makes you different from anybody else? And what have you that you did not receive? If, then, you received it, why do you boast, as if it were not a gift?' (1 Cor. 4:7). This concern to preserve the unity the Spirit had created, accounts for so much in the life and teaching of the early Church. It accounts for the determination of the Jerusalem leaders that there must be no independent Samaritan church growing up without the age-old split from Judaism being healed (Acts 8). It accounts for the decision of the Council of Jerusalem that the issue of circumcision must not be allowed to split the Church (Acts 15). It accounts for the constant visits of the apostle to the Gentiles back to the Jerusalem church (Acts 18:21, 20:16, 25:1 etc.), and his organisation of a great collection for their benefit, little though he could have approved of their theology (Rom. 15:26, 1 Cor. 16:1, 2 Cor. 8:1ff). It accounts for Paul's repeated call to the Christians at Philippi to pull together and stand together (Phil. 1:27, 2:1ff, 4:1–3). It explains why Paul will not allow that there are specially illuminated, 'gnostic' Christians at Colossae:

the divine mystery of the gospel is an open secret, and Paul warns 'every man, and teaches every man in all wisdom so as to present every man mature in Christ' (Col. 1:26,28). John does the same, with his emphasis that, 'You all have knowledge . . . you do not need anyone to teach you' (1 John 2:20, 27). This unity in the Spirit bridges the gap between Jews and Gentiles once they become Christians (Eph. 2:15) and breaks down the hostility between people of different colours and backgrounds.

Unity at Antioch

There is a splendid example of this in the church at Antioch (13:1ff). Its leadership was corporate, unlike that of most modern churches; it comprised an equally unusual feature, prophets and teachers in the leadership together – and they are not always the easiest of bedfellows. But more amazing still is the composition of this group. There is Barnabas, who used to be a rich, landowning Cypriot Levite: Symeon, called 'Swarthy', who was clearly a black man; Lucius of Cyrene, no doubt a Jew from the dispersion in North Africa; Manaen, who was educated in court circles alongside Herod the tetrarch; and Saul of Tarsus, the Jew from the Levant who had studied under Gamaliel. What a varied leadership! Their very names speak volumes for the unity which the Spirit creates. Christ's will for his Church, that they should be one (John 17:21), was being carried out in the Christian community at Antioch. That is why Paul was so angry and distressed when he heard of the divisions in the Christian church at Corinth.

Disunity at Corinth

The first three chapters of 1 Corinthians are dominated by this problem. Thinking of the faith as though it were a philosophical position, and of those who had come to preach to them as if they were travelling intellectuals, led the Corinthians to imagine themselves as judges between the various emphases they heard. The catch cries of 'I belong to Paul', 'I belong to

Peter', 'I belong to Apollos' and perhaps 'I belong to Christ' (1:12) were merely subtle forms of self-advertisement. Paul hammers this savagely. The gospel is not analogous to philosophical wisdom; it is folly to the worldly. Its teachers are not like travelling philosophers: they are co-operating labourers in God's vineyard, and one plants while another waters, but God is the only one who can make anything grow (3:6). The Corinthians are not in the privileged position of judges between theological niceties. To think they are, shows that they are governed not by the Spirit but by the attitudes and outlook of their unregenerate days (3:1,3). Disunity is utterly repulsive to Christ. The Church can no more acquiesce in being divided than Christ or baptism can (1:13). God has built his Church into a temple for the Spirit of God to indwell (3:16). The thought is that the Spirit of God whose glory filled the temple of Solomon, then shone out through the temple of Jesus' life (see John 2:18–22), now resides in the Christian community. Though he does not develop the metaphor, Paul would, I think, agree with the fuller details to be found in 1 Peter: individual Christians are spiritual stones which go to make up the spiritual temple which is built on Christ (1 Pet. 2:5). At all events he is very strong in this passage in 1 Corinthians 3. The man who spoils the temple of God by encouraging disunity will be destroyed by God (3:17). That is how highly Paul rates the unity of the Christian Church.

The Spirit brings reconciliation

Reconciliation is closely allied to this concept of unity. It is well brought out in Ephesians 2:14,18. A great wall separated Jew from Gentile in the ancient world: the law. This was graphically symbolised by the notice in the outer court of the temple threatening death to any Gentiles who went beyond that point. The 'unclean' might not enter the sanctuary of the Lord. That barrier bred enmity. Jews despised and hated Gentiles: despised them because they did not belong to the elect; and hated them because they lorded it over God's chosen people. Gentiles returned the compliment with interest, as can be seen by the references of Martial, Horace and Juvenal to the Jews. Yet in Christ that barrier has been broken down, along with the far bigger wall separating both Jew and Gentile from God. Both have been reconciled in one Body by Christ on the cross. Indeed, by incorporation into him the two have become one new humanity. The peace of the Messianic Age belongs both to those who once were outsiders and to those who prided themselves on being the elect. 'For through him we *both* have access by one Spirit to the Father' (2:18). That is no mere theological idealism. We see it happening in a crucial passage in the Acts, the conversion of Cornelius. There his reception of the 'one Spirit' convinces Peter, the orthodox Jew, that Cornelius, the Gentile soldier, has been accepted by God into his family on just the same basis as the original disciples. The Spirit brings intractable barriers down. The Spirit reconciles men who were at variance. This is a standing characteristic of his work in the Church.

The Spirit makes fellowship

Shared relationships

A third and closely allied way in which the Holy Spirit manifested himself in the early Church was through fellowship. Indeed, the Spirit is constitutive of Christian fellowship. On two occasions we actually read of 'the fellowship of the Holy Spirit', once in the grace of 2 Corinthians 3:13 and once as the ground for Paul's plea that the Philippians should stand united (Phil. 2:1). The phrase may mean 'the fellowship which the Holy Spirit gives' or 'joint participation in the Holy Spirit' which all Christians enjoy. Actually, these two are not far apart, for the Holy Spirit gives a share of *himself* to all believers, so all alike are partakers of the Spirit. The quality of this fellowship is best gauged by the early chapters of Acts. The new converts, having responded to the offer made by Peter of forgiveness and the Spirit, were baptised, and 'devoted themselves to the apostles' teaching and fellowship, the breaking of bread and prayers' (2:42).

Shared possessions

Their fellowship was no mere glow of warm feeling. It involved communalism of living, financial sacrifice and sharing, the care of those in need, and making time just to be together (2:44f). You would find them revelling in each other's company, sharing their possessions, praising God in the temple, regular at the meetings for prayer, vigilant to see that widows and other defenceless folk in the Christian community did not get overlooked in the share-out of money and food. In 4:32 we find the same picture. 'Now the company of those who believed were of one heart and soul, and no one said that any of the things which he possessed was his own, but they had everything in common . . . There was not a needy person among them, for as many as were possessors of lands or houses sold them and brought the proceeds of what was sold and laid it at the apostles' feet; and distribution was made to each as any had need.'

Christian communalism

It is one of the ironies of history that a movement which professes to follow a penniless carpenter-rabbi and his needy bunch of disciples; a movement which cherishes among its foundation documents an image of communal living like this, should have become so opposed to communism and so closely associated with capitalism's deification of personal possessions! Of course, Christianity can have no truck with communism's atheism and indifference to truth and the value of persons; but their communalism of possessions is very much more Christian than our glorification of wealth and our obsession with individualism. No doubt the primitive attempt at communal living at

Jerusalem was a failure, but what a glorious failure! Until there is a real sharing of money and possessions, an equitable distribution of resources and living conditions in so far as the Christian Church can achieve it, unbelievers are unlikely to remark on the quality of our fellowship. Real *koinōnia* in the Holy Spirit means that we cannot stand apart from those with whom we have this fellowship, no matter what it costs. I am told that some years ago President Nyerere of Tanzania sent out a copy of these verses in Acts on communal living to all the clergy, with the brief appended comment: 'That is the policy of the President.' There was a man who from Christian principle was attempting to apply communalism of possessions to a developing African state. He was an example to Western, capitalist Christendom.

Christian caring

The Jerusalem experiment was a failure. The church went broke, and richly merited the name in which they gloried, the *ebionim*, God's poor. A few years passed. The Gentile mission sprang into being and produced a flourishing church at Antioch, hundreds of miles away. This church received a prophetic warning from a Jerusalem prophet Agabus, that there would be a widespread famine. So what did they do, these Gentile Christians of Antioch? They did not even wait till the famine happened; on the word of the Jerusalem prophet (whom they might well have thought was prejudiced!) they had a collection; each of the disciples contributed according to his means; and they sent it to Jerusalem by the hands of Saul and Barnabas (11:28ff).

This seems to me a most remarkable thing. They could well have said, 'Those Jerusalem folk are a long way away; what do we owe them, anyway? Let us make sure that our own church members are all right when the famine comes, and not bother our heads about them.' They might have said, 'Those fools at Jerusalem will be taught a lesson by this famine. They will learn the hard way that when you realise your assets and share out your capital it does not last very long. They will learn some business sense for a change. And a good thing too.' They might have said, 'We don't see why we should do anything to help those most unsatisfactory Christians (if the name is not too good for them) at Jerusalem. Their theology is narrow; their ritualism is offensive; and they even attempt to mount a counter mission and force circumcision and food laws on our mixed church at Antioch.' They could have made these strictures, and with no small justification. But they did not allow theological differences, differences of churchmanship, differences in church organisation, and sheer distance to prevent them from making a most moving and eloquent expression of fellowship in the Spirit. It is hardly surprising that such a quality of life could find no parallel in antiquity, and drew many into the Christian fellowship.

The Spirit enables worship

Quality of worship

A fourth way in which the Spirit showed his presence in the Church was in their worship. The earliest disciples were led by the Spirit not only to a sharing of possessions but to a tremendous depth of worship. They 'broke bread from house to house' or 'at home': this seems to indicate house communion services. They ate their meals with generosity of disposition and exultation (a word which Luke uses to characterise the joy of the messianic community as it delights in what Christ has done for them, what they are now experiencing of his goodness, and what will await them at his return). They were notable for their praise of God even when threatened or in prison (4:24ff, 16:25). Indeed, praise is one of the special results of the Spirit coming on them (Acts 2:47, 3:8,9). They were to be found in the formal worship of the temple as well as the warm informality of the home meetings. They were regular in synagogue worship:

sometimes in a great Jewish centre like Antioch in Pisidia (13:14ff); sometimes in a place like Philippi, which had too few Jews to form a synagogue. The tiny congregation went down to a prayer place by the river, and Paul and his company joined them to such good effect that they led Lydia to faith (16:14).

Elements in worship

When we find the Christians organising their own worship, the Spirit of the Lord is often mentioned. In Acts 13, before the first missionary journey, we find the Church united in worship (and probably liturgical worship at that – *leitourgountōn*, 13:2) and showing their earnestness by fasting. It is in such a context that the Spirit could make known his leading. Perhaps he inspired a prophet to call for Barnabas and Saul to be set aside for special service; perhaps it was a conviction that he impressed upon the hearts of those present. At all events the mission from Antioch was born in that time of worship where the Spirit of God was so signally present. Paul expects visitors to a church where the people are gathered together for worship, and are open to the Spirit speaking directly through prophets in the assembly, to be conscious that God is in that place, and to be constrained to worship too (1 Cor. 14:25). The Book of Revelation springs from John's being in the Spirit on the Lord's day – doubtless in the context of worship (1:10). And in chapter 4, and repeatedly throughout the book, we find the author joining in worship in the Spirit before the throne of God (4:2,5ff).

Spiritual worship

True worship is in the Spirit, as Jesus made clear to the Samaritan woman (John 4:24). This passage is often misunderstood; as if it means that locality does not matter in worship, and that our human spirits have an affinity with God's Spirit. But this, as G. S. Hendry has pointed out in *The Holy Spirit in Christian Theology* (p. 32), is the precise opposite of the truth. 'Spirit' for John, as for Paul, is the opposite of 'flesh', and 'flesh' stands for all our fallen humanness. To say that God is Spirit, and that the only way to worship him is in Spirit and in truth, is first and foremost to slam the door in the face of our approach to God in our own strength or goodness. How can 'flesh' approach God who is 'Spirit', how can sinners approach the Holy One? They cannot. But the good news is that God has opened a way. God has made himself accessible in the Word become flesh, and he is now to be worshipped in the place where he has revealed himself, i.e. Jesus Christ, who proclaimed to the woman, 'I who speak to you am he.' Hendry concludes, 'God actively seeks men to worship him in spirit and in truth, by making himself accessible to them in his Son, who is truth incarnate, and by the mission of the Spirit, who is the Spirit of truth. The worship of God in spirit and truth is, therefore, Trinitarian worship; it is to worship God through Jesus Christ, in the Holy Spirit.'

Prayer in worship

Before we leave this aspect of the Spirit in the Church, we ought not to neglect the classic case of Acts 4:23ff. Peter and John have been released from prison, after being grilled by the Sanhedrin, and told not to say any more about the resurrection of Jesus. They returned to the Christian fellowship, and their immediate action was significantly different from what would happen in most Christian circles today. We might organise a petition for civil liberties, or approach our Member of Parliament, or at least appoint a committee to look into the matter of these unwarranted threats by officialdom. They did nothing of the kind. They gave themselves to prayer. This seems to have been a mixture of liturgical and free prayer. The prayer as recorded is dependent to a very large extent on Psalm 2, and to it they appended their brief request. But they did not pre-scribe to the Almighty what he should do. They did not ask for protection. They spread the matter before the Lord and asked him to 'behold' it. They claimed his sovereignty over every threat of man. And they asked for boldness in proclaiming the gospel of Jesus. 'And when they had prayed, the place was shaken in which they were gathered, and they were all filled with the Holy Spirit and spoke the word of God with confident assurance' (4:31). Such was the reality of the Spirit's presence in their worship.

The Spirit inspires Scripture

Closely associated with the Spirit's presence in worship is his inspiration of the Scriptures. As we have seen, the prophets of old claimed to have been sent and inspired by the Spirit of the Lord. Jesus himself set his seal on the Spirit's inspiration of Psalm 110, for instance, 'For David himself said by the Holy Spirit' (Mark 12:36). We find the same attribution of the Old Testament to the inspiration of the Holy Spirit in Acts 1:16, 4:25 etc., and it is entirely in keeping not only with Christian but with Jewish orthodoxy when we find the blanket claim in 2 Timothy 3:16 that 'All Scripture is inspired by God.'

The Spirit inspired the Old Testament Scriptures

We never get any nearer to an explanation of the divine inspiration of the human writers than in 2 Peter 1:20f where the author tells us that prophecy came from God, not from the prophet's own ideas. It came as the human writers were moved or carried along by the Holy Spirit. This is a fascinating maritime metaphor in the original Greek, suggesting the way a ship is carried along by the wind. The prophets raised their sails, so to speak (they were obedient and receptive) and the Holy Spirit filled them and carried their craft along in the direction he wished. The writers were not robots but men; men of their time, men of varied backgrounds and intellects, prejudices and outlooks. But those men were yielded to the leading of the Holy Spirit in such a way that he could speak through them. Co-operation between the human author and the divine Spirit is perhaps the key word; there is no suggestion that the personality or individuality of the writer was suppressed in any way. The Holy Spirit did not use instruments; he used men, holy men, through whom he could speak to people in ages yet unborn. 'Whatever was written in former days was written for our instruction,' wrote Paul. 'The prophets who prophesied of the grace that was to be yours . . . inquired what person or time was indicated by the Spirit of Christ within them when they predicted the sufferings of Christ and the subsequent glory,' wrote Peter (1 Pet. 1:10ff). It was therefore to the inspired Scriptures of the Old Testament that the early Christians went as they wrestled with the meaning of Christ and his work. The passages they found particularly illuminating, and their handling of them, have been superbly set out in books such as C. H. Dodd's *According to the Scriptures* and F. F. Bruce's *This is That*. That inspiration by the Spirit, is, of course, why the Old Testament became the Bible of the early Christians. It was not only that they took it over with their original Jewish heritage; they were persuaded that the Old Testament pointed forward to the days of salvation brought in by Jesus, and that it is impossible to understand Jesus or his salvation except against the background of this Old Testament. The Spirit that had been active in the prophets was the Spirit which had become embodied in Jesus.

The Spirit inspired the New Testament Scriptures

It was, however, impossible to leave the matter there. Had not Jesus promised the Spirit to his followers? The Spirit who would teach them and lead them into all the truth about him? And had that Spirit not become their inalienable gift from the day of Pentecost onwards? Then did it not follow that the same Holy Spirit who inspired the prophets to point forward to Jesus, no less inspired them as they bore apostolic witness to Jesus? This was undoubtedly the belief of the apostles. Peter, in the passage 1 Peter 1:10–12 already referred to, not only declared that the

Spirit of Christ inspired the prophets to look forward to the Messiah, but claims that the good news, fulfilling what the prophets had said, was brought to his readers by the apostolic witness and 'the Holy Spirit sent down from heaven'. The same Holy Spirit who was active in the prophets was active in the apostles. There was, therefore, no anachronism when 2 Peter 3:16 sets Paul's letters alongside the other Scriptures. They had to wait another three hundred years for the formal promulgation of the books of the New Testament in precisely the form we have them today, but from the days of the apostles themselves it was quite clear to the Christians that the Holy Spirit who inspired the prophetic writings was also standing behind the words of Jesus and his apostles. Paul could claim to have the very mind of Christ, to proclaim not the word of men but of God, and to teach not merely in broad outline but in detailed words imparted by the Spirit of the Lord (1 Cor. 2:16, 1 Thess. 2:13, 1 Cor. 2:13). Hence his abrupt challenge to any who thought themselves 'inspired' to recognise and abide by what he said (1 Cor. 14:38). Hence his expectation that his letters would be read in the Christian assembly at worship, alongside the inspired writings of the Old Testament (Col. 4:16).

The Spirit is encountered in the Scriptures

It is, therefore, in the Scriptures of the Old and New Testaments, with Jesus as the centrepiece, that the Spirit is most readily to be encountered. That is why Bible reading both in church and for the individual, occupies so prominent a place in Christianity. There is no sniff of bibliolatry about it. It is simply the fact that the Spirit who inspired the Scriptures is to be met there. We read them in order to gain illumination from him and be transformed by him into greater likeness to our Lord. 2 Corinthians 3 is the classic chapter for the role of the Spirit as illuminator of the Scriptures. It is when we turn to the Lord the Spirit that the veil is taken away from the eyes of our understanding. One sees once again the aptness of Bishop John

Taylor's name for the Spirit as the go-between God. He is the one who inspired the Scriptures in the first place. He is the one who interprets them to the humble, seeking reader.

The Spirit speaks through preaching

There is one point that ought to be added to the way the Spirit manifests himself through the Scriptures. He does so through another enterprise undertaken in the context of the worshipping congregation by one or more of its members, namely preaching. Acts 4:8 is typical: 'Then Peter, filled with the Holy Spirit, said . . .' and he launched into his address.

Preaching – a pathway for God's power

As we have seen in chapter 6, it is part of the work of the Spirit to convict a person of his need, and to make Christ attractive to him; this very often takes place in the course of preaching, particularly biblical preaching. One of the great weaknesses in contemporary Christianity is the poverty of preaching. Many clergy consider it a chore, and many congregations complain if it lasts more than ten minutes. There seems to be little expectation that the Spirit of God might be present and active, to take home the words that one would hope have been prepared and prayed over in his presence, so that the message (or some part of it) becomes luminous, indeed life-changing, for one here and another there in the congregation. But that is in fact what happens when there is prayerful, believing, biblical preaching, delivered in the power of the Spirit and in dependence on God to use it. Time and again after preaching people have said to me, 'I felt you were speaking precisely to me' or asked, 'How did you know about me when you said such and such?' That is the work of the Holy Spirit. I may know little or nothing about their needs: but he who searches the hearts does, and he takes the preached word and applies it to the needs of those present.

I remember a student once discovering this while he was actually preaching. He did not previously have great confidence in the value of preaching, and he certainly did not think he was much good at it. But he had prepared this sermon on prayer with great care and much prayer, and he got up in fear and trembling to preach it. To his amazement he found that the people in this downtown city congregation were gripped by the Word of God, and one non-churchgoer who had been dragged into the service by another student had to go out because he was so convicted by what was said. That student will never again doubt that the Spirit of God can use the preached word. Now he is ordained he is not likely to scrap the sermon in favour of more music or discussion. There is room for music, room for discussion, but the Holy Spirit uses preaching in a quite special way.

Preaching – a shared enterprise

And it is by no means a one-man effort. The congregation can 'meet' the preacher by the way they respond, the way they support him in prayer, the way they assess what is said, and the way they worship. They create the atmosphere in which the Spirit of God has ease of communication, if I may put it that way. I well recall an evangelistic service in the North of England at which I preached. I *knew* that God was going to lead many people to Christ in that service by the time we had got halfway through, long before we reached the sermon: the sense of worship was so real, the love and dedication to Christ so obvious. It was moving to stand in the aisle for half an hour afterwards and meet a steady flow of individuals who had been brought to the service by friends; and those same friends had stayed with them to help them on in the early days of their Christian life after many of them that night committed their lives to Christ and asked his Spirit into their hearts. No wonder many of the Barthian theologians maintain that the Bible is not so much the Word of God, *tout simple*; but that it *becomes* the

Word of God when the Spirit uses the Word preached or read to create an encounter with the hearts of men and women.

The Spirit enlivens the sacraments

The Spirit in baptism and eucharist

If the Spirit of God is active in the Word in the Church, he is no less concerned to bring life through the sacraments. It seems probable that there is an allusion in John 3:5, 'born of water and the Holy Spirit', to Christian baptism, and in John 6:53, 'unless you eat the flesh of the Son of Man and drink his blood, you have no life in you', to the eucharist. If so, it can scarcely be accidental that the Spirit is mentioned emphatically in both contexts. In John 3, the 'born of water and the Spirit' in verse 5 is an expansion of 'born from above' in verse 3, and it is the Spirit in regeneration that is the subject of the subsequent discussion. Similarly in chapter 6, alongside the extremely harsh sayings about literally 'munching' his body and his blood goes the assertion in verse 63, 'It is the Spirit that gives life, the flesh is of no avail; the words that I have spoken to you are Spirit and life.' Clearly, the Spirit is vital to effective baptism and meaningful communion.

Vehicles for blessing

There is a lovely passage in 1 John 5:7,8 which seems to indicate that the Spirit uses the sacraments to assure his people that they belong and to act as physical vehicles of spiritual blessing. 'The Spirit is the witness, because the Spirit is the truth. There are three witnesses, the Spirit, the water and the blood; and these three agree.' This letter of John is written, among other reasons, to combat Docetism, an early heresy which maintained that the heavenly Christ was too holy and spiritual to be soiled by permanent contact with human flesh. The heresy had a number of variations, but they would all have repudiated the idea that the Christ of faith could have been identified with the Jesus of

Palestine. But John's point in these verses is that that identification is essential to the gospel. God really became man, and Jesus came not with water only (his heavenly nature? his baptism?) but with blood (his human nature? his crucifixion?). Whatever the precise meaning of this difficult phrase, John is saying that in Jesus the divine did become accessible to human touch and sight. And the same continues to be true! The sacraments of the water and the blood (and there must surely be at least an *allusion* to baptism and the Lord's Supper in those words) are used by the Spirit to bear witness to us of the reality of our salvation, and of the fact that we are indeed sons in the heavenly Father's family. More, they are the physical bearers of spiritual blessing, for the Spirit can and does work through the sacraments in the Church, just as he worked through the life of Jesus of Nazareth.

But not magic

But just as one could look at Jesus, listen to him, and touch him in the days of his flesh without gaining any benefit from him or even realising who he was, so it is with the sacraments. They may be bare signs, or they may be vibrant with the life of the Spirit: it depends, not a little, on the receptivity and faith of the recipient. Certainly churchmen are not to sit back confident that they must be all right with God because of their sacraments. 1 Corinthians 10 is written to that situation. The Corinthians seem to have been regarding their sacramental life as a sort of talisman which would allow them to engage in idolatry and fornication with impunity. Paul reminds them that the Israelites of old had their counterpart to the Christian sacraments and relied on them for security – but in vain. They went in for fornication and idolatry like the Corinthians, and 'God was not pleased; for they were overthrown in the wilderness'. The sacraments in the Church are a means of grace and an objective, palpable ground of assurance. But they are not magic.

The Spirit inaugurates mission

Another mark of the Spirit in the Church is mission. It has been so from the first days of Christianity, as we saw in Chapter 5. Outreach to others is the complement to fellowship within the Christian family. The Spirit's activity in the worship and fellowship, the Scriptures, the preaching and the sacraments of the Church must be balanced by driving out its members in mission to a needy world: '*ite, missa est*'. There can be nothing exclusive about the Christian gospel. The Church, when it is truly the Church, can never be a cosy club for insiders. It must always see itself as the family of God gathered for mission. Accordingly, we find repeatedly in the early Church that the sequel to worship is evangelism.

Spiritual worship leads to mission

We will glance briefly at a few examples, since we have already examined the nexus between the Spirit and mission in some detail. But it is noteworthy how in Acts 2, after recording the worship and fellowship of the early believers, we read, 'And the Lord added to their number daily those who were being saved' (2:47). Again, after the prayer meeting in chapter 4 we read that, 'they spoke the word of God with boldness . . . and with great power the apostles gave their testimony to the resurrection of the Lord Jesus, and great grace was upon them all'. In the passage in 1 Corinthians which we have noted earlier, the expected result of Spirit-filled worship is the conversion of people who come in. In the case of the Antiochene church of Acts 13, it is the same pattern; mission follows hard on the heels of Spirit-led worship. The point is important, because there are few such powerful evangelistic agencies as a Christian fellowship at worship, where the various gifts of the Spirit are being exercised in love and harmony by people who are consciously under the leadership of that same Spirit. And this brings us naturally to a final important mark of the

Spirit in the Church, namely interdependence in the body of Christ.

It is a lesson they had not digested at Corinth, and Paul spends three chapters in teaching it to them.

The Spirit builds up the Body – in love

A dynamic church

Corinth was a richly gifted church. And they rated very highly among these gifts the ability to speak in tongues. The value they set on it was very understandable from either a Hebrew or a Greek background. One has only to think of the *ruach adonai* coming with supernatural violence upon Saul so that he danced like a dervish, or upon Ezekiel so that he was carried away to another place, to sympathise with the Corinthians in supposing that extraordinary manifestations like this were the sure mark of the Spirit's activity. In the Greek world it was the same. Even that great intellectual Plato could write in the *Phaedrus*, 'It is through *mania* (ecstasy due to divine possession) that the greatest blessings come to us' and in the *Timaeus*, 'No one in possession of his *nous* (rational mind) has reached divine and true exaltation.' The nonrational was the mark of divine inspiration: the more *pneuma*, the less *nous*. The Corinthians would have rated in ascending order of value the teacher (in reliance on his rationality), the prophet (who spoke under divine inspiration but intelligibly), and the man who spoke in tongues (whose inspiration was marked by unintelligibility).

A serious danger

A vital, dynamic church; a highly talented church, with freedom and openness and freshness. But the Corinthian church was in serious danger. To suppose that the more a man loses self-possession the more inspired by God he must be, is to deny God his place in the rational. To suppose that non-personal irruptions of *ruach* are the mark of inspiration is to forget that it is the Spirit of *Jesus* with whom we are dealing. Any such depersonalisation of the Spirit is also disparagement of the ethical, as if it does not much matter how you behave so long as you have this mark of divine inspiration upon you. If this particular gift is prized above all others, it easily leads to a cult of experience, and to excessive individualism (jealousy in those who have not got the gift, pride in those who have). In the midst of all this, Christian love can easily disappear.

Paul's response

How does Paul handle this difficult situation, a situation which could easily wreck all interdependence in the Christian community, and set the various members in jealous competition for spiritual gifts? He faces it head on.

1 Corinthians 12:1–3

In verses 1–3 he explains the relation of the Holy Spirit to ecstasy. First, he reminds them that not all ecstatic speech is Christian. They knew it in their unregenerate days of worshipping Bacchus or Attis. They had shared in feasts in honour of demons (10:19f), and had fallen under their influence. Indeed, the force of the word used in the Greek here, *apagomenoi*, indicates that they had actually experienced demon possession: they had been 'taken out of themselves' in frenzied speech as they worshipped idols that themselves were dumb and gave no answer to the prayers of suppliants. Justin spoke of pagans being 'chased with the scourge of evil demons' (1 *Apology*, 5), and Lucian speaking of the power of love, says, 'A sort of god (literally *demon*, the same word that Paul uses) carries us away (*agei*) wherever he wills, and it is impossible to resist him' (*Dialogues of the Dead*, 19:1). This is the sort of supernatural power which the Corinthians had experienced in their pagan days, driving them on in their worship of idols. It is salutary to remember that Muslim devotees in the Sudan speak in tongues no less than Christians in Guildford or Cleveland!

It is not easy to be sure quite what was happening when people cried out in church, apparently under inspiration from above, that 'Jesus is accursed'. It seems almost inconceivable to us that any Christians should even count it a possibility to curse Jesus. But we know at least three types of situation where it actually happened. The Roman governor of Bithynia, Pliny, tells the Emperor Trajan of his attempts to stamp out Christianity in the Province about A.D. 112, and of the way in which 'some who were or had been Christians . . . invoked the gods and cursed Christ, none of which things, it is said, genuine Christians can be compelled to do' (*Epistles* 10:96). If some cursed Jesus under the pressure of persecution, others did so through rejecting the historical Jesus who died in agony on a cross of shame; instead, they concentrated their devotion on the heavenly Lord, the risen Christ. Cerinthus made just this division, and was severely taken to task by the church fathers such as Epiphanius and Irenaeus. Again, there were the Ophites, a heretical Gnostic Christian sect who required their members to curse Jesus (Origen, *Contra Celsum* 5:1, 28). This shows that it was not unheard of for professed followers of Christ to curse Jesus. Probably some of the ecstatic Christians at Corinth, carried away by the champagne of religious experience, separated the historic Jesus from the Spirit-giving Christ: a similar sort of thing seems to have happened in the community to which 1 John was writ, where 'liars' were saying that Jesus is not the Christ (1 John 2:22). At all events, Paul used this shocking happening to teach the Corinthians a most important lesson. The really crucial mark of the Spirit's presence is not religious fervour or even speaking in tongues (which can arise from demon possession or psychological conditioning as well as from the Spirit), but the confession that Jesus is Lord. In other words, it is the *content* of the Christian proclamation which matters. The man who walked the streets of Palestine is exalted to the throne of the universe; the Jesus of history cannot be divorced from the Christ of faith. Once again we see, as in chapters three and four, that the Spirit of Christ bears witness to the historical Jesus. The one we encounter as Spirit is the Spirit of *Jesus*: there are other spirits, and it is all too easy to be deceived by them (1 John 4:1ff).

Incidentally, there is good reason to suppose that 'Jesus is Lord' was the earliest baptismal confession. It was certainly something every believer could say; it was the irreducible minimum of Christian faith. Paul is concerned to show the Corinthians that genuine Spirit-possession is not marked out by tongues but by the unambiguous confession that Jesus of Nazareth is Lord; Lord of the universe, and Lord of your life. That is the first and foremost criterion of the Spirit's authentic presence. And it was something that was not restricted to certain Corinthian Christians with particular gifts who despised others as not being *pneumatikoi*, 'Spirit-filled'; but was rather the basic condition of being a Christian at all, embodied in the baptismal confession! Paul gives another great mark of authentic spirituality, and we shall come to it in verse 7. But this one is fundamental to the whole of the subsequent discussion.

1 Corinthians 12:4–6

In verses 4–6 Paul goes on to make a most important point. He contrasts the variety of the gifts with the unity of the Giver. Note the repetition in 'the same Spirit . . . the same Lord . . . the same God', compared with the triple 'there are varieties . . .' in these verses. We have here the oldest trinitarian (or, to be more accurate, triadic) formula in the whole of the New Testament. It is thoroughly Hebraic. St. Paul is not so much thinking in Greek terms of three 'persons' in one Godhead. He is thinking, as a true Israelite, of God in action. One and the same God acts in three different ways. It is therefore important to examine the difference between the three words Paul uses to describe the variety of God's action. The answer is simple enough linguistically: *charisma* 'gift', *diakonia* 'service', and *energēma* 'empowering' are self-explanatory. But the interesting thing is the way the apostle has paired them up. The gifts of grace, *charismata*, are linked with the Spirit; the acts of service with the Lord Jesus; and the requisite power with God the Creator. In other words, the spiritual gifts I have are *gifts* imparted by the supreme gift of grace, the Holy Spirit himself. They are not possessions of my own to use as I please. They are lent by him. And what are they for? Not for personal pride or gratification. Not for showing off, or comparing myself with others who have less or different gifts. No. They are intended for service of others, *diakonia*, after the pattern of the one who was uniquely endued with the Spirit, and supremely the Servant of the Lord. And when this service leads to success, when it helps anyone else, that is not because of my talents or my holiness; it is simply due to the empowering given by God who called all things into being from the beginning of time, and sustains them by his might.

1 Corinthians 12:7–11

We shall be examining verses 7–11 in some detail in chapter 10. Here it is sufficient to notice that Paul carries his argument a stage further by telling the Corinthians that the Spirit gives gifts to all members of the Church; that these gifts have various and concrete manifestations in the differing endowments of different members; and that it is all for the common good. This brings us to the second and complementary truth about the criteria proper to distinguishing a genuine gift of the Spirit. The first we saw in verse 3. We must ask, 'Does it point unmistakably to Jesus as Lord?' The second meets us in verse 7: 'Does it benefit and build up the Christian community?' The content of the message and the community of God's people are the two important questions that the apostle bids us ask if we are in doubt about the validity of some spiritual claim or experience.

In these crucial verses, then, Paul has shown us the unity of the Spirit's working through a wide variety of gifts. He grounds his argument in the very nature of God's being and action in history. Because God himself is diversity-in-unity, and has revealed himself that way throughout his saving acts in history, so is the Church where he is active. One God is the source of these various manifestations of the one Spirit in the body of the one Christ, the Church. These manifestations of God at work are called *energēmata* 'workings', where the emphasis is on what God does (12:6,10), *charismata* where the emphasis is on the gracious gift of his sovereign distribution of these capacities (12:4,9,28), and *diakoniai* to remind his readers that all gifts are intended for service of others (12:5). Thus there are indeed varieties of gifts, but it is the same Spirit who distributes them. There are indeed varieties of ways of serving the Lord, but it is the same Lord we all serve. There are indeed varieties in the way the Father is active in us, but every capacity and the strength to make good use of it are his alone. There is therefore no room either for boasting or jealousy. These gifts have no necessary link with holiness of life nor with power in service: they are gifts of the Spirit, not graces of character. And they are intended for the building up of the whole Christian community in service to the common Lord.

1 Corinthians 12:12–31

From verse 12 to the end of the chapter Paul uses a graphic illustration to expound the purpose of the Spirit's gifts. He sees the Church as Christ's Body, in which all the Corinthians (12:27) and indeed all believers throughout the world (1:2) are members. All are incorporated into this one Body of Christ. It is God the Father who appoints us our place to fill and gives us gifts to do it with (12:18,24,28). It is the Holy Spirit who makes us members of that Body. 'By one Spirit we were all baptised into one Body – Jews or Greeks, slaves or free – and were all made to drink of that one Spirit' (12:13). Paul is insisting that the one Spirit of God baptised all Christians into this one Body, whatever their background, nationality and gifts. Some of them had impressive gifts like tongues;

some of them did not (12:30). But all alike have been immersed in the sea of the Spirit; all alike have had his living water irrigating their parched lives (such seems to be the meaning of the two metaphors in verse 13). There are particular problems of detail in this famous verse to which we shall turn in a later chapter. But it is clear from the context that the apostle is not referring to a baptism by or in the Spirit which only *some* of them possess; he is insisting that they *all* have it, just as they are all members of Christ, and sons of the heavenly Father. The thought is trinitarian through and through. Indeed, it is shocking, and is intended to be so. We too easily gloss over the shattering half-expressed analogy in verse 12, with which he opens this section of the argument. Had he said, 'Just as the Body is one and has many members, and all the members of the Body, though many, are one Body, *so it is with the Church*,' the point would have been clear – and unremarkable. There would even have been parallels in Stoic thought. But he says something quite unparalleled in religious literature anywhere. He says *'so it is with Christ'*. What does he mean by this enigmatic statement?

He is making the Corinthians sit up and take notice. The Church is no earthly society. It is the embodiment of Jesus the Messiah. Whatever the Church is, it is by virtue of the power and presence and action of its Lord. Christ is the one in whom all believers are incorporate. Christ is the very air they breathe. It is perhaps significant, as Professor Eduard Schweizer has often remarked, that the title 'Christians' only appears in the New Testament upon the lips of pagans! Paul's favourite title for the Church is men and women who are 'in Christ'. If they are different, it is because Christ is in them and they are in Christ. That is the important thing about the Church. That is why Paul speaks not about the Church but Christ as being the Body to which we all belong. And by their divisive and arrogant spirit, these Corinthians were spoiling the harmony not of the Church, so much as of Christ.

Very well then. All the Corinthians have the Holy Spirit. And the gifts they revel in are gifts of his ordaining. Their individual role may be that of ear or eye, hand or foot in that Body. The point is that they are there as a result of God's appointment and their equipment is that of the Spirit's giving.

Next, Paul deals with two separate tendencies within the Body of Christ. Some members have less outstanding gifts, and they are tempted to feel that they are inferior members in the Body. Paul encourages them in verses 14–20. How awful it would be if the Body consisted of just one great eye! If all had the same gift, the harmony of 'unity-in-diversity' would give way to dreary uniformity (12:19,20); moreover they would be tacitly blaspheming God who arranged each of the organs in the Body as he saw fit (12:18). Let them take heart. An inferiority complex is out of place in the household of God. He knows what he is doing with the diverse gifts he imparts. All members of the Body are necessary and interdependent.

In the verses which follow, Paul addresses himself to those who suffer from a superiority complex. They are reminded that all members have a part to play, but that God delights to give special honour to the less showy parts; 'the parts of the body which seem to be weaker are indispensable, and those parts of the body which we think less honourable we invest with the greater honour' (12:22f). If those with the less spectacular gifts are slighted, the whole Church is impoverished.

This is the point which Paul labours to bring home to them in his closing words as he applies his analogy directly to them. Once again, he has often been misunderstood. When he says 'if one member suffers, all suffer together; if one member is honoured, all rejoice together' he is not saying anything at all about Christian sympathy. His point is altogether more penetrating to Corinthian pride. He wants the more arrogant members of the Body there to realise that if any one member, however mean and ordinary his service, is inhibited from making that service, *then the whole Body suffers*! If, on the other hand, one member is honoured by being able to render its proper service acceptably, then the whole Body is honoured. The truth that the whole Church is the loser if it is not so constituted that all members get the chance to make their God-given contribution to its life and worship was as surprising and unacceptable to the Corinthians as it is to us. But that is what Paul is asserting throughout this chapter. Always for him the Body of Christ is primary, and the individual member secondary. This is the precise opposite of the Corinthian – and our own – atomised way of thinking. The Corinthians had to learn that they were not individually 'little Christs' with all the gifts, but rather, members of Christ with some gifts. Nobody was unnecessary, and nobody self-sufficient: they needed each other in the Body of Christ.

1 Corinthians 13: the centrality of love

It is at this point that Paul contributes his masterly chapter on love. We do not know if it was composed before he wrote this letter, by himself or by someone else. At all events it is highly appropriate here. 'Seek the greatest gifts,' is his final injunction in chapter 12, and the greatest gift the Spirit can impart to us is not tongues or prophecy, healing or the ability to work miracles, but love, *agapē*. The ancient world knew all about *philia*, friendship, and about *erōs*, passionate love; but it did not know anything about the love which is determined not by the worthiness of the recipient but by the goodness of the donor, the love which seeks the good of all men irrespective of their merits and of personal attraction. The world had to wait for Jesus Christ before it saw love like that. And then a new word, *agapē*, was added to the vocabulary of love in order to describe it. And as we have already seen, 'Jesus' could without loss be substituted for 'love' throughout 1 Corinthians 13. This love, which can never be worked up by human effort, is the supreme gift of the Holy Spirit to his people. 'God's own love is poured out into our hearts through the Holy Spirit who is given us' (Rom. 5:5).

There can be no higher gift than this, and that is why it is inserted in the middle of this three-chapter discussion of spiritual gifts. Unless people meet the risen, loving Christ mediated through me by the Spirit, it is immaterial that I can speak in tongues, or have prophetic insight, or the gift of wisdom and spiritual understanding, or mountain-moving faith: I may dole out all my possessions and even face the ultimate sacrifice of martyrdom, but unless the loving Jesus is encountered in me through all this, nothing is achieved. What a rebuke to those Corinthians, proud of their various gifts – what a rebuke to us, too. In this marvellous chapter the love of Jesus is set alongside the vices of the Corinthians. It is the opposite of the pride in spiritual experience which 'puffed them up' (4). It is the opposite of that emphasis on particular gifts which made the recipients proud and the aspirants jealous (4). It is the opposite of that selfish exercise of special gifts for personal gratification which Paul calls 'seeking one's own' (5). The Corinthians were seeking the 'higher way' of spiritual experience. Paul sets before them the 'lower way', as they might think it, of love; the love of Jesus the Servant, who was never puffed up and never selfish in the exercise of his gifts. All was for others. Thus he returns to the theme at the end of chapter 12, where 'the common good' dominated the exercise of gifts, a theme which he will develop in chapter 14. For a loving self-giving for others is the way of Jesus; it is the way of the Spirit; indeed, it is the very life of heaven itself, for in the day when all our earthly gifts are past, when prophecy has found its fulfilment, when tongues are taken up into the song of the redeemed in heaven, when we know even as we are known, faith is turned to sight, and hope fulfilled in ultimate possession by the Beloved – then love remains. The redeemed in heaven will still be united in that glad self-offering to the Lord and to the brethren which marked the highest flights of their spirituality on earth when they were brought by the Spirit most closely into conformity with the love of Jesus the Servant.

Make love your aim!

Well might Paul therefore implore the Corinthians at the end of this memorable chapter, 'Make love your aim' (14:1). His plea is taken up by John Wesley in *A Plain Account of Christian Perfection*, in a passage which will appropriately close this chapter.

> Another ground of these, and a thousand mistakes, is the not consid-ering deeply that love is the highest gift of God – humble, gentle, patient love; that all visions, revelations, manifestations whatever, are little things compared to love; and that all the gifts above mentioned are either the same with it or infinitely inferior to it.
>
> It were well you should be thoroughly sensible of this – the heaven of heavens is love. There is nothing higher in religion – there is, in effect, nothing else; if you look for anything but more love, you are looking wide of the mark, you are getting out of the royal way. And when you are asking others, 'Have you received this or that blessing?' if you mean anything but more love, you mean wrong; you are leading them out of the way, and putting them upon a false scent. Settle it in your heart, that . . . you are to aim at nothing more, but more of that love described in the thirteenth of Corinthians. You can go no higher than this till you are carried into Abraham's bosom.

8

The Spirit's Baptism

1. THE SPIRIT AND BAPTISM

One of the most lively debates about contemporary spirituality concerns what is often called baptism 'in' or 'by' the Holy Spirit. Broadly speaking, there are three attitudes towards it.

Is the Spirit's baptism water baptism?

First, there are those who identify baptism in the Holy Spirit with water baptism *tout simple*. If a person has been baptised with water in the name of the Trinity, then he must be considered as a child of God, an inheritor of the kingdom of heaven, a person equipped with the Spirit of God. Those who take this view believe that the sacrament does not merely symbolise but actually effects the change from darkness to light, from the power of Satan to God, from death to life. They rightly stress the objective nature of Christ's incarnation and atonement which are, as it were, made over to us in baptism. They rightly stress that we are saved not because of anything that we do, but because of what has been done for us by Christ independent of any of our efforts and fancied merits, and long prior to any response that we may make. They properly point to the one baptism shared by Christians throughout the world as the really significant way of marking allegiance to Jesus and fellowship with all others who share the baptismal bath.

159

But where this view is weak is in the whole area of personal response, of faith, of allegiance. There are millions of people who have been baptised in infancy without their knowledge or consent; they have been 'done' surreptitiously in a parish church on a Sunday afternoon when nobody but the family was present. They neither believe in the Christian story themselves, nor do those who brought them to baptism, except perhaps in the most general, not to say superstitious terms. They do not practise the Christian religion. They do not go to church. They do not believe the creeds. They do not know anything of the life-changing power of the Holy Spirit. The question is forced sharply upon us: in what sense is it meaningful to speak of such people as Christians despite the fact that they have been baptised with water in the name of the Trinity?

Is the Spirit's baptism conversion?

The second main view is this. Baptism with the Holy Spirit is identical with conversion. When a man repents and believes in Christ, when he makes his life over to the Lordship of Jesus and receives the Spirit of the risen Christ into his personality, he is thereby baptised with the Holy Spirit. This view, common in Protestant and Evangelical churches, is strong where the previous view was weak, and, conversely, weak where the previous view was strong. Its strength lies in its stress on personal response to the grace of God in Christ. Personal repentance and personal faith are crucial if the Holy Spirit is to baptise us into Christ.

But what about water baptism, on this view? It is either thought to be largely irrelevant (after all, what does the symbol matter if you have the reality?) or merely the mark of man's repentance and faith. Assuredly, baptism is integrally connected with repentance and faith, but is that all there is to it? Is it entirely something we do, and not at all something that God does to or for us? If so, it is very odd that the New Testament does not talk about a man baptising himself; instead, baptism is always something that is done for him by another. Clearly, we shall have to look a bit closer at the meaning of baptism in the New Testament before we can accept this identification of conversion with baptism in the Spirit. And even if we were convinced, it would still pose problems, this Protestant view. It is too cerebral, too intellectual. How about the children of believing families? Must they remain alienated from the Spirit of God until they make an act of personal faith? Is the Church merely the body of those who can exercise active belief? Has the Church no room for those who are too old, too young, or too mentally ill-equipped to believe the good news and entrust themselves to Christ? Must all such people be cut off from the Holy Spirit?

Is the Spirit's baptism a two-stage initiation?

The third answer to this question 'What is baptism in the Holy Spirit?' comes with a divided voice from two very dissimilar backgrounds.

The Catholic view

On the one hand, some Catholics, seeing the inadequacy of supposing that water baptism of infants must necessarily produce new birth by the Spirit, have argued that it is not baptism alone, but baptism accompanied (normally years later) by the imposition of hands in confirmation, which imparts the Holy Spirit. Distinguished Catholic theologians like Thornton, Mason, and Gregory Dix have taken up this view. They have drawn attention to two passages in the Acts where the Holy Spirit was given through the imposition of apostles' hands on the heads of folk who had been baptised but had not received the Holy Spirit. In Acts 8 the Samaritans receive the Spirit through the hands of John and Peter; in Acts 19 some disciples of John the Baptist receive him through the ministry of the apostle Paul. Accordingly, they believe that through confirmation by a bishop who is (it is hoped) in direct line with the apostles, people receive the Holy Spirit in a full and distinctive way at confirmation. The phrase 'baptism in the Holy Spirit' is not normally used by those who think in this way; but they clearly advocate a two-stage Christian initiation. Stage one, baptism, is incomplete; stage two, confirmation, brings the Holy Spirit into a person's life.

The Pentecostal view

Curiously enough, Pentecostal Christians are in the habit of using precisely the same verses to support their claim that Christian initiation is a two-stage affair. Coming, for the most part, from a Protestant background, they are inclined to take a person's conversion as stage one, and a subsequent over-powering experience of the Holy Spirit, which is normally (though not necessarily) accompanied by speaking in tongues, as stage two. It is this second stage which is commonly called by Pentecostals and neo-Pentecostals 'the baptism in the Holy Spirit'. It is seen as the indispensable step to spiritual power and a full Christian life. Although Pentecostalism as a denomination dates only from the first decade of the twentieth century, and neo-Pentecostalism (the spread of Spirit-baptism teaching and practice through other denominations) has only become prominent since the middle of that century, the roots go back a long way. John Wesley had taught a 'second work of grace' in the believer subsequent to justification. The worldwide Holiness Movement which includes the Keswick Convention, and boasts such influential names as Finney, Torrey, Andrew Murray and Watchman Nee, espoused this two-stage view of what makes a man a Christian. The nomenclature differed, but whether you spoke of 'entire sanctification', 'the gift', 'the blessing', 'the second blessing' or 'the baptism with the Holy Spirit' made little difference except in detailed description of the contents of the experience. In all cases it meant a new quality of Christian experience distinct from conversion; an experience which for some made Christian living at the previous level look so pale and shoddy that it was hardly worthy of the name Christian at all. And whether the recipients laid special claim to sanctification of life, as the early Methodists did, or to an experience of the Spirit marked by speaking in tongues, as the Pentecostals did, made little difference in practice. For those who possessed the experience inevitably came to think of themselves as an 'in' group, the people who had arrived; and those who did not share that experience were, inevitably, regarded as in some sense second-class Christians. After all, they hadn't got the baptism in the Holy Spirit . . .

In the light of these very divergent views, let us go back to the Bible and try to understand the broad sweep of its teaching on baptism.

2. THE SPIRIT AND BAPTISM IN THE NEW TESTAMENT

'Baptism' in the New Testament

A new word

The word *baptisma* is specifically Christian. It is not found before its appearance in the New Testament. The main lines of New Testament teaching about baptism are fairly clearly to be seen from the way in which this word is used. It is applied frequently to the baptism of John, which is called a 'baptism of repentance' (Luke 3:3, Acts 13:24). John's baptism looked forward to the coming kingdom, which the Greater than John would introduce. Those who were prepared for God's kingly rule to be exercised in their lives 'came together in baptism', as Josephus put it, determined to live a life of virtue and piety (*Antiquities*, 18:116f). It was baptism 'with a view to forgiveness of sins' (*eis aphesin hamartiōn*), so the evangelists tell us (Mark 1:4, Luke 3:3). It did not confer forgiveness, but it pointed the way, and it was because of this deeply seated link with forgiveness that early Christians were sometimes embarrassed that Jesus should have been baptised. Hence the conversation recorded in Matthew 3:13ff where John hesitates to baptise Jesus and Jesus says, 'Let it be so now; for thus it is fitting for us to fulfil all righteousness.' It seems that Jesus identified himself with sinners in the dramatic act of baptism, though he had no sins of his own to repent of. He was later to identify himself far more profoundly with sinners when he took responsibility for them on the cross. Indeed, it is interesting to notice that Jesus on two occasions alludes to his death in the metaphorical terms of 'baptism' (Mark 10:38, Luke 12:50). It was the cross that would make possible that forgiveness of sins to which repentant Israelites looked forward when they went down to the Jordan to be baptised by John. Repentance, forgiveness, membership of the messianic community – there was a further gift to which the baptism of John looked forward, though it could not confer. John made it abundantly clear that his baptism with water was a preparatory rite; Jesus would baptise with the Holy Spirit. And this promise began to be fulfilled on the day of Pentecost.

The 'once-for-allness' of baptism

We get some further idea of the way in which early Christians regarded baptism by noticing the use of *baptisma* in the writings of Paul and Peter. Paul says that we Christians were buried by our baptism into Christ's death, so that just as Christ was raised from the dead by the glory of the Father, so we too might walk in newness of life. In the context he is talking about justification, and the fact that it does not lead to lawlessness in behaviour. He says, in effect, that it cannot do, for they are baptised into Christ's death and resurrection. Baptism (along, of course, with the faith, repentance and allegiance to Jesus) has united Christians with Christ. They share his death to sin; they share his risen life. Baptism is, in fact, the sacrament of justification. The same point is made in Colossians 2:12. Paul is arguing that the Colossians do not need any additional saviour figures. They have Christ, and not only 'in him the whole fulness of the deity dwells bodily' but they themselves 'have come to fulness of life in him'. How did this come about? 'You were buried with him in baptism, in which you were also raised with him through faith in the working of God who raised him from the dead.' He goes on to say that, 'God made us alive with him, forgiving us all our trespasses, having cancelled the bond that stood against us with its legal demands; this he set aside, nailing it to his cross.' Now this is no second experience that Paul refers to: it is Christian baptism, the one baptism that they all share as Christians. Baptism is one of the seven constituents of Church unity to which the apostle can confidently refer in Ephesians 4:5. 'One Lord, one faith, one baptism . . .' Baptism is *the* mark of Christian belonging, the badge which all God's people have in common whatever their differences. The New Testament knows nothing of believers in Jesus who do not get baptised (though, of course, someone like the penitent thief did not have the opportunity). Neither does it know anything of Christians who get themselves rebaptised. For baptism is the sacramental expression of Christian initiation.

Personal commitment in baptism

If the use of the word *baptisma* does not support any two-stage idea of Christian initiation, it does not lend any support, either, to the notion that baptism in water inevitably saves a person irrespective of repentance, faith, obedience, and commitment to Christ and his Church. 1 Peter 3:21 goes out of its way to make this clear. Peter has been using the story of the ark in the flood, through which Noah and his family were saved, as a picture of Christian baptism. 'Baptism, which corresponds to this, now saves you,' he says. But as if conscious of the misinterpretation to which his words could be liable, he continues, 'not the putting away of the body's defilement' (i.e. the physical washing will not achieve anything by itself) 'but the pledge of a good conscience towards God, through the resurrection of Jesus Christ . . .' The word translated 'pledge' is variously interpreted. It may refer to the 'question' asked of those to be baptised; it may mean 'appeal' to God for a good conscience; it may even mean 'decision' for God arising out of a good conscience. But in any case it speaks of the genuine commitment on our side. And the allusion to the resurrection of Christ to God's right hand hints at the power released in the life of the baptised when the candidate does not merely go through a ceremonial washing, but turns in obedient repentance and faith to Jesus Christ. That sort of baptism saves us.

The distinctiveness of baptism

This distinctively Christian word *baptisma*, then, is associated with repentance, entry into the kingdom, forgiveness of sins, reception of the Spirit, and union with Christ in his death and risen life. It does not allow us to suppose that there is a baptism for Christians subsequent to conversion, nor does it permit us to think that a merely external submission to the rite affects anything. Baptism appears to be the expression in an outward ceremony of the new birth, justification, becoming a son of God, call it what you will; it is the mark of the new life, and that new life involves the other crucial constituents of repentance, faith, and reception of the Spirit of Christ who alone can make us new people.

'Baptise' in the New Testament

'Baptise' in the world

When we turn to the verb 'baptise', a similar picture meets us. Unlike the noun *baptisma*, the verb *baptizō* was used in pre-Christian Greek. It meant to immerse, and was used literally of 'scuppering' a ship, 'sinking' in the mud, and, in the passive, 'to perish', 'to be overwhelmed'. It would be attractive to suppose that this idea of being immersed and dying was carried over into the theology of Paul in Romans 6 and Colossians 2, but this cannot be proved.

'Baptise' in Judaism

The word was also used in pre-Christian Judaism, and indeed assumed considerable importance. For converts to Judaism, baptism was a significant part of initiation. Sacrifice was also required, along with circumcision for male members of the household; but all proselytes, male and female, adults and children, were baptised. They washed themselves in a bath of water, and saw this as washing away their Gentile impurities; so much so that the rabbis regarded the baptised proselyte as 'a newborn child'. He had a new status. Moreover, his baptism enabled him to enter symbolically into the event that was crucial in Israel's salvation history – the Exodus. We have a reference to this in 1 Corinthians 10:2 where Paul is alluding to the Old Testament prototypes of the Christian sacraments. He reminds the Corinthians, who seem to have been relying on their baptism and the eucharist as if they were of magical efficacy, that the Old Testament folk had their sacraments too, and these did not save them when they became disobedient. 'They all baptised themselves into Moses in the cloud and in the sea' – that is to say, at the Exodus; and 'they all ate the same spiritual food and drank the same spiritual drink', but nevertheless many of them perished in the desert for their disobedience and idolatry. This strange phrase, 'baptised into Moses', is the nearest parallel we find to the prevailing New Testament description of a Christian as someone who is baptised into Christ. The idea is primarily one of commitment to the figure who is active in salvation, Moses in one case and Christ in the other; but with Jesus there is a further connotation, for he is seen as the head of the new humanity in whom believers become incorporated.

'Baptise' in Paul

Apart from the evangelists, the only New Testament writer who uses the verb 'to baptise' is Paul, and it is instructive to see what he makes of it.

First and foremost, baptism derives its meaning from God's saving act in Christ. 'Christ loved the Church,' we read, 'and gave himself up for her in order that he might set her apart for himself, having cleansed her through washing by water with a word' (Eph. 5:25f). Though the word 'baptise' is not used here, the meaning is plain, and we have clear allusion to the bathing of the candidate in water, his response in the word of confession (cf. 1 Cor. 12:3), and both depending upon the self-sacrificing love of Jesus who went to the cross to make our cleansing possible. Again, the discussion of disunity in 1 Corinthians 1 is settled by Paul reminding them that they were baptised into the name (i.e. the ownership, the possession) of Christ who had been crucified for them (vv. 12–15). As we have seen, Jesus had looked forward to his sacrificial death as the supreme baptism, and Paul, looking back on the cross, emphasises the link. Baptism brings a man into contact with the saving work of Christ.

Baptism and justification

Accordingly we are not surprised to find that baptism is linked with justification in Romans 6:3f and 1 Corinthians 6:11. Many Evangelical Christians see justification by faith as the very antithesis of the sacrament of baptism. Paul sees them as the outside and the inside of the same thing. Consider these three points.

Firstly, baptism, like justification, is *done for us*. No man can justify himself. No man can baptise himself. In contrast to the proselyte baptism of the Jews when the candidate washed himself, Christian baptism is always in the passive. It is something done for you by another, as if to remind you that your salvation is entirely a matter of grace, and not something to which you make any active contribution.

Secondly, baptism, like justification, is *once for all*. It is unrepeatable. You can no more be rejustified than you can be rebaptised. Both ideas make nonsense. Baptism speaks of Christ's death once and for all on that cross for our forgiveness. Justification speaks of our account settled, of the verdict of the Last Day which we can know here and now – acquitted. Both have finality. Indeed, the sacrament of circumcision had this purpose in the Old Covenant. Abraham 'received circumcision as a sign of or seal on the righteousness by faith which he had when he was still uncircumcised' (Rom. 4:11). Abraham is a prototype of the true believer. God met him in undeserved grace, and offered to give him the ends of the earth for his inheritance and seed like the stars of heaven. Abraham responded in faith and obedience, and was given the rite of circumcision as a physical sign of the right standing he now enjoyed with God and as a seal on the whole transaction, to which he could look back with confidence in days when he was tempted to doubt. Baptism is like that: a gracious gift to believers, as a sign of their right standing with God and a seal on the whole transaction between divine grace and human faith.

And thirdly baptism, like justification, speaks of *incorporation into Christ*. That is the whole point of this remarkable phrase we repeatedly meet of 'baptism *into* Christ' – the Greek word *eis* is utterly explicit. Through the whole complex of repentance, faith and baptism a man is brought *into* Christ, so that from now on his position can be described by Paul's favourite definition of a Christian, as someone who is 'in Christ'. Yes, baptism speaks of incorporation into Christ. And so does justification. It is quite wrong to imagine that justification is some cold legal status conferred upon us by God reckoning Christ's merits to our account; far from it. Christ acted for us decisively and sufficiently through his cross and resurrection; as a result of that action we can be justified, acquitted, reckoned to be right with God but only as we are incorporated in Christ, united with the Righteous One, accepted in the Beloved. Hence the first half of Romans 5 can be so strong on justification: Christ for us. The second half of that chapter is all about the New Adam and our incorporation in him: us in Christ. The two belong together. For justification has incorporation into Christ as its corollary and rationale. This is made very clear in the concluding words of 2 Corinthians 5, where Paul insists that God made Jesus actually *to be sin* for us, Jesus who knew no sin; in order that we might *be the righteousness of God* – an almost inconceivable exchange. But Paul does not leave it there, for to do so would rightly merit the charges of injustice and legal fiction on God's part. He adds the crucial phrase '*in him*'. It is only in Christ that we are made right. God was in Christ, justifying me: I am in Christ, justified. Justification, like baptism, speaks of incorporation into Christ.

The sacrament of initiation

If it were necessary to stress even more emphatically the role of baptism as the sacrament of Christian initiation, we could turn to the end of Galatians chapter 3. In successive sentences Paul can say 'Christ came that we might be justified by faith', 'In Jesus Christ you are all sons of God through faith', and 'As many of you as have been baptised into Christ have put on Christ' (verses 24,26,27). Being justified by faith, becoming sons of God, and being baptised into Christ are three ways of describing the same thing – the beginning of the Christian life. And to conclude the paragraph, by taking us back to the great paradigm of justification by faith, Paul reminds his readers, 'If you are Christ's, then you are Abraham's offspring, and heirs according to promise.' Just as Abraham believed God's promise, obeyed his call, was justified by faith in God's grace, and received the sign and seal of circumcision – so with the Christian.

The parallel is exact. God has had only one way of saving people throughout all the ages. He did not save them by their works in Old Testament days, and by faith in New Testament days. He has been constant throughout history, accepting into close relationship with himself men and women from every age who were willing to turn from their evil ways, cast themselves on his mercy, and enter a recognisable community through an outward sacrament – circumcision in the old days, and baptism in the Christian era. Indeed, in a remarkable passage in his letter to the Colossians, Paul brings the sacraments of the Old and New Covenant together round the cross of Christ which alone gives them efficacy. 'In Christ you were circumcised with a circumcision made without hands . . . and you were buried with him in baptism': and all of this because Christ triumphed over the forces of evil in the cross (Col. 2:11–15).

Baptism – one-stage initiation

Baptism then, and not baptism plus a subsequent confirmation or 'baptism with the Spirit' is what marks a man as a Christian. It is the unrepeatable sacrament of Christian beginnings, just as the communion is the sacrament of going on with Christ in his Church. Of course, baptism is not to be seen as the bare external rite. The Bible is full of attacks on the merely outward (see Ps. 51:10, Rom. 2:28, 1 Cor. 10:1–11, Mark 7:14ff, Ezek. 18:31, 36:26, Isa. 1:10ff etc.). Baptism includes the idea of sonship, of entry into the kingdom, of incorporation into Christ, of reception of his Spirit, of justification. Sometimes one word is used, sometimes another; but the whole complex belongs together. There are three strands which taken together make a person a Christian. There is the human side – repentance and faith. There is the divine side – reception of the Spirit, adoption into the family of God, forgiveness of sins, justification. There is the churchly side – baptism into the body of believers. And all three belong together and are necessary parts of initiation. If you start asking 'Which is the most necessary?', it is a silly question, but I suppose the answer would

have to be – the divine side. If you ask which is the least important, that would be an even more silly question, but I suppose
the answer would have to be – the churchly side. But whichever
order they come in (and experience shows that, as Augustine
realised long ago, baptism sometimes precedes regeneration,
sometimes follows it, and sometimes never leads to it for lack
of faith on man's side and the gift of the Spirit on God's), the
three belong together in the plan of God as surely as loving
companionship, sexual relationship and children belong
together in God's plan for marriage.

What, then, of 'two-stage' passages?

If this is so, what are we to make of those passages in Acts
which speak of a two-stage initiation?

At first sight there are two such passages: Acts 8 where the
Samaritan believers did not receive the Holy Spirit immediately, and Acts 19 where a handful of disciples, who had been
followers of John the Baptist declared themselves unaware of
the existence of the Holy Spirit, but subsequently received him,
spoke with tongues and prophesied. In addition we might add
the conversion of Saul of Tarsus, where there seems to have
been a three-day gap between his surrender to Christ on the
Damascus road and his baptism and filling with the Holy
Spirit. But before we lay too much stress on these passages, it
is worth noticing a general point. Luke appears quite uninterested in providing a theology of Christian initiation. Those
who have gone to him for tidy theological schemes have been
disappointed. Sometimes reception of the Spirit follows
baptism (e.g. Acts 2:38ff); sometimes it precedes baptism (e.g.
Acts 10:44–48); and sometimes a man is baptised who has no
part nor lot in the Christian thing, and whose heart is still fast
bound in wickedness (Acts 8:21). Luke is so little concerned to
write a handbook on Christian initiation that he does not even
tell us whether Apollos received Christian baptism from

Aquila and Priscilla, who took him in hand and instructed him when 'he knew only the baptism of John'. Nevertheless, in the very next chapter, Luke gives us this remarkable excursus on the rebaptism of a dozen disciples of the Baptist at the hands of Paul! Professor Dunn would argue, in his *Baptism in the Holy Spirit* that the reason is plain: all that really matters is the possession of the Holy Spirit, and Apollos possessed the Spirit already, so was not rebaptised, while the disciples of John at Ephesus had not received the Spirit and so were given full Christian initiation. He may be right; but I rather doubt it. His claim that Apollos was full of the Holy Spirit is precariously based in the text. The phrase *zeōn tō pneumati* in Acts 18:25 could mean 'burning hot with the Holy Spirit', but could also mean 'fervent in spiritual disposition', which is the probable meaning in the only other place it occurs, Romans 12:11. It has often been observed that Paul is more interested in the interior work of the Spirit, assuring believers, transforming their lives, and so on; whereas Luke is more interested in the broader picture of the coming of the Spirit on the Church, his external manifestations in prophecy and tongues, and his direction of the Christian mission. It would certainly be a mistake to try to base a doctrine of theological necessity upon passages in Luke's writings which were designed to describe the various stages which seemed to him significant in the spread of a work for God.

With this note of caution in mind, let us examine the three passages in question.

St. Paul's conversion?

It would be very precarious to found a doctrine of two-stage initiation on the three-day delay in Paul's conversion experience. As we have seen from his own writings, he was clearly a one-stage man, for whom justification and sonship were symbolised and sealed in baptism and reception of the Spirit.

Luke, too, sees the whole three-day experience as one. Thus in the account he gives of Paul's conversion before the Jerusalem Jews (Acts 22:10ff), the Ananias incident is recalled along with Paul's commission and baptism; while in his other account of it, before Agrippa (Acts 26:12ff) there is no mention of the three-day wait, the role of Ananias, or even of baptism. The one unified emphasis which confronts us in all three accounts, as well as Paul's allusions in his own letters, is of a radical, life-changing encounter between Saul of Tarsus and the risen Jesus.

The Ephesian dozen?

What does the text really say?

Equally, there is no ground for supposing that the events of Acts 19 are meant to advocate a two-stage initiation for Christian people. It is clearly an exceptional instance: only a handful of men are involved, a mere dozen 'disciples'. The word to be sure, usually denotes Christians, and Paul initially mistook them for Christians. But he soon found out his mistake. They seemed to possess none of the marks of the Spirit's indwelling. So he asked them, *not*, as the Authorised Version rather carelessly put it, 'Have you received the Holy Ghost *since ye believed*?', as if the Greek warranted some great space between their belief and their reception of the Spirit; but, 'Have you believed and received the Holy Spirit?' – the participle 'believing' being contemporaneous with their 'receiving'. It is unfortunate that many Pentecostal writings still rely on this simple mistranslation of the Greek original for their teaching on a two-stage experience. I have before me, as I write, a little book by Don Basham, *Ministering the Baptism in the Holy Spirit*. He is associated with the Full Gospel Business Men's Fellowship, a leading Pentecostal agency, and explains Acts 19:2 as follows. 'Have you received the baptism in the Holy Spirit since you accepted Jesus Christ as your Saviour?' Not

only is there nothing in the verse about 'accepting Jesus Christ
as Saviour' nor about 'receiving the baptism in the Holy Spirit',
but the time reference indicated by the English 'since you
accepted . . .' has no warrant in the Greek. It is rather surprising to read in his Introduction, after three errors in the exposi-
tion of one verse like this, the claim that 'the Holy Spirit led him
(i.e. Basham) into presenting almost word for word the message
this book contains'. Such exegesis and such claims are not
helpful.

Were they really Christians?

The passage goes on to make it crystal clear that these disciples
were in no sense Christians. They were followers of John the
Baptist, baptised by him (v. 3) who had then made their way
hundreds of miles north-west to Ephesus. They had clearly not
been in touch with John's later testimony to Jesus, for they
needed to be informed by Paul that the Coming One whom
John predicted was in fact Jesus. They had neither heard of
Jesus, nor believed in Jesus, nor been baptised into the name of
Jesus, and they were quite uninformed about the Holy Spirit.
Uncharacteristically the old King James' Version is likely to
mislead us at this point. According to it, they reply to Paul 'We
have not so much as heard whether there be any Holy Ghost'
(v. 2). This is certainly a possible way to take the Greek, but it
would have been difficult for anyone who listened, however
inattentively, to John the Baptist to be in doubt that he was
interested in the Holy Spirit! It is much more likely that the
original should be translated, 'We have not even heard if the
Holy Spirit is available.' Not only did John the Baptist speak of
the Holy Spirit as the future gift of the Coming One, but as
John the Evangelist observed concerning a statement of Jesus,
'As yet the Spirit had not been given, because Jesus was not yet
glorified' (John 7:39). The followers of John at Ephesus did not
know if the age of the Spirit had broken in yet. It is rather hard
to suppose that men who were disciples of the Baptist, who did

not know about Jesus or the Holy Spirit, can be called Christians and made models for a two-stage initiation! The fact seems to be that these men were not Christians at all, and their initiation into Christ followed the preaching by Paul. They were baptised in the name of the Lord Jesus. They had Paul's hands laid upon them. They received the Spirit in a very manifest way, for they spoke in tongues and prophesied. Very much one-stagers . . .

The Samaritan converts?

Why the delay?

Which brings us to the remaining passage, Acts 8. However you choose to interpret it, it leaves you with problems. Philip preached the gospel to the Samaritans. Multitudes responded. Evil spirits were cast out; lame folk were healed; and much joy marked the city. Simon the magician is then brought before our eyes. He had set himself up as a great power from God, but saw himself outclassed, and 'even Simon himself believed, and after being baptised he continued with Philip, and seeing signs and great miracles performed, he was amazed'. At this point Peter and John came up from Jerusalem to see what was going on, and they prayed that the Samaritans might receive the Holy Spirit, 'for it had not yet fallen upon any of them, but they had merely been baptised into the name of the Lord Jesus'. Why the delay?

An exceptional case

The Pentecostal answer, and the answer of many Catholics, is the same. The Samaritan believers needed the laying on of apostolic hands in confirmation to make them full members of the Church (on the Catholic view) or to baptise them with the Holy Spirit (on the Pentecostal view). Quite apart from the mutually contradictory theologies built by Catholics and Pentecostals on this passage, it has to be pointed out that

nowhere else in the New Testament is the laying on of hands
seen as the decisive act in Christian initiation. To be sure, it
sometimes has a place, as passages like Acts 19:6 and Hebrews
6:2 make clear; but nobody laid hands on the apostles at
Pentecost to confirm them – or to equip them with the Holy
Spirit; nor on Cornelius, nor on the Ethiopian eunuch, nor the
converts on the day of Pentecost nor almost every other
recorded conversion! If Acts 8 is taken as justification for
regarding either confirmation or baptism with the Spirit
through the laying on of hands as the second essential stage in
becoming a Christian, then on the showing of the New
Testament itself, there are precious few Christians! No, this
incident at Samaria was not typical, and Luke records it
because it is not typical. He has something important that he
wants to show us by it, but unfortunately he has failed to make
his point abundantly plain!

A mark of solidarity?

One view propounded by Professor Lampe and owing a good
deal to the writings of Conzelmann is that Luke is at great pains
to stress the links between the apostolic church at Jerusalem on
the one hand and the spreading circles of Christian outreach on
the other. There is a lot of evidence to support this view. In this
particular incident, accordingly, Lampe sees Peter and John
being sent by the Jerusalem church 'not to administer confirmation to the Samaritans, but to confirm their baptism by
Philip, and to incorporate them, by the sign of solidarity, the
laying on of hands, into the community of the Pentecostal
Spirit; so that the Samaritan converts, too, became a sort of
extension of the Jerusalem church'. This view, though attractive, does not quite fit the evidence. Saul's conversion was, on
any showing, a major advance for Christianity, yet it was
Ananias, who had no close links with Jerusalem, so far as we
know, who laid hands on his head. And in the even more climactic turning to the Gentiles in the first missionary journey

(13:46) we hear of no hands being laid on anyone's heads, but faith, the growth of the Word of the Lord, joy and the Holy Spirit.[1]

The dawning of reality?

Another view has been propounded by Professor Dunn in his *Baptism in the Holy Spirit*. He thinks that the Samaritans never really believed at all; their attention was fixed on Philip, not on Christ. Simon, though baptised and said to be believing, was clearly not a Christian, as Dunn rightly observes. He suggests that the rest of the Samaritans were caught up in a wave of

---

[1] Professor Lampe comments in *St. Luke and the Church at Jerusalem*: 'I don't think that my view that the Samaritan mission became a sort of extension of the Jerusalem church through the action of Peter and John is invalidated by what you say. Luke is keen to show that the major developments in the Church's mission were brought about under the wing of Jerusalem, but he knows that this was done in a variety of ways. At Samaria it had to be by this special action by the heads of the Jerusalem apostolate, because Philip's baptisms clearly needed authenticating and ratifying. Paul was given the same sign by Ananias. The presence of Peter and John was not required: no schism had to be bridged in Paul's case. But Luke emphasises that Ananias was an established Jewish-Christian disciple (Acts 22:12; 9:10), i.e. a representative of the primitive community; and he brings Paul to Jerusalem and to fellowship with the apostles there as soon as possible after the Ananias episode. There was no need for hands to be laid on Gentiles at 13:46 or anywhere else in that mission, for Paul and Barnabas were authorised by the Antioch church, which had itself been authenticated by Barnabas as an envoy of Jerusalem (11:22ff). Paul was himself, according to Luke, an envoy of Jerusalem, reporting back as often as possible. The only people, after Paul himself, who needed authentication were Apollos, through instruction by Paul's associates, and the Ephesians who were possibly Apollos' converts.' As will be seen from the text, I do not share Professor Lampe's view in every detail, and I do not think that Luke was as keen on authentication as he does. Nevertheless the account he gives may be the correct one, and certainly makes some sense of the diverse phenomena in Acts.

emotion and believed Philip rather than Christ, on the basis of the Greek construction *pisteuō* with the dative rather than the more usual *pisteuō eis*. However, there are other cases where *pisteuō* with the dative denotes saving faith (e.g. Acts 16:34, 18:8), so we cannot give too much weight to that point. And the healings, the joy, the exorcisms which marked their belief at Samaria strongly suggest that it was real Christian faith all right. Why, then, did God withhold his Holy Spirit on this unique occasion?

The healing of a split?

I believe the answer lies in the centuries old split between the Jews and the Samaritans. 'The Jews have no dealings with the Samaritans' or perhaps 'refuse to use vessels in common with the Samaritans', as St. John had remarked (John 4:9). If the Holy Spirit had been given immediately upon profession of faith and baptism by the Samaritans this ancient schism might have continued, and there would have been two churches, out of fellowship with each other. Acts 15 shows how carefully a decisive split between Jewish and Gentile Christianity was avoided by the early Christians. Acts 8 seems to stress that a similarly disastrous split was avoided at Samaria. God did not give his Holy Spirit (or, perhaps, the supernatural manifestations of that Spirit in tongues and prophecy?) to the Samaritans at once: not until representatives from Jerusalem came down and expressed their solidarity with the converts by praying for them and laying their hands on them. Then they received the Holy Spirit; indeed, the use of the imperfect tense, *elambanon*, may be significant; they received repeated manifestations of the Holy Spirit. It was not so much an authorisation from Jerusalem or an extension of the Jerusalem church, as a divine veto on schism in the infant Church, a schism which could have slipped almost unnoticed into the Christian fellowship, as converts from the two sides of the 'Samaritan curtain' found Christ without finding each other. That would have been the denial of the one baptism and all it stood for. It was for this reason, I believe, that God made delay on this occasion. Acts 8 is recorded precisely to show the abnormality of a baptism which does not lead to reception of the Holy Spirit. The two, this passage implies (and the rest of the New Testament states explicitly), belong together. Indeed, Simon Tugwell puts it very well when he writes, 'This does not mean that the New Testament has no interest in other manifestations of the Spirit. Obviously it has! All that is being claimed is that baptism is the appointed locus, the appointed "visibility" of reception of the Spirit. We should neither exaggerate this claim, as sacramentalists have tended to do, nor reduce it, as Evangelicals and especially Pentecostals have tended to do. There is a great diversity of ways in which the Spirit works in us; the one thing that is common to all and is the bond of our unity, is baptism' (*Did you receive the Spirit?* p. 85f).

New Testament teaching on baptism in the Holy Spirit

'In' and 'by'

It is perhaps surprising that there are so few references in the New Testament to baptism in or by the Holy Spirit. There are in fact only seven. Before we look at them, it is worth clearing up the phrase I have just used, 'in or by' the Holy Spirit. In Greek the word *en* can either mean 'in' or can denote the instrumentality through which something happens, 'by'. It is not possible to decide finally whether baptism with the Holy Spirit refers to the Spirit as the one in whom we are immersed, or as the one by whom we are baptised into sharing the fortunes and destiny of Christ. The evidence leans a little towards the latter interpretation, as we shall see.

Six N.T. references to baptism in the Spirit

There are just seven places in the New Testament where this phrase is used. And six of them refer to the baptism which John the Baptist promised that the Coming One would bring. In contrast to his own water baptism, Jesus would baptise with the Spirit. That is the plain meaning of Mark 1:8, and its parallels in Luke 3:16 and Matthew 3:11. John 1:33 is similar, and we have already examined it: 'He on whom you see the Spirit descend and remain, this is he who baptises with the Holy Spirit.' Acts 1:5 is equally explicit. Jesus reminds them of John's words, 'for John baptised with water, but before many days you shall be baptised with the Holy Spirit'. This promise of Jesus was fulfilled a few days later, when the Spirit which had 'rested' on Jesus came and 'rested' on them, filling them, and enabling them to speak in other tongues. The sixth reference comes in Acts 11:16. Peter is explaining the Cornelius incident to his critics at Jerusalem. 'As I began to speak, the Holy Spirit fell on them (i.e., Cornelius and his household) just as on us at the beginning. And I remembered the word of the Lord, how he said, "John baptised with water, but you shall be baptised with the Holy Spirit." If then God gave the same gift to them as he gave to us when we believed on the Lord Jesus Christ, who was I that I could withstand God?' Peter is referring to an incident as significant for Christian advance as the conversion of the first Samaritan believers: the Gentile 'godfearer' Cornelius has been grafted into God's family. And just as God withheld his Spirit from the Samaritans until the Jewish Christians were willing to heal the breach with them and make one Church; so now God gives his Spirit to Cornelius and his family before Peter can make any appeal for repentance and faith, so as to cleanse all traces of pride and superiority out of Peter and teach him not to despise Gentiles and call them common or unclean. It is one of the high points in Acts, where the Spirit of God breaks through human apartheid. That is why it is recorded no less than three times. That is why Peter recognises it as the Gentile equivalent of Pentecost. Jesus has baptised not only Jews and Samaritans but Gentiles with the Spirit promised long ago by John. The same gift is for 'them' as for 'us'. There is no distinction among those who have repented (11:18), believed in the Lord Jesus (11:17) and received the same Holy Spirit, baptising them into union with Christ.

The seventh reference

In these six references so far we have an unambiguous picture presented. John baptises with water as a mark of repentance; Jesus will baptise with the Holy Spirit, to bring men into the blessings of the New Covenant. This became possible on the day of Pentecost, when the disciples who had already submitted to John's baptism were baptised by the Holy Spirit. It was the Holy Spirit who baptised Jews who had companied long and deeply with the incarnate Christ; it was the same Holy Spirit who, to the amazement of Peter, baptised Cornelius into Christ, Cornelius who neither knew about nor knew the incarnate Christ. In both instances baptism with the Holy Spirit initiated men into the blessings of the New Covenant. And exactly the same thing is taught in the seventh and final reference to baptism in the Holy Spirit in 1 Corinthians 12:13. 'By one Spirit we were all baptised into one body – Jews or Greeks, slaves or free – and all were made to drink of one Spirit.' Paul could hardly put it more plainly, nor indeed more polemically. For many of his Corinthian readers prided themselves on gifts of healings, tongues, prophecy, faith and so forth, and despised others, setting themselves apart. How they would have loved to claim that only the healers, only the tongues speakers were baptised in, or by, that Spirit. But Paul demolishes that claim before it is uttered. It is the one Spirit who enables men to make the baptismal confession, 'Jesus is Lord' (12:3). And it is the one Spirit who baptises believers into the one body of Christ – whatever the differences between them. The one baptism by the one Spirit is as decisive a unitive factor as the one Father who inspires all his children alike, and the one Lord Jesus whom they all serve (12:4f). It is not certain whether the '*en*' is locative or instrumental. It could mean that all are immersed in one Spirit, but since it goes on 'into the body' that would be very harsh, and the instrumental use is highly likely here and in the other references we have looked at. The Corinthians were all baptised by the one Spirit into the one body of Christ. And, for good measure, Paul sees the Spirit not only as the one who plunges them into Christ, but as the one who comes within them like a draught of cool water, or irrigation on parched soil: 'You were all made to drink of one Spirit.'

Christians not told to be baptised with the Spirit

What this evidence shows is two facts of considerable doctrinal importance. First, nowhere are *Christians* subsequent to the day of Pentecost said to be baptised with the Spirit. Pentecost was the anointing, the 'Christing' of the original disciples. They had had Jesus alongside them. They now had the Spirit of Jesus within them. And the gift of the Spirit, made on that first Whit Sunday, has never been withdrawn. The Spirit is available for all who repent and believe and are baptised into Christ. The converts on the day of Pentecost found this: 'Repent, and be baptised every one of you . . . for the forgiveness of sins, and you shall receive the gift of the Holy Spirit' Peter had promised them. They did repent, and they found it true. The two distinctive blessings of the New Covenant were theirs at once. Cornelius found the truth of this; so did the Corinthians; and so have Christians down the ages. Indeed, 'if any man does not have the Spirit of Christ, he is no Christian' (Rom. 8:9). So baptism with the Holy Spirit is not a second-stage experience for some Christians, but an initiatory experience for all Christians. Without it we are not Christians at all.

Christians not told to wait for the Spirit

The second important thing is this. Christians are never told to wait for or pray for the baptism in the Holy Spirit. Of course not, for they are already baptised by the Spirit. The original disciples were indeed told to wait for the coming of the Spirit, but this was before Pentecost, before the distinctive experience of the Spirit of Jesus, internalised within the believer, was open to all. Ever since Pentecost there has been no need for 'waiting meetings' for baptism with the Holy Spirit. This is our Christian starting point, not our goal.

3. FALSE LINGUISTICS: GENUINE EXPERIENCE

The experience of 'baptism in the Holy Spirit'

If this is what the New Testament teaches about baptism in the Holy Spirit, how is it that so many zealous Christians use the term in a quite different sense? Why do they refer it to some second experience? It is in that word 'experience' that the answer lies. They have had an overwhelming experience of the Spirit of God; an experience that has changed their Christian lives as decisively as wrestling with God by Jabbok changed Jacob's. They then attach this label to the experience. Graham Pulkingham's experience is a celebrated and not atypical example. In *Gathered for Power* he tells us of the Liberal circles of Episcopalianism in which he had been brought up, of his appointment to The Church of the Redeemer, Houston, of his powerlessness in the face of the depressed condition of the church and the neighbourhood, and of his longing for a deeper experience of God. He tells us how he met David Wilkerson of *Cross and Switchblade* fame, and went with him to a home for rescued prostitutes which David's organisation looked after. 'It was here that I received the baptism with the Spirit,' says Pulkingham (p. 75). Abruptly Dave Wilkerson told him to kneel down, and Pulkingham recalls, 'I knelt and they came across the room hurriedly. When their hands touched my head something inside of me leapt with gladness, and even the unusual manner of their prayer was not offensive – it was loudly proclaimed in languages that were entirely foreign to me.' Almost immediately 'all awareness of the men and their prayers, of the room, and even of myself was obliterated by the immense presence of God's power. He was unmistakably there, and my inner response was like the clatter of a bamboo wind chime in a gale; the very foundations of my soul shook violently.' He bowed low before the greatness of God, and wept at his own unworthiness. 'We can go now; the Baptiser's here,' said Dave to his companion, and they departed, leaving Graham alone with God.

That is how Graham Pulkingham describes the experience of God which revolutionised his Christian life. There followed a new gladness, a new power in ministry, in healing, in preaching, a liberty in prayer and worship, a crossing of denominational backgrounds, and a wonderful experiment (which is still going on) in community living after the apostolic fashion which so struck a commercial broadcasting company in the States that they made a documentary of it. How could Pulkingham call the experience which triggered off such mighty revolutions in all he had known as Christianity by a lesser name than 'baptism in the Holy Spirit'?

The description 'baptism in the Holy Spirit'

It is very understandable for Christians with experiences of God like Graham Pulkingham's to call that experience 'baptism in the Holy Spirit', but all the same it is mistaken. This is not how the New Testament relates baptism and the Spirit. Always, as we have seen, the baptism in the Spirit is an initiatory experience. The Spirit of God brings people into the family of God, and it is utterly confusing to speak of the Spirit baptising people who already have the Spirit. It is a confusion which leads to several unfortunate results.

Distortion

First, it either has to neglect or to distort what the New Testament has to say about the Spirit and baptism. Take Dennis

Bennett's *The Holy Spirit and You* as an example. He quotes the
'one baptism' of Ephesians 4:5 and continues, 'yet it is clear that
in the New Testament this "one baptism" divides into three. In
1 Corinthians 12:13 Paul says, "In one Spirit we were all baptised
into one body . . . and were all made to drink into one Spirit."
This refers to the spiritual baptism into Christ which takes place
as soon as Jesus is received as Saviour. This was followed by the
baptism with the Holy Spirit, in which the now indwelling Holy
Spirit poured forth to manifest Jesus to the world through the
life of the believer. Either before or after the baptism with the
Holy Spirit there was the outward sign of baptism with water.'
There appears to be some confusion here! Not one baptism, but
three. And in order to differentiate them, they require explana-
tory glosses: '*spiritual* baptism into Christ', 'baptism *with the
Holy Spirit*' and '*the outward sign of* baptism with water'. As we
have seen, God has joined these three together in significance,
however they may differ in the time at which they are experienced. Baptism in water is the sacramental symbol of repentance and faith on one side and the gift of the Spirit on the other.
The whole thing belongs together. We therefore do despite to the
New Testament if we use the phrase 'baptism with the Holy
Spirit' to refer to a second experience for Christians.

Confusion

Once you do use the phrase in this way, you immediately find
yourself in deep theological trouble. Because it is plain from
such verses as Romans 8:9 that all Christians have the Spirit.
How is it, then, that they have the Spirit on the one hand, but
have not received the baptism with the Spirit on the other? All
very confusing and contradictory. In successive sentences
Dennis Bennett says, 'Because you have received Jesus, you
already have the Holy Spirit, so no one needs to "give" Him to
you' and 'Jesus is living in you and he is ready to baptise you in
the Holy Spirit as soon as you are ready to respond' (p. 56). What
he intends is clear enough; he calls 'baptism with the Holy Spirit'

a deep experience of God which involves speaking in tongues. 'We have shown that speaking in tongues is indeed a common denominator in examples of the baptism in the Holy Spirit given in the Scriptures' (p. 57). In other words, for Bennett, though he is by no means a hardline neo-Pentecostal, speaking in tongues seems to be an essential part of the baptism with the Spirit. It was just what the charismatics at Corinth thought; just what necessitated those three chapters 1 Corinthians 12–14, with their stress on the one Spirit although he manifests himself in various ways in the body of Christ into which all Christians are baptised.

Division

A third most unfortunate consequence which follows from regarding this deep experience of God, often marked by the ability to speak in tongues, as 'baptism in the Holy Spirit' is divisiveness. The New Testament makes it very plain that a man who has the Spirit of God is very different from one who does not. You are either 'in the Spirit' or 'in the flesh'. But charismatics tend to transfer this strong Christian dualism, this 'either/or', to the experience they have labelled 'baptism in the Holy Spirit'. Those who have had the baptism are 'in', and those who have not had the baptism are 'out'. Hence the divisiveness which the charismatic movement has often brought to churches. There are, of course, various reasons for this division; the unspirituality of many of the ordinary members of the congregation and their unwillingness to be open before God and their brethren; a sense of having arrived by some neo-Pentecostals, and so on. But much of the trouble is due to this use of the phrase 'baptism in the Holy Spirit'. For baptism means beginning; it is the initiatory Christian rite, and it speaks of the initiatory Christian experience. If believing Christians are told they must be baptised with the Spirit, it inevitably suggests that they lack him already, that they have not yet begun. But they *have* begun! They are in Christ, justified, adopted into God's family, recipients of his gracious Spirit. The unintended arrogance of the division of

Christians into those who have been baptised in the Holy Spirit
and those who have not would be enormously eased if charismatics rejected the unscriptural use of this term 'baptism in the
Holy Spirit' to describe a second experience for those who are
already Christians. It is contrary to the usage of the New
Testament, confusing in the extreme, and contributory to division among the one people of the Spirit.

A plea for careful language

It is greatly to the credit of some thoughtful Christians within
the Catholic charismatic movement, that they have perceived
and avoided this danger of taking over uncritically the
Pentecostal description of 'baptism in the Holy Spirit' to
describe the renewal they have received. Even Dr. Gordon Fee,
in his most careful study of the Holy Spirit in St. Paul, allows
himself an Appendix to his book *Paul, the Spirit and the People
of God* entitled 'Spirit baptism and water baptism in Paul'.
While he does not make the mistake of seeing 'Spirit baptism'
as a second stage initiation, but identifies it with conversion, he
persists in using this unhelpful language setting baptism in
water over and against baptism in the Spirit, which the apostle
Paul never does. Paul's only reference to the Spirit baptising, in
1 Cor. 12:13, is clearly linked with the earliest Christian confession at baptism (in water!) that 'Jesus is Lord' (v.3). By way of
contrast, Fr. Kilian McDonnell, O.S.B., writing on the theological basis of the Catholic charismatic renewal, grasped the
nettle which had proved too prickly for his fellow Roman
Catholic, Simon Tugwell, in chapter 5 of *Did You Receive the
Spirit?* He integrates every experience of the Spirit with the one
baptism. 'The charismatic renewal has its theological foundations in the celebration of initiation, and calls for a renewal of
baptismal consciousness broadly conceived, that is, "that we
might understand the gifts bestowed on us" (1 Cor. 2:12). A
feature of the renewal which causes confusion is the use of the
phrase "baptism in the Holy Spirit". For historical reasons

many Catholics in the renewal have adopted this phrase, already current among classical Pentecostals, to describe the experience through which they came into a new awareness of the presence and power of the Spirit in their lives.

'But there is a problem in the use of this phrase, as it could be taken to mean that only those who have had a particular kind of experience of the Spirit have really been baptised in the Spirit. This is not the case, since every valid and fruitful Christian initiation confers the "gift of the Holy Spirit" (Acts 2:38), and "to be baptised in the Holy Spirit" is simply another scriptural way of saying "to receive the Holy Spirit".

'Hence, many prefer to use other expressions to describe what is happening in the charismatic renewal. Among other alternatives which have been proposed are: "release of the Spirit", "renewal of the sacraments of initiation", "actualisation of gifts already received in potentiality", and "a manifestation of baptism, whereby the hidden grace given in baptism breaks through into conscious experience". These are all ways of saying that the power of the Holy Spirit, given in Christian initiation, but hitherto unexperienced, becomes a matter of personal conscious experience.' He goes on to show that this conscious experience may develop gradually or through a crisis experience: 'both the growth pattern and the crisis pattern should be looked upon as authentic ways of realising the grace of initiation at the conscious level'. If all those within the renewal would use language with the same care as this Roman Catholic theologian, a great deal of confusion and heartbreak would be avoided.

The reality behind the inaccurate description

The new wine

On the other hand, if the language which neo-Pentecostals use for their experience is unfortunate, this is not the case with the experience itself. It is tragic that many Christians have robbed themselves of blessing because they distrusted, feared or despised this movement. They have been satisfied with a low level of spirituality. They have not allowed God to release them in prayer and praise and personal relationships, from the imprisonment of age-long inhibitions. They have not expected to see God at work in conversions, in changing tough lives, in healing, in explicit guidance. They have forgotten that the manifestations of the Spirit in the New Testament had an uncomfortably concrete nature. Much of the division in the churches that has come with the Pentecostals, has not been the fault of the Pentecostals themselves, but of the narrow, fearful, unspiritual Christianity in whose lukewarm waters many of us have for so long been willing to stay, terrified to launch out into the deep of experience of God. In an age when the Spirit of God is breaking up the fallow ground and the man-made barriers all over the world and irrespective of denomination, it would be ironic indeed if we missed what he has for us because we refused to get below the false linguistics in which the Pentecostals customarily express their living experience of God. Let those who want to retain the New Testament link between baptism in the Spirit and water baptism, justification, adoption – becoming a Christian, in fact – make very sure that it is the full New Testament concept of baptism which they espouse; a plunging beneath the waters of the Spirit, an inundation with him, a vitality produced by him that could cause folk to wonder if we were drunk. Have we that power in prayer, that strength over temptation, that growing Christlikeness, which marked the communities of Christ in New Testament days and of which the one baptism was the outward bond?

The old wineskins

When in the sixteenth century this tension between tradition and experience, between churchly Christianity and new life in Christ was felt so acutely, the Reformers did not say, 'Away with church structures. Down with water baptism, because it clearly does not bring new birth. All that matters is justification.'

Instead, they spoke of 'improving on' their baptism, by which they meant ensuring that they had the reality as well as the symbol. If they lived in our day they would show themselves too good scholars, I fancy, to use the phrase 'baptism in the Holy Spirit' in the way many Pentecostals do; they would retain the biblical sense of the word as the divine element in Christian initiation. But they would want to go all the way with the Pentecostals in emphasising the deep experience of God. They would call on us today to 'improve on' our baptism, and make sure that we are not merely immersed in the Spirit symbolically through our baptism, but actually in our lives. It is to this full surrender to the Lord who is Spirit, this openness to his sweeping through our lives, that the Pentecostal movement is recalling the Church of God. If the Church fails to heed, then the new wine may regretfully be found to require new bottles.

9

The Spirit's Fulness

Two initial surprises about 'fulness'

It has been characteristic of holiness movements throughout Church history to claim that the fulness of the Holy Spirit depends on conformity with their particular shibboleth. The terminology changes: 'perfection', 'brokenness', 'full surrender', 'sanctification' have all been used, but 'the fulness of the Holy Spirit' is perhaps the most contemporary and explicit in its claim. It is a commonplace in Pentecostal and neo-Pentecostal literature that while all Christians share to some extent in the Holy Spirit, only those who have been 'baptised in' the Holy Spirit can know his fulness. The fulness of the Holy Spirit which comes from his personal, permanent and full in-dwelling, is intended to equip us for service, and is obtained only by this crisis experience of 'baptism in the Holy Spirit'. Indeed 'Spirit-filled' is often used by charismatic people to describe someone who shares their experience, in contradistinction to run-of-the-mill Christians. What does the New Testament say about the fulness of the Holy Spirit?

Surprisingly, it says nothing at all. The Greek word for fulness, *plērōma*, is applied to many things in the New Testament, notably to both Christ and the Church; but never to the Holy Spirit. This is not an important point, because the idea may be present without the word; but it does show how ill-based in Scripture is any attempt to make the 'fulness of the

Holy Spirit' into a doctrinal war cry, as if it were a most important and neglected biblical emphasis.

The second noteworthy point is that the verb 'to be filled with', *pimplēsthai*, is almost exclusively Lucan. Apart from two occasions in Matthew, all its other twenty-two occurrences are in Luke's Gospel or Acts. The adjective 'full' has a wider spread, but of its sixteen appearances eleven are in Luke or Acts. It is clear that this is a favourite word of Luke's. In addition we ought perhaps to mention the normal word for 'to fill', *plēroun*, but this is only twice used of the Holy Spirit (Acts 13:52, Eph. 5:18) and twice loosely associated with him (Rom. 15:13f, Col. 1:8,9).

Two main uses of 'fulness'

The words are used in two main ways.

A general description

One is to denote the general characteristic of a person, 'full of the Spirit'. The supreme exemplar for this use is, of course, Jesus (Luke 4:1), but after Pentecost it is occasionally applied to Christians by Luke. The qualifications sought in the Seven of Acts 6 were that they should be 'full of wisdom and the Holy Spirit'. Among them Stephen is described as 'a man full of faith and the Holy Spirit', and the point is re-emphasised at his martyrdom (7:55). Barnabas is the only other man so described (11:24): 'He was a good man, full of the Holy Spirit and of faith.' Luke seems to be using this phrase of a man's governing characteristic, his controlling disposition. Thus we read of a man 'full of leprosy' (Luke 5:12), that is to say gripped by the disease. We read that Elymas was 'full of all deceit and villainy' (13:10) and understand that he was controlled by these evil impulses. The meaning of 'full of the Holy Spirit' is therefore not hard to fathom. It signifies someone who is habitually governed and controlled by the Lord the Spirit, just as Jesus was.

There is no suggestion that this state is due to any particular ritual or experience.

A sudden filling

The second way in which the notion of being filled with the Spirit meets us in the Scriptures is quite different. It does not refer to the settled characteristics of a lifetime but to the sudden inspiration of a moment. The instances where it occurs are as follows, and they are most interesting because sometimes they bear what we might call a 'charismatic' character, and sometimes a 'non-charismatic' one. But the strangest of all is the first, John the Baptist. For the promise to Zacharias is that 'he shall be filled with the Holy Spirit even from his mother's womb' (Luke 1:15). Now a statement like that does not chime in with anybody's ready-made theological pattern, and what a healthy thing that it does not! For God is God. He is free to act in accordance with his sovereign will and purposes. If he determines to fill the Baptist with his Spirit from his mother's womb, who are we to cavil? However, it is worth remembering that here and in the two references which follow, we are not dealing with the full Christian experience of the Holy Spirit, made possible only after the death and glorification of Jesus, but something much more akin to the *ruach adonai* of Old Testament days. Great though John the Baptist was, he pointed forward to the kingdom but was not a member of it, and did not enjoy the distinctive blessing of the kingdom, the presence of the Spirit of Jesus within him (Matt. 11:11).

Perhaps the emphasis on John's being filled with the Spirit from his mother's womb was due to the fact that the New Testament sees him as 'the voice of one crying in the wilderness, "Prepare the way of the Lord."' His was a prophetic function, and prophets were equipped with the Spirit of the Lord so that they could proclaim the Lord's word. This is what is meant when Elizabeth (Luke 1:41) and Zacharias (1:67) are said to be filled with the Holy Spirit. In both cases the purpose is made explicit: it is so that they may prophesy. The Spirit comes upon them, fills them, and enables them to give inspired utterance.

The five post-Pentecost references

But it is the passages subsequent to Pentecost that primarily concern us. Can we discern from what is said about people who are filled with the Spirit in the Acts any clear guidelines for our day?

There are just five instances.

The *first* is on the day of Pentecost, where the 'tongues as of fire' came upon the disciples and 'they were all filled with the Holy Spirit'. What was the result of this first, crucial filling? They spoke in other tongues, they burst out in praise to God, and they preached the gospel boldly and effectively through their spokesman, Peter. The Spirit equipped them with power for service, filled their mouths with praise, and enabled them to speak in tongues. In emphasising these characteristics of the filling with the Holy Spirit, the Pentecostals are perfectly correct. When they extrapolate from this incident and assume that filling with the Holy Spirit must always have the same results, they make a serious mistake. When they assume that the filling with the Spirit is a single unrepeatable experience which puts people on a plateau from which they never thereafter descend, they make an equally serious mistake – though not as serious as those earth-bound Christians who do not believe that there is any plateau of spirituality to be scaled. For what do we find in the *second* reference to being filled with the Spirit?

It comes in 4:8, and concerns Peter. Already filled though he was on the day of Pentecost, he is again filled with the Holy Spirit, and for the very important purpose of bearing witness to Jesus. No tongues, no praise, no never-to-be-repeated experience, but bold preaching. Jesus had told them to expect the Spirit to equip them for impromptu witness of this sort (Matt. 10:19f) and Peter was experiencing the fulfilment of it, as countless Christian witnesses have ever since. It was a special infilling to meet a special opportunity.

Third, the infant Church was deeply engaged in intercession (4:31). They cast themselves in utter dependence upon God. The result was that 'they spoke the word of God with boldness'.

It is this emphasis on witness which characterises the *fourth* reference to a man being filled with the Holy Spirit. This time it is Saul of Tarsus. Ananias comes to him, at the Lord's behest, to enable those blind eyes to be filled with light and that empty life to be filled with the Holy Spirit (9:17). We read that he received his sight, was baptised, took food and was strengthened, and then that he went out in courageous testimony to Jesus in the very city where he had planned to arrest all the followers of Jesus he could find.

The *fifth* reference is in 13:9. Elymas, relying on magical powers, is contesting with the apostle Paul for the soul of the Roman proconsul of the island of Cyprus, Sergius Paulus, over whom he seems to have exercised considerable ascendancy. As if he wants to contrast the power of the Spirit of God with the power of magic, Luke records that Saul was filled with the Holy Spirit, that Elymas suddenly found himself blind – the one who had set out to lead others had to be led by the hand – and the proconsul came to faith. No doubt the miraculous blinding of Elymas had a lot to do with persuading him of the power of God, but what we are told really astonished him was 'the teaching of the Lord'. Once again, the filling with the Holy Spirit is directly related to witness-bearing.

There is one further occasion in Acts where, we saw, a different word is used for being filled. In 13:52 we read that the disciples in Pisidian Antioch were filled with joy and with the Holy Spirit. The context is illuminating. It is one of witness-bearing and persecution. They are fulfilling the role of the Servant in being a light to the Gentiles to bring salvation to the ends of the earth (13:47). They are suffering the fate of the Servant in widespread rejection and opposition. Appropriately, they enjoy the equipment of the Servant, the Spirit himself.

Conclusion

If we look back over these references to being filled with the Spirit, what may we conclude? Surely that Christians should be full of the Spirit, as Jesus was (Luke 4:1), as Stephen was (Acts 6:5), as Barnabas was (11:24), as the Seven were (6:3). As Christians this should be our regular state, but we can look for special fillings of the Spirit in special circumstances, particularly when we have the opportunity to witness for Christ. It is right to stress that on the day of Pentecost being filled with the Spirit showed itself in speaking in tongues, and that in the Elymas incident it showed itself in a miracle. These things have too often been forgotten by 'non-charismatics'. But it is also important to remember that bold witness, a united prayer meeting, humble administration, and courageous joyful testimony in the face of persecution are no less marks of people who are filled with the Spirit of God.

'Be filled with the Spirit'

The meaning of Ephesians 5:18

In the light of all this, what are we to make of the command in Ephesians 5:18 that we should not get drunk, but should be filled with the Holy Spirit? One could plausibly give a Pentecostal interpretation to this injunction. The comparison of the Spirit's effects with those of drunkenness take us naturally back to what was being suspected at Pentecost; and the references to singing to the Lord, giving thanks always, and understanding his will, which figure in the immediate context, could all refer to charismatic gifts of the Spirit. However, a more careful examination of the context suggests otherwise. Paul is giving here instructions for Christian behaviour. The light of the gospel shines in dark places, and therefore Christians must be careful of their behaviour, quick to snap up

opportunities of service, anxious to discern and follow the
Lord's leading. They must not derive their stimulation from
drink; excess of that can bring a hangover. But no amount of
the Holy Spirit can have that effect! When filled with him
people are full of joy, full of thanks to the Lord, and ready to
submit in love to other members of the Christian Body. He
then goes on to give examples – husband and wife, master and
servant. While not excluding the possibility that Paul may be
thinking of some particular spiritual gift, it is pretty plain that
his command is for all Christians irrespective of their gifts. All
are commanded to be filled with the Spirit so that they may
fulfil their lightbearing function in society. Once again we
see, sketched out in the broadest terms, the essential New
Testament conviction that the Spirit is for mission. The cor-
rectness of this interpretation of Ephesians 5:18 is supported,
it seems to me, by the two loosely related passages which I
alluded to earlier.

Two supporting passages

In Romans 15:13 in a context exclusively concerned with
mission to the Gentiles, Paul prays that they may have God's
full measure of hope, joy and peace in believing, as they are
empowered by the Holy Spirit. It is clearly the ethical qualities
of the Spirit which he associates with the filling. Similarly in
Colossians 1:8,9, where Paul gives thanks for their love in the
Spirit and prays that they may be filled with the knowledge of
God's will in all wisdom and spiritual understanding – it is in
order that their lives may bring credit on the Lord, that they
may be fruitful, increase in knowing God, and be strengthened
to endure hardship patiently as they bear witness to God's
delivering them out of darkness and putting them in the
kingdom of the Son of his love. In so far as this is an allusion
to any filling with the Spirit, the distinctively charismatic con-
notations of the term are notably absent and the ethical implications of the Spirit of Jesus very much to the fore. To be filled

with the Spirit means to allow Jesus to have the fullest control in our lives that we are conscious of. In so far as we do that, we will always be finding new areas of self-centredness to surrender as the Lord who is Spirit possesses us more and more fully. To such submission all Christians are called. And it is no once and for all transaction: 'go on being filled with the Spirit' is the meaning of the original.

Baptism and fulness

Thus, while baptism in the Spirit is the initial experience of Christ brought about by the Spirit in response to repentance, faith and baptism, the fulness of the Holy Spirit is intended to be the continual state of the Christian. It is not a plateau on to which you are ushered by some second stage in initiation, a plateau which separates you from other Christians who have not had the same experience. The New Testament gives no support to that view whatsoever. In plain language, we are meant to be progressively filled with the Spirit of our Saviour Jesus Christ. That position can be lost, through disobedience (e.g., Acts 5:3, 9, 7:51). It can also be regained, through repentance and asking God to fill us afresh. God gives his Spirit to those who obey him (Acts 5:22) and to those who ask him (Luke 11:13).

I discovered this shortly after my conversion when I surrendered to his Lordship a prized area of disobedient selfishness: after the battle and the surrender I was flooded with joy and peace and a sense of his power. Call that a second blessing if you will. But do not let it rest there. I have had many a similar experience since then as I have grown in knowledge of the Lord and living in the Spirit. A second blessing becomes ossified if it is overstressed. Let us look for a third, and a hundred and third as we press on along the upward path for the purpose for which Christ has laid his hand on us.

Any doctrine of a special spiritual state defined as 'the fulness of the Holy Spirit' is very hazardous indeed, and has little to support it in the New Testament. It may be worth enquiring why this should be so.

Danger in exclusive claims to 'fulness'

The Galatian error

In the first place, any exclusivist doctrine of a fulness of the Holy Spirit subsequent to conversion, and deemed to be essential to high quality Christian living, has to face the strictures of Paul against similar positions in his letters to the Galatians and the Colossians. Certain teachers in Galatia were maintaining that unless you kept the Jewish law and got yourself circumcised you were either a very second-rate Christian or no Christian at all. The whole burden of his passionate letter to them is that Christ and Christ alone is the way of salvation. It was through faith in Christ, 'placarded before them as crucified', that the Galatians entered into the realm of the Spirit: and now, by adding a further requirement to Christ (namely law-keeping) they were implying that Jesus was insufficient. The whole thrust of his letter is a repudiation of that calumny on Christ. Savagely, he wishes they would go and mutilate themselves (5:12).

The Colossian errors

At Colossae, it was not legalism but a syncretistic philosophy that was causing the trouble. It was being urged that Jesus is merely one of the mediatorial beings who brings us to God, that he offers us part of the fulness of the Godhead, that he is an effective though not an exclusive agent in redemption. Paul's answer to this is sharp and decisive. Christ alone, who is both the agent in creation, and the one who sustains it, can redeem men and women in virtue of his death on the cross (Col. 1:14–20). Far from thinking of Jesus as a partial intermediary between God and man, they must realise that in Christ dwells all the fulness of the Godhead in bodily form, and that they are complete in him (2:9). That claim is very precise and very exclusive. The locus of God's fulness is 'in him' and in him alone. It is not disseminated among various celestial figures, as the Colossian heretics taught: 'all the fulness' is to be found in him. Moreover, there is a strong and a weak word for 'Godhead' in Greek, and it is the former that Paul uses. There is a word which denotes permanent residence and another which means temporary stay, and it is, once again, the former that he uses. As a final fling he adds 'in bodily form', that is to say, in the historical Jesus who lived and died and rose and was presented to them as the one meeting place of God and man. It is plain that Paul will have no truck with any doctrine which makes Jesus merely the precursor of some further spiritual blessing. The man who said so emphatic a 'no' to the cry of 'Jesus *and* circumcision' or 'Jesus *and* philosophical knowledge' or 'Jesus *and* angelic mediators', would assuredly find no place for a doctrine which says, in effect, 'You must have Jesus *and* the fulness of the Holy Spirit for a high-octane Christian life.' Indeed, he goes on to remind the Colossians that so far from needing to be initiated into further mysteries and spiritual visions (2:18ff), so far from needing further spiritual resources (1:15–20), they have everything they need in Christ, who embodies the divine fulness: 'and you have come to fulness of life in him' (2:9). In the face of this, it is difficult to maintain that Paul would give any support to a second blessing doctrine which advocated a fulness additional to Christ.

The Corinthian errors

Furthermore, if we make exclusive individual claims to possess the fulness of the Holy Spirit, we run into the dangers so evident at Corinth. These are, I suppose, five-fold.

In the first place, their whole attitude was gnostic. It claimed a form of knowledge which made them superior to ordinary Christians. Knowledge, Paul had to remind them, puffs up; love builds up (1 Cor. 8:1).

Second, like the Gnostics, the Corinthians were not interested in any future resurrection or kingdom; they had their
fulness now, they had already entered upon their reign (1 Cor.
15 and 4:8ff). 'I wish you had entered on your reign,' replied the
apostle tartly; 'then perhaps I could share it with you!' He then
reminds them that apostle though he is, he shares the suffering,
the rejection and the costliness of discipleship which marked
his Lord. They need to remember that the truly Christian life is
marked by the cross as well as by the resurrection. The ultimate
fulfilment lies with Christ in heaven, and any claim to fulness
now is an illicit anticipation of God's future.

Third, the Corinthians, with all their claim to fulness and to
having entered on their heavenly reign, were distressingly defec-
tive in Christian behaviour. Party strife, litigiousness, immorality of a dimension unheard of in paganism, coupled with greed
and disorder in the assemblies, marked their lives. No wonder
Paul has to castigate them as carnal Christians. And yet here
were the very people who possessed these gifts of tongues, miracles, faith, healing and the like which convinced them that they
were the favoured children of heaven and had already become
full! It is still an observable fact that those who speak most
about being full of the Holy Spirit are often governed by other
spirits, such as arrogance, divisiveness and party spirit, disorder, lack of love and criticism. It is hard to see how a person can
be full of the Spirit if these glaring failures of character persist.

Fourth, the Corinthians were extremely experience-
orientated. They were fascinated above all with the supernatural gifts of the Spirit. It was tongues and miracles that thrilled
them most. And part of the thrust of Paul's reply is to demol-
ish the division between 'natural' and 'supernatural' which they
delighted in. For example Harold Horton in his book, *The Gifts
of the Spirit*, maintains the usual Pentecostal position that there
are nine gifts of the Spirit, no more and no less (1 Cor. 12:8ff),
and as he says of his book, 'stress is laid throughout on the
hundred-per-cent supernatural character of each and all of the

Gifts' (p. 8). However, neither Paul nor the rest of the biblical writers countenance this dichotomy between 'natural' and 'supernatural'. Just as the Bible will not allow any disjunction between creation and redemption (they both hang together as complementary aspects of God's self-disclosure) so it does not know any disjunction between the natural and the supernatural. All truth is God's truth; all gifts are his gifts; nature and grace both stem from one Author. The notion of the natural and the supernatural is Greek and not Christian, and to prize the so-called supernatural gifts of the Spirit above the natural is to affront the God who became incarnate in Christ. Yet that is precisely the mistake the Corinthians were making, and it is often enough repeated today among Christians who discount the 'helpers, the administrators, the teachers' of 1 Corinthians 12:28ff, in favour of the 'workers of miracles, healers, speakers in tongues'. They have yet to learn interdependence in the Body of Christ, and it is to this that Paul calls them in chapter 12 of the Epistle.

This leads naturally into *the fifth danger* in the Corinthian position. It was excessively individualistic. So is much of the talk these days about the fulness of the Holy Spirit. It is implied that this is a personal quality which can be had in independence of the rest of the Christian community. Now while it is true that there need to be Christians of outstanding leadership and dedication to God who will draw others after them, it is significant that whenever the New Testament uses the word 'fulness' it is in a corporate, not an individualistic sense. We have noted Colossians 2:9 where 'the fulness' is attributed to Christ; it continues 'and you (plural) are complete (or "filled full") in him'. Similarly in Ephesians 1:23 the Church with all its variety-in-unity, is said to be Christ's *plērōma*, his 'fulness' or 'complement'. Moreover, in Ephesians 3:17ff, when Paul prays for the growth of his Ephesian friends, he asks that they *together with all Christians*, may be rooted and grounded in love and be filled with all the fulness of God. In the classic verse, Ephesians 5:18, it is to be remembered that the command to be filled with the Spirit is in the plural. In other words, it is not very meaningful, and certainly, not very biblical, to speak of the fulness of the Spirit in a merely individualistic sense. God is concerned for the variety-in-unity of the body of Christ indwelt by the Spirit. The fulness of the Holy Spirit, like salvation itself, is corporate no less than individual.

Warnings

For all these reasons we should do well to be cautious of claiming to have the fulness of the Holy Spirit. Such a claim is often immature and individualistic, sometimes almost gnostic in its exclusiveness towards other Christians, dangerously liable to add something to the sufficiency of Christ, often disproved by ethical failings, and resting upon the non-Christian disjunction between the natural and the supernatural. But we should be in a far worse case if, in reaction against the imprecise phraseology and indifferent theology of some Pentecostals, we failed to emulate their real dedication to Christ, their sacrificial living, and their faith in the reality of God and his willingness to speak, to empower, to heal and to deliver us from bondage to evil spirits. So long as contemporary Christianity remains powerless, earthbound, sceptical and oblivious of the spiritual battle and the need to watch and pray, so long the Pentecostal emphasis will continue to challenge and reprove those whose theology is perhaps better based, but whose knowledge and experience of the living God is so much less.

A church full of the Spirit?

An existing church

I want to finish this chapter with a brief sketch of a church I visited back in the sixties where I was sensitive as rarely before to the fulness of the Holy Spirit. It belonged to none of the recognised denominations. People had flocked into it from a

variety of other churches where they had been neither warmed
nor fed; the spectrum included liturgical churches like the
Roman Catholic, the Anglican and the Lutheran; and also
Mennonites, Methodists, Baptists, Brethren and Pentecostals.
But most of them had come from no church; they had been
converted here. The building was packed three times a Sunday.
Five hundred or so assembled, overflowing from the seats on to
the floor. The welcome as people came in was remarkable –
warmth and embraces everywhere. 'Greet one another with a
holy kiss' was literally carried out. The service took some two
hours, and passed like a few minutes. The people really sensed
what it was to be one Body in Christ. The minister and his
assistant took a part in the service, but not a dominant one.
They sat inconspicuously with others, and were dressed in ordinary clothes. Street people and tramps, professors and house-
wives mixed joyfully and naturally in the worship. All age
groups, both men and women, were represented, with the
majority under thirty rather than over it. There was no choir:
the congregation sang from its heart to the Lord. It was an
unforgettable experience to sing the praises of God with this
congregation. We were lifted out of ourselves in the worship of
the Lord. There was a period of singing in tongues, and the
variety in the sound was matched only by its harmony and the
unanimity with which it began and ended, almost as if at the
signal of a conductor; but there was no conductor – at least, not
a human one. One person sang in a tongue, and then interpreted in song. The interpretation exactly fitted the tune she
had just sung in tongues, and the sound of her voice was simply
out of this world. I gathered later that her ordinary singing
voice is quite unremarkable. The content of the interpretation
was a call to the congregation to pray for the Jehovah's
Witnesses who were meeting in a big convention in the city at
that time. The whole thing was inspired by love, not by a
censorious spirit, and the congregation began to pray for
the Jehovah's Witnesses in response. Despite the heat and

congestion in the building, the congregation listened with rapt attention to a forty-five minutes sermon, and clearly wanted more. The minister then invited people to question the preacher and raise difficulties or suggestions, so that the communication should not be one way. Another twenty minutes of dialogue ensued, and this was obviously appreciated. More singing, more worship, most generous giving in the offering, and the service came to an end. But people did not rush away. In one part of the church a Christian in tears sought counsel; in another, a believer who had been healed rejoiced with his friends. Outside, the people enjoyed each other's fellowship for nearly an hour before departing. They felt that God was in the whole place, and they were right. I met some of the people who had given up their homes and were living in extended families. About a hundred of the congregation did this; they had all things in common like the early Church; their whole lives were bathed in prayer and service to one another and to others who dropped in. They knew from experience how hard this could be, and how easily they could give way to self-centredness and division. But still the households grew in number and in quality of life. Children as well as parents, young people as well as older ones, chose to live together in this way. They did not form a household on mere human affinity, but as they sensed themselves moved by the Lord who is Spirit. Sometimes there was a re-grouping. Sometimes the family split, amoeba-like, so as to add new members. It is perhaps too soon properly to assess this radical departure from the nuclear family pattern which has dominated the West for so long. So far as I could see the children did not suffer; the mothers had more help; the rough edges in character were smoothed away in the intimacy of common life; and the warmth of fellowship could only be sustained by a depth and intensity of prayer which is unknown among most of us, coupled with an honesty in confessing faults to one another to which most of our Christian fellowships are complete strangers. If there was one place where, it seemed to me, the patterns of Christian communal living and worship as indicated in the New Testament were being carried out, it was here. I have rarely experienced such depth of fellowship, and never such unity, dedication and joy in corporate worship. Here, if anywhere, was a church which could claim to be full of the Holy Spirit.

Travelling – not yet arrived!

But that was not so. They would not have claimed it for themselves. They were too honest to suppose they had arrived, and, surprisingly, too ecumenically concerned to be self-satisfied or self-sufficient. They had a great sense of the Church catholic, and were struggling to find a means of expressing it. Witness the fact that when there was a big movement of the Spirit among the counter culture and large numbers of flower people came to faith in Christ, they alone of all the churches in the city made room for these barefooted, unwashed brothers and sisters in Christ and made them so much at home that they became indistinguishable from other members of the congregation. No, they would not claim for their church or for themselves individually that they were full of the Spirit, and in that they would be right. For they still had a long way to go: there was, for instance, considerable tension and awkwardness in personal relationships among the leadership of that church. As at Corinth, sharp personal differences went hand in hand with a remarkable richness in gifts and worship. If God waited until a church or an individual was perfect before filling them with his Spirit, he would wait for ever.

A subsequent visit two years later to that church showed a rather different picture. There had been divisions among the leadership; a strong 'shepherding' regime had taken over, and the original pastor had graciously moved aside and gone to found a church elsewhere (which soon numbered 600!). Much that was good remained, but undeniably some of the glory had departed. This incident caused me to reflect how unwise we should be ever to claim that a church is full of the Spirit of God.

It may be, for a time. But we dare never presume. And if ever 'fulness' is seen in a static way, if 'Spirit-filled' is claimed as a description of our personal Christian life or of our church, we are in a perilous situation. For we need to go on opening ourselves up as far as we possibly can to God the Holy Spirit. But we must never forget that we are citizens of two worlds, children of two families; we are both in Christ and in Adam, and so we remain until we die. God's fulness awaits the last day, when our salvation is complete, and we are delivered for ever from the evil which haunts us and twines its tendrils among the very roots of our being. Not until then shall we be totally free of evil, totally full of the Filler. The Christian path until then is plain; it is also difficult. It does not consist in making great claims for our state of fulness, nor of vying in the evaluation of our gifts. It means that with St. Paul we shall say, 'Not that I have already arrived, or am already perfect. But I press on towards the goal for the prize of the upward call of God in Christ Jesus' (Phil. 3:12,14). The mature Christian might well covet the simple inscription found on the grave of a Swiss mountain guide: 'Died climbing'.

10
The Spirit's Gifts

In chapter 7 we examined some of the ways in which the Spirit manifests himself in the Church, and we ended in the troubled waters of 1 Corinthians 12 where Paul was urging this richly talented church to use their gifts for the benefit of the whole Body of Christ, rather than vie with one another in selfish indulgence of their gifts. This prompts the question, what were these *charismata* on which the Corinthians laid such stress?

For many centuries these chapters have been passed over in comparative silence by the churches, but since the rise of the Pentecostal movement in the twentieth century, and its spread into the main denominations, the subject has come into great prominence wherever the Holy Spirit is discussed. Since the Pentecostal movement, in all its varieties, lays such stress on the *charismata*, let us examine them one by one. The usual Pentecostal position is that there are nine such gifts, set out for us in 1 Corinthians 12:8–10. They are 'a word of wisdom, a word of knowledge, faith, healings, prophecy, discernment of spirits, different kinds of tongues and interpretation of tongues'. They can conveniently be grouped into three areas, the gifts to *say* (prophecy, tongues, and interpretation); the gifts to *do* (healings, miracles, faith); and the gifts to *know* (discerning of spirits, knowledge and wisdom).

1. Gifts of Utterance

The gift of tongues

First, the gift of tongues. This is the ability to speak in language that the speaker has not learnt, that he does not understand, and that is incomprehensible to the hearer. I say 'language' with some hesitation, for while some charismatics claim that they speak in a definite human language, others do not, but regard the gift as a 'Holy Spirit language' designed to enable both men and angels to worship God in greater depth and with greater release in their inner being – rather like the love language of a happily married couple, which may not *mean* anything when the words are analysed; but which *denotes* the intimacy and trust of the couple concerned. The latter view would chime in well with research on speaking in tongues[1] which concludes that glossolalia is fundamentally not a language, in spite of superficial similarities. It is a sort of pseudo-language, a form of precognitive speech, which is not filtered through the mind's orderly arrangement of syntax and vocabulary. It would also accord well with Paul's hints in 1 Corinthians 14:7–11. He gives three analogies.

Three analogies

First, from inanimate musical instruments. If the flute or the harp give no meaningful variation in notes, nobody will understand, and nobody will do anything about it. Uninterpreted tongues are like these musical instruments played at random in contrast to prophecy, which is both intelligible, and rouses us to action.

Second, he turns to the human tongue itself, and makes the same two points. If I do not enunciate clear words, I am not

---

[1] W. J. Samarin, *Tongues of Men and Angels*, Macmillan, 1972.

understood, and I achieve nothing. Paul in this analogy is making a play on the word 'tongue'; the Greek word can mean either the part of the body, or the 'language' of 'tongues'. And he is gently rebuking the Corinthians for their cult of the unintelligible. For to them 'speaking in a tongue' spelt unintelligibility; to Paul the tongue, as part of the body, was essentially associated with intelligibility, or else it achieved nothing at all.

Third, he gives an illustration from other languages, making the same two points as before. If I speak in a foreign tongue people will not be able to understand me or respond to my communication – unless it is interpreted. I shall sound like a barbarian to them. That was a particularly wounding shaft to the Corinthians, who, as Greeks, despised the foreigners whose languages sounded like a meaningless jabber of 'bar-bar-bar' – hence the pejorative name they gave them of 'barbarians'. Each of these three points made by the apostle to discourage the uninterpreted use of tongues in church seems to indicate that the phenomenon of tongues was not a language as such but rather the deeply felt love-language of the Corinthians to their Lord.

Languages?

However, there are so many well-attested examples of 'tongues' being understood by someone present who happens to belong to another language group and knows the tongue in question, that it is probably best to give the fullest possible breadth to Paul's phrase 'different kinds of tongues' and to conclude that whereas some glossolalia may be speaking in a language unknown to the speaker but intelligible to somebody who knows the particular language employed, other 'tongues' may not be a particular language at all but will rather be the effusion of the deepest longings of the heart released by the Spirit of God in prayer, praise or song.

Tongues, then, may be a language, or it may not, depending on circumstances and the particular gift of God to the individual. Incidentally, it is wrongly translated 'tongues of ecstasy' in some of the modern translations of the Bible, notably the *New English Bible*. There is nothing necessarily compulsive or ecstatic about it. It is (as those who have the gift well know) under the control of the speaker – otherwise it would have been pointless for Paul to bid the tongues-speakers to control themselves in church if an interpreter is not present.

The purposes of tongues

What, then, is the purpose of this gift? St. Paul gives several. First, it enables a person to speak to God in prayer: 'he speaks not to men but to God; nobody understands him, but he speaks mysteries in his spirit (or perhaps, "in the Spirit").' Thus the apostle in 1 Corinthians 14:2. He is maintaining that the gift of tongues opens a new dimension to our prayer life. He actually longs to pray whereas before it had been an effort. Time seems unimportant, and it will be nothing out of the way for him to spend an hour or two in communion with his Lord. Today, the gift of tongues produces precisely the same effect; a genuine liberty in prayer.

Second, tongues enable us to praise God at a depth unknown previously. This is certainly a major emphasis in the Acts of the Apostles. In the house of Cornelius the new converts 'spoke with tongues and glorified God' (Acts 10:46). On the day of Pentecost this was very much the same. The crowd realised clearly enough that these men were praising God for his wonderful works, even though they suspected that drink might be the cause (Acts 2:11–13). Perhaps Paul's references to singing spiritual songs to the Lord (Eph. 5:19, Col. 3:16) allude to singing in tongues; certainly this is a most beautiful and harmonious phenomenon, and elates the soul in worship to a remarkable degree. But whether the singing is in us tongues or not, it is an undeniable fact that when people receive this gift of tongues they find themselves free to praise and thank and adore and glorify their heavenly Father as never before. In charismatic prayer meetings praise is usually the dominant element; in the run-of-the-mill evangelical prayer meeting this is not normally the case. We should not be surprised by this. Every religious revival throughout the history of the Church has been accompanied by singing. When God's Spirit is at work within, men must give vent to their emotions in songs of praise. The charismatic renewal has produced a whole new genre of songs and choruses which have spread all over the Christian world. Such is the natural outworking of what the Lord the Spirit has worked within.

Third, tongues edifies the individual (1 Cor. 14:4). This is not surprising, if it releases the inhibitions which keep us from prayer and praise of God. To be sure, Paul in this chapter is concerned to contrast speaking in tongues, which only edifies the speaker, with prophecy, which also builds up the church. But it is illicit for that reason to deny that tongues speaking does edify the individual, as many commentators infer. No, it is one of the ways of growth in the Christian life for those who have been given this gift. Tongues is given, like the other manifestations of the Spirit, for our profit (1 Cor. 12:7).

Further value in tongues

Perhaps one of the areas of profit that we may need to be reminded of in an over-cerebral age is this: it allows the human spirit to pray, even when the mind is unfruitful because it cannot understand (1 Cor. 14:14). Many people pray in tongues while driving a car or washing up – their mind can be employed elsewhere. Clearly, therefore, tongues is a valuable gift for private edification. It can bring a profound sense of the presence of God, and lead, as a result, to a release from tension and worry, and a deepening of love and trust. As the Holy Spirit leads the believer in such prayer, there is often a deep sense of being in harmony with God.

There are other ways in which the private use of tongues can edify. Many people find it a real help in bearing physical pain or mental distress. It is a valuable adjunct to intercessory prayer, especially when we do not know what to pray for. Romans 8:26–28 must not be construed exclusively of charismatic prayer, but equally certainly must not exclude it. We are promised that when we do not know what to pray for as we should, we may look to the Spirit for his aid; that he will intercede within us with groans too deep for words; that the Father understands what the Spirit prompts us to pray, even though we do not; and that such prayer is certainly according to the will of God and therefore it will be taken up and used in his purposes of good for those who love God.

Perhaps one of its most important uses is in spiritual warfare. When there is an oppressive sense of evil present, when a ministry of deliverance is being engaged in – then prayer in tongues proves to be a powerful instrument for the Lord the Spirit to use. In Ephesians 6:18 Paul concludes his description of the armour a Christian needs to wear against satanic attack with the injunction to 'pray at all times in the Spirit'. This includes praying at the inspiration of the Spirit in words we understand and in words we do not (1 Cor. 14:15). There is, therefore, great value in the private use of tongues. But the public use of this gift in the congregation has no value, indeed it can be a disturbing distraction, unless someone is present who has the gift of interpretation. For it simply will not be understood. 'I thank God that I speak in tongues more than you all; nevertheless in church I would rather speak five words with my mind in order to instruct others, than ten thousand words in a tongue' (1 Cor. 14:19).

Uninterpreted tongues

If tongues is of no value for the edification of the church unless it is interpreted, it is even more useless in evangelism. It will cause the outsider who happens to be in the assembly to think the Christians are mad (1 Cor. 14–23). It would be quite wrong to suppose that tongues was used evangelistically on the day of Pentecost. It is sometimes imagined by non-charismatics that

Pentecostals believe this, but such is not the case. Harold Horton explains succinctly, in his *The Gifts of the Spirit* (p. 152):

> The notion that the Gift of Tongues was a miraculous bestowal of foreign languages to the early apostles that they might preach the gospel to every creature is an error that could only be held by those who have never taken care to examine all the Scriptures on the subject. Peter was the only one, according to the record, who preached the gospel on the day of Pentecost, and he employed not other tongues but the universally understood Aramaic, or the equally universally understood Greek.

The 'other tongues' was the praise of God by the disciples, not their preaching of the gospel. The varied language groups present were, it would seem, given the gift of interpretation on this occasion, so that they heard the praises of God in their own languages.

Indeed, not only are uninterpreted tongues disastrous in evangelism; they may even denote the judgment of God upon the Christian community. Such seems to be the thrust of 1 Corinthians 14:20ff. After pointing out the futility of uninterpreted tongues in church, Paul continues: 'Brethren, do not be children in your thinking; be babes in evil, but in your thinking be mature. In the law it is written, "By men of strange tongues and by the lips of foreigners will I speak to this people, and even then they will not listen to me, says the Lord." Thus, tongues are a sign not for believers but for unbelievers.' The reference is to Isaiah 28:11,12. The point is that Israel spurned the message of the prophets, delivered as it was in clear unambiguous speech. And so God, by way of punishment, had to speak to them through the strange, unwelcome tongues of the Assyrians. These tongues came to them because they were 'unbelieving'. They did not believe what the prophets had said, and they did not obey. The tongues of the Assyrians were, therefore, 'a sign to those who did not believe'.

The tongues bespoke God's separation from his people, not his presence; they denoted his judgment, not his pleasure. When God speaks intelligibly it is to reveal himself to his people. When he speaks unintelligibly, it is to hide himself. So in their preference for the unintelligible tongues over the straightforward prophecy the Corinthians were sailing dangerously near to the judgment of God. So far from boasting, they should beware of an unrestricted use of this medium in public worship, and especially when pagans were present.[2]

---

[2] It is sometimes suggested that this reference to Isaiah 28:11f merely indicates that tongues are a sign of God's rejection of unbelievers, i.e. outsiders; pagans approaching the assembly and hearing only tongues do not hear the gospel, but only receive a sign that God rejects them, confirming them in unbelief; whereas through the use of prophecy they may be converted. This is attractive, but it forces 'this people' from the prophecy to refer not to God's disobedient people but to pagans, and makes no sense of 'and *even then* they will not listen to me, says the Lord'. Perhaps a more probable suggestion is that of J. P. M. Sweet in *J.T.S.* 1966, pp. 240–57. He thinks it likely that the 'spiritual men' at Corinth, the *teleioi* of verse 20, were arguing that 'tongues is a sign for believers'; it was a slogan to denote their spiritual superiority. Paul retorts by asking them to listen to Scripture (v. 21). He quotes a text from Isaiah 28 which looks as if it may well have been used by Christians in anti-Jewish apologetic. Laughed at by the Jews for glossolalia (cf. Acts 2:13), Christians had turned to this text for vindication. But in verse 22 Paul turns the tables on the Corinthian advocates of Isaiah 28:11,12. The verse does nothing to substantiate their claims to spiritual superiority because they could speak in tongues; it is no 'sign for believers'. It is rather a sign against (the dative being taken as a dative of disadvantage, which is possible) unbelievers. It hardens unbelievers in their rejection of the gospel, giving colour to their view that the Christians are mad. By way of contrast, a word of prophecy pierces to the very soul of the visitor.

This is ingenious, it seems to me, but has one fatal weakness, which brings me back to the interpretation I have advanced above: Sweet's view makes no sense of 'prophecy is not for unbelievers but for believers'. So he has to maintain that the phrase 'not for unbelievers' is

Even here, however, human mistakes can be mercifully over-ruled by God. There are on record several examples of people coming to faith in Christ through hearing their own language spoken by someone in a Christian assembly who had never learnt it.

The nature of the tongues at Corinth

This whole discussion of the gift of tongues in 1 Corinthians 12 and 14 has caused some remarkable exegesis, not always rooted in the text. Thus it is often argued that 'tongues' in these chapters must mean 'foreign languages'. This makes nonsense of the passage. How, for example, could you pray in a foreign language without your mind being involved (14:14)? Why should God give a person a foreign language in order to commune with him (v. 2)? How could speaking in a foreign language edify you (v. 4)? If you speak in a foreign language, why pray that you may be able to translate it (v. 13)?

---

put in merely 'for rhetorical balance'. It is hard to evade the plain meaning of the passage, particularly in its context here and in Isaiah; that if the Corinthians insist on the unrestrained use of tongues in evangelistic meetings they not only drive away those who are enquiring about the faith but risk falling under the judgment of God. In any case it is illegitimate to argue from these difficult few verses that the 'tongues' in 1 Corinthians 14 must be languages, because languages were indicated in Isaiah 28:11. Paul is indeed referring to the foreign language spoken by the Assyrians who came in judgment upon Israel. But the point of his comparison is the unintelligibility and the judgment of those tongues, not that they were foreign. Mallone rightly observes: 'The precognitive language of the Corinthian tongue speaking was a judgment on those who did not believe, simply because, without interpretation, they could not understand. But clear speech, prophecy or tongues with interpretation leads to the conviction and conversion of unbelievers. Paul pleads with the Corinthians to stop playing with tongues in a childish manner which leads unbelievers to think they are mad.' (*Those Controversial Gifts*, p. 87).

Again, it is sometimes argued that 1 Corinthians 12–14 is exclusively about the public use of this gift, and that it is therefore illegitimate to apply any part of these chapters to the private exercise of glossolalia in prayer which marks most charismatics. But Paul is well aware that tongues-speaking is primarily directed to God, not to men (14:2) and that the tongues speaker edifies himself by the use of this gift, while at the same time he does not edify the Christian Body unless it is interpreted. But it is clear that Paul is reflecting both on the public and the private use of this *charisma* in 1 Corinthians, and is regulating its public use to occasions when it is interpreted.

The importance of the tongues at Corinth

The importance attached to tongues in many circles requires a few further observations on St. Paul's discussion of the subject in these three chapters.

In the first place, there is no suggestion that Paul envisages tongues as dying out when spiritual maturity arrives. 1 Corinthians 13:10 is contrasting the partial nature of our gifts and understanding in this life with their perfection hereafter when nothing but love will matter. Knowledge and prophecy will have received their fulfilment. Tongues will cease to be necessary. The partial has disappeared, fulfilment has arrived. But to argue, as some do, that by 'when the perfect comes' Paul is looking forward to the completion of the New Testament Canon, after which tongues will be unnecessary, is a flagrant example of rejecting the plain sense of the passage in the interests of a dogma.

Second, there is no suggestion that tongues is a sure mark of being spiritual. There seem to have been those in Corinth, as there are today, who maintain that nobody is baptised in the Holy Spirit unless they speak in tongues. This Paul roundly condemns. Not only does he tell them that they have all been baptised in the Spirit, tongues speakers and non tongues speakers alike (12:13), but he tells them too that anyone who can make the most basic Christian confession, 'Jesus is Lord', can only do so under the leading and inspiration of the Holy Spirit (12:3). There is no ground whatever in these chapters for spiritual elitism based on speaking in tongues.

Third, Paul would most strongly disagree with those who maintain that every Christian should speak in tongues. He makes it plain that it is a gift which is at the disposal of the Holy Spirit. He distributes this gift, like others, as he sees fit (vv. 7,8). 'Do all speak in tongues?' manifestly expects the answer 'no', as it does when he asks, 'Are all prophets?' (12:29, 30).

Fourth, the gift of tongues, like other gifts, is not seen by Paul as a badge of spiritual maturity. It is not something of which the recipient has any right to be proud. It is, unfortunately, compatible with gross sins such as were prevalent in the Corinthian church. And it is primarily intended for the common good (v. 7). It is therefore to be used sensitively and with reserve, not flaunted at inappropriate times (14:23). Paul is willing (or keen? the *thelō* in verse 5 could mean either) for them all to receive this gift, but he stresses that its use must be subordinated to the interests of intelligibility (v. 19) and the helping – not the hindering – of others in the congregation (vv. 16,17). Paul makes it clear in these chapters that tongues is not one of the most important gifts of the Spirit and should not be thought of as ushering the recipient into Christian maturity. Millions of spiritually mature Christians have never spoken in tongues, and millions who have are not spiritually mature.

Finally, Paul is well aware that the gift of tongues could easily be abused and become a danger rather than a blessing in the Church. It could lead to pride and divisiveness; it could lead to a theology of two-stage initiation; it could distract attention from the main purpose of the Holy Spirit,

to make us Christlike. It could contribute to a fascination
with a gift rather than the Giver, and with the bizarre rather
than the ethical. It could cause grave embarrassment
when used in the wrong context. It could become a projec-
tion of a private ego-trip on the other members of the congregation and lead to chaotic disorder and the accusations
of lunacy, if not controlled and interpreted. Worst of all, it
could lead to an uncritical value being set on tongues whatever their provenance, and Paul is clear that some of his
Corinthian friends speak in tongues that are not at all given
by the Holy Spirit but are a relic of the demonic influences
upon them in their pagan days. Having said all this,
however, he does not forbid but gently encourages the use
of this precious gift of God both privately and in the congregation, granted the overarching principle of the exercise
of Christian love.

The gift of interpretation

An exercise in faith

So much for tongues. Interpretation of tongues is a gift
which can be dealt with more briefly. It is the ability to give
the sense of what has been said in an unknown tongue,
when this has been exercised in the congregation. Just as the
Spirit leads one person to speak in a tongue he does not
understand, so the same Spirit leads either him or someone
else present to interpret what has been said or sung. It is not
an exact translation. The interpreter does not normally
understand the tongue that has been used any better than
the rest of the congregation. But he feels the Spirit impel-
ling him to speak, not a translation but an interpretation.
This is very much an exercise in faith. When he gets up to
speak he does not know more than the very first words of
what he is going to say. He must trust the leading of the
Lord the Spirit.

Problems

The whole subject of interpreting tongues is most obscure and open to abuse. It is not possible for others to have any objective criteria for checking that the interpretation is genuine, and it is not possible to ensure beforehand that the apostolic injunction will be obeyed, that nobody is to speak in tongues in church unless someone is present who can interpret.

The best safeguards against abuse of this gift will include the following. The interpreter will normally be somebody whose own life and Christian maturity has won respect in the local congregation. The interpretation will be in line with the *mood* of the original tongue. The interpretation will not reflect any tendency or prejudice of the interpreter's own. The interpreter will have a modesty and openness to correction by others, should there be a general sense that his interpretation is not correct. And, conversely, one of the surest signs of authenticity is when the congregation as a whole sense the rightness of what is being said.

Why, it may be asked, if the whole subject is so fraught with peril, should God choose to use this extraordinary combination of tongues and interpretation for the edification of his people? The answer may lie in the partnership which tongues and interpretation necessitates. If this is indeed a gift to build up the Body, then it is appropriate that its exercise should involve members of that Body moving forward tentatively in dependence on God and on each other. They may well not always get it right. But that, too, can lead to the edification of the congregation in patience, mutual correction and love. Spiritual gifts are heady wine: there are sure to be mistakes and imbalances. But granted love within the Body, humility in those who exercise the gifts, and a reverent discrimination in those so gifted, growth will take place. Without risk, without experiment, there can be no life or growth. What Paul is pleading for at Corinth is risk coupled with control and love.

Tongues and interpretation

Those who have the gift of speaking in tongues are exhorted by Paul to pray for the gift of interpretation (14:13). Though some people have the gift of interpretation who cannot themselves speak in tongues, this is unusual; for the most part it is those who already have tongues who gain this further gift of interpretation. And it is obviously highly desirable, for the edification of the church, when tongues are used in worship; and also for the edification of the mind of the individual Christian when praying in tongues – for as we have seen, his mind remains unfruitful although his spirit is lifted up in prayer to God.

It seems clear from 1 Corinthians 14:5 that although tongues is an inferior gift to prophecy (the ability to speak direct from God to a situation) because it edifies only the individual and not the church; nevertheless tongues and interpretation together are the equivalent of prophecy. Like prophecy they are a divinely inspired message; and like prophecy the two gifts, taken together, are intelligible and therefore touch the minds as well as the spirits of those present. The interpretation need not always come in words. Sometimes it comes through a picture given to a member of the congregation. Sometimes the tongue unlocks a confession from some member. It can be very varied. Even so, Paul's preferences in the matter are plain. 'Desire to prophesy', is his conclusion of the matter, 'and do not forbid speaking in tongues' (1 Cor. 14:39)!

Guidelines

If, then, we are to take 1 Corinthians as our guide, we must recognise that tongues, along with interpretation, can be a genuine gift of the Spirit of God to certain people, and Paul expected the gift to be used in private devotions for the edification of the believer, and in public when the two gifts could be employed together. He is careful to regulate this latter practice, however, in his concern for greater order in the disarray of Corinthian worship: 'two or at most three, and that in turn; and let one interpret' is his injunction. There is clearly a note of caution in Paul's advice. He is not happy at the way in which things are going at Corinth, with their infatuation with tongues. He knows it can be a real gift of the Spirit of God, and therefore while regulating it carefully he does not forbid it. But he also knows, I fancy, that glossolalia could be psychologically induced. He also realised, as many Pentecostals do, that there is a demonic counterfeit to tongues speaking. In the Corinthian assembly men were saying 'a curse on Jesus' and were using the tongues of their old pagan days which they had learnt in idol worship. Tongues, in fact, is a phenomenon which is widely disseminated and is observable in many cultures, ancient and modern. It is no exclusive mark of the possession of the Holy Spirit; but the Holy Spirit can take it and use it. But because of its very ambivalence, because of its incomprehensibility, because of its selfishness, because of its liability to abuse, and because of its non-ethical and sub-personal character the apostle was most unwilling to concur with the Corinthians' estimate of it as the best and most valuable of the gifts of the Spirit. It is perhaps not accidental that every time he mentions tongues and their interpretation, they come last on his list, not first, as the Corinthians would undoubtedly have rated them.

The gift of prophecy

A fresh outpouring

The third of the gifts of speech is prophecy. Prophecy had been dead in Israel for centuries, but blazed into life again with the coming of Jesus, the prophet of Nazareth, the prophet like Moses (Matt. 21:11, Acts 3:22, 7:37). Jesus came to fulfil not only the Torah but the prophets (Matt. 5:17), and his fulfilment did not only show itself in a burst of prophecy round his birth and in John the Baptist but continued among his people after his death. Indeed one would not be far wrong in asserting that Christian prophecy was born on the day of Pentecost, when the remarkable invasion of the Spirit of God convinced the disciples that they were witnessing the fulfilment of Joel's prophecy, 'and upon my servants and my handmaidens in those days I will pour out a portion of my Spirit, and they shall prophesy' (Acts 2:18). The last phrase, 'and they shall prophesy', is not in the original of Joel; it is a Christian gloss. But it shows very clearly that they were conscious of the prophetic Spirit among them, and saw this as a direct overflow of the Spirit which had indwelt their Master and a fulfilment of the hopes of the Old Testament that all God's people should prophesy (Num. 11:29). Christian prophecy could be delivered by men or women (Acts 31:9, Rev. 2:20, 1 Cor. 11:5). The four prophesying daughters of Philip the Evangelist made a tremendous impact on the Church at large and were a model well into the second century; indeed, even in 1 Corinthians where Paul is very concerned to regulate glossolalia and avoid any excesses which could bring the Christian cause into disrepute, he does nothing to discourage the woman prophet from speaking in the assembly; rather the reverse (11:1ff).

Widely diffused

Prophecy was very widely disseminated. There were prophets not only in Jerusalem and Caesarea, but in Antioch (Acts 11:27, 13:1), Rome (Rom. 12:6), Corinth, Thessalonica (1 Thess. 5:19,20) and the churches of Asia Minor (Rev. 1:3). Both Luke and Matthew indicate that Jesus anticipated a continuation of prophecy among his followers (Matt. 10:41f, Luke 11:49). It was a gift very highly valued, whether it was exercised by a single individual, or, as certain passages suggest, by a prophetic group of believers (Acts 13:1, Eph. 2:20, 3:5, 4:11, Rev. 10:7, 22:6,9). It is easy to see why it was so prized: for prophecy meant domination by the Lord the Spirit. In prophecy God was communicating directly through men and women. The prophet shared with the apostle in being an agent of revelation; but prophets were inferior to apostles because they did not and could not go behind or beyond the apostolic testimony to Jesus – after all, they were not, as the apostles were, eyewitnesses of the final revelation of God, Jesus, come in the flesh.

Prophecy, then, was valued, because through it God spoke directly to his people. He had done so through the prophets and prophetesses of the Old Testament days; he had done so through 'the prophet of Nazareth', that 'prophet like Moses', Jesus himself; and he continued to do it through inspired individuals or groups bearing testimony in words not of their own contriving to Jesus, the risen fount of all wisdom and knowledge.

New Testament prophecy, therefore, was highly valued. If genuine, it was God's Holy Spirit speaking directly through some member to a particular congregation. These men and women were therefore in direct continuity with the Old Testament prophets. And yet there was a double difference.

On the one hand the New Testament prophecy seems to have been given for a particular situation only: there is no hint of such prophecies being applied across the universal Church. In this way they differ from the Old Testament prophecies which have a wider degree of authority because of their application to all believers everywhere, not merely to the situation in which they originated. They form part of the canon of Scripture.

Moreover, New Testament prophecy was clearly marked by encouragement rather than judgment, which was the major emphasis of Old Testament prophets. This is highly appropriate, of course, in view of the church's situation. They were living, as we saw above, 'between the times'. A prophet who speaks encouragement to a church which is already in the end times and is journeying towards the fulfilment, is clearly in a different situation from one commissioned by God to call down judgment on ancient Israel and her neighbours.

What is Christian prophecy?

It is not easy to be clear precisely what early Christian prophecy was. It could vary from the predictions of a man like Agabus, the mysteries of the Book of Revelation (a remarkable example of early prophecy, see Rev. 1:3), to the indication of a Christian for a particular office (1 Tim. 4:14), testimony to Jesus (Rev. 19:10), and use in evangelism, edification, consolation, or teaching (1 Cor. 14:3f,24f,29f). What was this varied thing, Christian prophecy?

First and foremost, it was a direct word from God for the situation on hand, through the mouth of one of his people (and on occasion, this could apparently be any Christian, including those not reckoned to be 'prophets', Rev. 10:7, 11:10). The other thing about it is that it was clear speech, which did not need any interpretation. Herein lay its great advantage over tongues. Because of its intelligibility, it used the mind of the speaker (that mind which lies fallow while he is speaking in tongues, 1 Cor. 14:14); it contributed to the edification of the whole Christian Body assembled for worship; it struck to the heart of unbelievers present who were amazed at the directness and relevance of what was said; it showed that God was indeed present in the congregation (1 Cor. 14:4, 24f). Therefore it was a gift to be sought and prized by Christians. Not all Christians have it (1 Cor. 12:29), but all are encouraged to pray for it, because it is so useful for other members of the Body of Christ (1 Cor. 14:1).

It is not ecstatic

Several misunderstandings commonly crop up at this point. The first is to call prophecy 'ecstatic speech'. It is much the same mistake as we saw in examining the use of the term 'ecstasy' for tongues. It is an accurate description if it means that the gift comes from a direct leading of the Spirit. It is inaccurate if it suggests a compulsive, excitable urge which cannot be resisted.

For there is no indication in the New Testament that prophecy is the product of spiritual excitement. And there is no indication that it is compulsive. Quite the reverse.[3] Paul can instruct some prophets to keep quiet, while others have their chance to speak. He can also restrict the use of prophecy in any one church gathering to two or three speakers (1 Cor. 14:29). This would be quite impossible if the gift were used independently of the will of the user: but it is not. It involves the use of his mind. It is subservient to his rational decision.

It is not the same as teaching

One commonly hears it said that prophecy is the same as preaching or teaching. This could only be maintained in defiance of the whole weight of New Testament evidence. The men of the first century knew preaching and teaching when they heard it, and they knew prophecy as well. The two were quite different. Prophets and teachers are distinguished in passages such as Acts 13:1, 1 Corinthians 12:29. It is one thing to prepare one's address in dependence on the Spirit, and to preach it in the power of that same Spirit; it is quite another thing to find the Spirit taking over and speaking directly from Christ through you, in words that you had never intended to use at all. In

---

[3] Interestingly enough, in the heyday of the Montanist movement, the claim was made that prophecy was something compulsive that could not be evaded. Montanus claimed that 'Man is like a lyre and I (i.e. the Spirit) rush upon it like a plectrum' (Epiphanius, *Haer*. 48:4. 1). Maximilla is said to have put it still more emphatically: 'The Lord has sent me as an adherent, preacher and interpreter of this affliction and this covenant and this promise; he has compelled me, willingly or unwillingly, to learn the knowledge of God' (*ibid*. 48:13. 1). This undue emphasis on compulsion gives full force, to be sure, to the inner sense of conviction that every prophet has; but fails to make room for the co-operation with God which is implicit in authentic prophecy. The balance of the New Testament teaching has been slightly but decisively altered.

Evangelism in the Early Church I pointed to a fascinating passage in the second century Bishop Melito of Sardis that has come to light among the Bodmer Papyri. In it this distinguished Christian teacher suddenly breaks out into prophecy, and Christ speaks through him directly. The change is startling. Melito is preaching: 'The Lord, having put on human nature, and having suffered for him who suffered, having been bound for him who was bound, and having been buried for him who was buried (i.e., in sin) is risen from the dead, and loudly proclaims this message.' Then comes the prophecy:

> Who will contend against me? Let him stand before me.
> It is I who delivered the condemned. It is I who gave life to the dead.
> It is I who raised up the buried. Who will argue with me?
> It is I, says Christ, who destroyed death. It is I who triumphed over the enemy,
> And trod down Hades, and bound the Strong Man,
> And snatched mankind up to the heights of heaven. It is I, says Christ.
> So then, come here all you families of men, weighed down by your sins
> And receive pardon for your misdeeds. For I am your pardon.
> I am the Passover which brings salvation. I am your life, your resurrection.
> I am your light, I am your salvation, I am your King.
> It is I who bring you up to the heights of heaven.
> It is I who will give you the resurrection there.
> I will show you the Eternal Father. I will raise you up with my own right hand.

By no stretch of the imagination could that be described as simply preaching or teaching. The Spirit has taken over, and addresses the hearers directly through Melito. That is the essence of Christian prophecy.

It did not die out

Another misunderstanding is to suppose that prophecy came to an end at the conclusion of the apostolic age. It certainly became less important for the Church as the New Testament

Scriptures gained in circulation and became recognised as authoritative teaching about Jesus. Clearly, there was nothing one could add to God's last word to mankind, Jesus the Word of God incarnate; and there was nothing fresh about him that could be added by men of the second and subsequent generation except through the medium of the apostolic testimony. So the sphere of prophecy became more restricted as the canon of Scripture became more clear; indeed, the need for it diminished, in so far as general teaching of the faithful was concerned. But to suppose that prophecy was no longer needed for the encouragement of the faithful, for the conviction of unbelievers, and for the guidance of the Church on specific issues, would be very wrong. For example, it was in response to a piece of Christian prophecy that the Jerusalem church escaped from the city prior to the fall of Jerusalem in A.D. 70 and took up residence in Pella (Eusebius *Hist. Eccl.* 3:5,3). In the sub-apostolic age, we find wandering prophets circulating round the Christian churches exercising a charismatic ministry, and complementing the work of the resident presbyters. Famous names like Ammia and Quadratus meet us among the prophets of the second century; and authors like Ignatius (*Trallians* 5, *Ephesians* 20), Polycarp (*Epistle* 5:2, and *Martyr. Polc.* 16), Hermas (*Mand.* 11) are well aware of the continuance of prophets in their day. The unknown writer against the Montanists speaks for main line Christianity of the second century when he writes, 'the apostle believes that the prophetic charisma should continue until the end of the age throughout the church' (Eusebius *H.E.* 5:17). As late as the fourth century Cyril of Jerusalem clearly thinks it possible (if unlikely!) that his candidates for baptism may receive the gift of prophecy (*Catechetical lectures* 16:12, 17:37).

It did become suspect

Although, therefore, prophecy continued, it became increasingly suspect and liable to abuse. The *Didache*, dating from perhaps the second quarter of the second century, has some sharp things to say about bogus and self-seeking prophets, as we shall see when we come to examine the gift of discernment. It is sufficient to note that prophecy was intended to continue in the Church, but that because of the dangers of abuse and subjectivism, and supremely because of the Montanist movement at the end of the second century, it virtually died out. Only a few years previously, Justin had been maintaining that there was no difference in degree of inspiration between the Old Testament and the New Testament prophets. Both bore witness to Jesus. That is why, he argues, the Jews have had no more prophets since the days of Christ, whereas the prophetic office has been much in evidence in the Church (*Dialogue* 51 and 82). Prophets were for the benefit of the people of God at large, and that is why Hermas wrote his *Shepherd* to the whole Church, just as John wrote his Apocalypse to the seven churches of Asia, symbolising the Church catholic.

The Montanist crisis

But with the Montanist movement, all that came to an end. Already there had been a tendency to identify the prophetic function with the office of the bishop (aided by the fact that some distinguished bishops like Melito and Polycarp were also prophets in their own right), but after the Montanist troubles this identification became absolute, and the bishop became regarded as the authoritative mouthpiece of divine teaching for his diocese. This swallowing up of the prophet in the bishop was disastrous for the Church, but in the circumstances it was understandable. For Montanus, an Asian bishop, claimed that he and his female associates, Maximilla and Prisca, were descendants of the prophetic tradition of early Christianity. So far so good. But when they taught (professing to be the mouthpiece of the Spirit) that the heavenly Jerusalem would immediately appear near Pepuza; when they claimed that they personally embodied the Holy Spirit; when they wrote off other Christians as carnal and proclaimed themselves alone as 'Spirit-filled'; when they refused to have their teaching tested by the Scriptures but regarded it as every bit as authoritative as the New Testament records – then the Church had to take action. That action was to reject the Montanists emphatically, and at the same time, to quench the prophetic Spirit in the Church. How much better it would have been for the Church at large if the Montanists had determined to submit to the authority of Scripture, and to resist the temptation to be exclusive and write off other Christians. How much better if the Catholics had stressed tests for the genuineness of prophecy rather than writing off the whole movement, good and bad, together. Apparently the Catholic leadership regarded the existence of prophets as a threat to the regular ministry of the Church. But this need not have been the case at all, when one remembers that men like Jude and Silas, Saul and Barnabas were both prophets and presbyters; and when some of the leading bishops in the second century, Ignatius, Polycarp and Melito among them, combined the office of a bishop with the gift of prophecy. If prophecy un-regulated by order could dissipate in individualism and end in sectarianism and heresy, order without prophecy could so easily turn a deaf ear to the leading of God and relapse into the peace of the graveyard. To 'charismatic' and to 'non-charismatic' alike, the total failure of communication over the Montanist affair is a tragedy that must not be repeated, if the Church values on the one hand her unity and on the other hand her vitality.

2. GIFTS OF ACTION

So much for tongues, interpretation and prophecy, the gifts of speaking. Now for the gifts of doing: healings, miracles, faith.

The gifts of healing

Jesus and the disciples

Jesus healed people; and he commissioned his disciples to do the same. It is interesting to recall that the word 'save' means in the original 'to heal' just as much as it does 'to rescue'. Undeniably, many of the needy people whom Jesus met in the days of his flesh were both spiritually put right with God and physically healed. Equally undeniably, there is less and less stress on healing as the ministry of Jesus runs its course. He deprecated men's quest for miracles and mighty works; and he was limited in performing them by lack of faith in the recipients. Moreover, on occasion he withdrew from promising healing situations, in order to concentrate on preaching (Mark 1:38, Luke 4:43).

When we consider the healing activity of the early Christians, there is similar need for caution. On the one hand the apostles are once commanded to heal during the course of the ministry of Jesus (Matt. 10:8 cf. the Seventy in Luke 10:9) but those who wish to take this as an all-embracing command for Christians today should pause at the next phrase 'raise the dead'. This does not happen at present. It will not do to turn such a question aside by reference to some very doubtfully attested raisings from the dead reported at third and fourth hand from Indonesia or the third world.

Healing in the Church

Both Peter and Paul, together with John and the apostles in general, were agents of divine healing in the early Church (Acts 3:7, 9:34, 5:12–16, 28:19). Healing is given a place here in the list of spiritual gifts in 1 Corinthians 12:9,28,30. It is, moreover, referred to quite frequently in sub-apostolic days. Justin spoke of men exercising gifts of healing in the name of Jesus in his day, and Irenaeus distinguishes true Christian teachers from false by their ability to heal. It is, therefore, a real gift of God to be exercised in and for the Body of Christ. A flood of books in recent years bears testimony to the recovery of this gift in many parts of the Church today. These books vary enormously in credibility and quality of theological and medical validation: among the best are Morton Kelsey's *Healing and Christianity:*

in ancient thought and modern times, Francis MacNutt's two books, *Healing*, and *Power to Heal* and John Woolmer's *Healing and Deliverance*. Undeniably many Christians today are waking up to the possibility of healing in a way they did not previously believe possible.

The same thing happened to Augustine. In his earlier life he had disparaged the notion of healing. But when he came to write *City of God* he tells us how his views changed 'once I realised how many miracles were occurring in our own day which were so like the miracles of old, and also how wrong it would be to allow the memory of these miracles of divine power to perish from among our people. It is only two years ago that the keeping of records was begun here in Hippo, and already, at this writing, we have nearly seventy attested miracles.'

In all probability the spread of the gospel was considerably furthered by the exercise of healing gifts. Our earliest witness outside the New Testament is Quadratus. Writing about A.D. 125 he knew people who had been healed by Jesus. 'But the works of the Saviour were always present, for they were true – those who were cured, those who were raised from the dead, who not only appeared as cured and risen but were constantly present not only when the Saviour was living but even for some time after he had gone, so that some of them even survived to our own time' (Eusebius *H.E.* 3.35). Irenaeus, writing some fifty years later, says 'Others heal the sick by laying their hands on them, and they are made whole' (*A.H.* 2.32). Origen, too, makes much of the ministry of healing. 'For those who need healing they use no other invocation than that of the supreme God and of the name of Jesus, together with the history about him. By these also we have seen many delivered from serious ailments, and from natural distractions and madness, and countless other diseases' (*Contra Celsum*, 1.6, 7.4).

There is no doubt that the ministry of healing was very

significant in the early Church. Yet we must not exaggerate its impact. Healers are not mentioned in the lists of workers in the church in Ephesians 4:11, or in the fuller list in Romans 12:6–8. In the Pastoral Epistles the tasks of Christian ministry are fully described, but there is no hint that healing is seen as one of them.

When healing does not come

James 5:14 certainly speaks of the healing power of God in answer to believing prayer and the anointing with oil (ceremonial or medical?) on the part of the Christian leadership. But quite clearly the healing is contingent, not universal. The apostles themselves were not always able to heal. God was not at their disposal to be manipulated as they willed. Paul himself had to leave his friend Trophimus sick at Miletus (2 Tim. 4:20). He could not, apparently, do anything about the illness of Epaphroditus (Phil. 2:25–27). He advised Timothy, when suffering from a gastric complaint, to use wine in its medicinal sense, and does not ask for supernatural healing (1 Tim. 5:23). He himself suffered from an eye affliction (Gal. 4:15) and was racked with a thorn in the flesh which God in his wisdom did not see fit to remove. The Lord gave, not healing, but the strength to bear the affliction (2 Cor. 12:7–9). It is important to remember this side of the biblical material, together with its great emphasis on 'weakness', when excessive claims are made by some Christians that it is never God's will for us to be ill. In a world where sin is not excluded from the permissive will of God (though it is obviously not his direct will for us), why should we think that we have the right to be rid of suffering? Paul had no such exemption. Neither have we. Suffering, sin, disease and death are all part of the fallen lot of mankind, and they will be with us until heaven. It is cruel to see the mental anguish that has been induced by well-meaning people who have raised the hopes of the sick that they would be physically healed, and then no such healing has come; the rejoinder has then been that the patient either had some unconfessed sin in the way,[4] or else that his faith was inadequate. The ensuing agonised heart searchings are not hard to imagine.[5] I do not know whether such therapists do more or less harm than the materialistically minded Christians of small vision, who do not believe that God could possibly heal without medical means. Of course he can. And of course he does. It happens all over the world. It happens with organic illnesses, such as tuberculosis and cancer, blindness and limb deformity, as well as with inorganic ailments. The point is that all healing is God's work. He is able to heal with or without medical means. It is no more 'spiritual' if the healing comes through the laying on of hands and prayer than if it comes through the hospital and drugs. But God does not always choose to heal us physically, and perhaps it is as well that he does not. How people would rush to Christianity (and for all the wrong motives) if it carried with it automatic exemption from sickness! What a nonsense it would make of Christian virtues like longsuffering, patience and endurance if instant wholeness were available for all the Christian sick! What a wrong impression it would give of salvation if physical wholeness were perfectly realised on earth while spiritual wholeness were partly reserved for heaven! What a very curious thing it would be if God were to decree death for all his children while not allowing illness for any of them! No, those who claim Christian immunity from illness not only fly in the face of facts and

---

[4] Sometimes, of course, illness *is* due to sin. Paul believed that some of the illness and even deaths at Corinth stemmed from their sins against the fellowship. On the links between healing and salvation, see my *The Meaning of Salvation* (1 Cor. 11:30, cf. James 5:16), Hodder, p. 218ff.

[5] Mark 9:29 points us away from the meaningless measuring of faith to something much more qualitative: the need for waiting on God in quiet confidence that he is in control.

conjure up false hopes; they are guilty of the same basic theological error as those who preach the possibility of sinless perfection in this life. Both are wanting to have here and now what God has kept for the life to come, where perfect wholeness and perfect freedom from indwelling sin will go hand-in-hand.

When it does

Healing, then, is a gift that God offers through some members of the body of Christ, to enable them to act as channels of his love and compassion to others. 'Have all the gift of healing?' asks the apostle. The answer, clearly, is 'No'. But those who have this gift are to use it for the benefit of others. It seems to be one of the good gifts of the Spirit which is increasingly being realised today, and Christians who had no idea that they possessed it are finding that they are being used in this ministry of healing. There have been large outbreaks of healings in two cathedrals, one in Africa and one in Asia, where I have personal friends who were present and witnessed them. They tell me of thousands who came, and many who were healed of blindness, cancer, lameness and other diseases, while many more came to a living faith in the Saviour.

Different gifts of healing

Sometimes healing is ministered through a particular individual whom God seems to equip with a particular charism of healing. I think of one friend, a humble man of God, now dead, through whom the most remarkable healing miracles regularly took place. I have had a colleague who, likewise, was especially so gifted, and many people who sought his help were healed from illnesses organic and emotional. But there are great dangers in the cult healing figure, and perhaps that is why Paul never personalises these gifts of healing in the three allusions he makes to them in chapter 12. It is *gifts of healing* which the Holy Spirit provides in his Church: not necessarily healers. I know one man who was used in healing only once in the course of a

long ministry: but in answer to his prayer and the laying on of
hands the patient who had been told he must spend the rest of
his life in bed, immediately got up and was instantly and permanently healed. In our Oxford congregation we often saw
physical, emotional and psychosomatic healings in response to
prayer and anointing with oil and the laying on of hands. We
did not have any member of the congregation who was a noted
'healer', but gifts of healing took place as the congregation – or
the small group – prayed in faith and expected God to act.
There was no triumphalist doctrine of healing in our midst. We
were all too acutely aware that God sometimes chooses to heal
and sometimes does not. We taught a theology of suffering and
its fruits, as well as a theology of healing. But when all is said
and done, healing frequently took place. I am sorry to admit
that I used not to believe it. Now I have seen it, I have experienced it in my own body, and I have been the channel of it, on
occasion, to others. The reality of this gift can only be doubted
by those who are not prepared to examine the evidence.
Equally, those who maintain that Christians should never, if
they are living close to God, suffer illness, and who maintain
that healing and salvation are always and properly inseparable,
do not match up to the evidence of Scripture, history or experience.

The gift of miracles

Acts of power

The next of the gifts of doing, namely 'the working of miracles', is very widely attested in the Bible. Miracles were common
in the Old Testament, in the life of Jesus, and in the Acts of the
Apostles. One thinks of prison doors opening to release a Peter
or a Paul; of Elymas the sorcerer being struck with blindness,
and so forth. If it is correct to read the plural *dunameon* after
energēmata in 1 Corinthians 12:10, then it can only mean that
Paul reckoned the ability to work miracles as one of the gifts of

the Spirit. However, the genitive singular (*dunameōs*) is read by several of the best MSS: the meaning would then be not 'the working of miracles' but 'the effects of power' – the outworking in Christian ministry of the divine power as believers accept and use the gift of the Spirit. Whichever is the right reading of that disputed text, the emphasis is clearly on power. Some men in apostolic days, and since, have been given particular endowments of God's power within them, enabling them to do what they would otherwise never have been able to contemplate. One need only think of the effects of Christ's power in men like Martin Luther in the sixteenth century or Martin Luther King in the twentieth to take the point.

John 14:12 – and Indonesia

Not a great deal is written about the gift of doing miracles in current Pentecostal literature. It gets nothing like the coverage of tongues, prophecy and healing. There was reference to the revival in Indonesia some years ago, however, about which stories were told of miraculous happenings to parallel anything that is recorded in the Acts of the Apostles. John 14:12 is adduced to indicate that Jesus expected his followers to do greater things than he had himself accomplished, and the matter is generally left there, apart from some more or less impressive personal anecdotes.

To glance at these in turn, there were strong political factors which affected the undoubted spiritual movement towards Christianity in Indonesia at the time; and personal acquaintances of mine who visited the country more than once told me that reports of miracles were greatly exaggerated. Distance, as ever, lends enchantment. John 14:12 need not necessarily refer to miraculous works at all; merely to the undoubted fact that Jesus during the course of his ministry had deliberately restricted himself to working in Israel. After his return to the Father (which is the whole thrust of the context) the disciples would achieve far more than he had himself done, because the

Spirit of Jesus, now no longer limited by a human body, but resident within their personalities, would empower them to be Christ's witnesses in word and deed throughout the whole known world. This power may well have been intended to include the miraculous, but the verse does not say so.

What sort of power?

When Paul spoke of the gift of *energēmata dunameōs* or *dunameōn*, he may have been pointing to the singular effectiveness God gives to some Christians to impress people by their words and deeds. That is, it would seem, what Jesus was meaning in the passage in John 14. He tells the disciples that the demonstration available to them of the reality of a Father they cannot see is the words (14:10) and the deeds (14:11) of Jesus. Similarly, he promises them that they will do greater works than this when he returns to his Father and sends them the Spirit. Their words and their deeds will be the evidence to men of all nations (not Israel only) of the reality of the Jesus who is preached to them, but whom they cannot see. It was this *dunamis*, this powerful impact, which struck men about the teaching of Jesus and his behaviour. Hearing his teaching in the Nazareth synagogue, his fellow countrymen were amazed and asked, 'Where does this man get his wisdom from, and his *dunameis*, his acts of power?'

I do not for one moment wish to minimise the supernatural power of which Paul is speaking. The word is certainly used in the Gospels to indicate the miraculous healings of Jesus and indeed the splendour of his Advent, as well as the impact of his words and deeds. I, for one, do not believe that the Almighty is shackled by 'laws of nature' (which are nothing more – nor less – than a massive series of observed uniformities). If levitation, for instance, can be practised in occultism and Eastern meditation, I see no reason why it should not be available to Christians through the Spirit. It is simply a question of exegesis. Does Paul mean that the Spirit enables some Christians to break what are normally taken to be physical laws? Or does it mean that the Spirit so takes control of the personalities of some Christians that their words and deeds have a particularly powerful impact for God?

Power – or powers?

If the singular, *dunamēos*, is the correct reading in 1 Corinthians 12:10, it is probable that we should accept the second of the above alternatives. This would accord well with Paul's claim that the Spirit empowers his words (1 Thess. 1:5, Rom. 15:19, 1 Cor. 2:4, 2 Cor. 6:7) and shines powerfully through his life (Phil. 3:10, Col. 1:11, Eph. 1:19f, 2 Cor. 12:9f). This is the true *imitatio Christi*, the impact made by Christ's Spirit when active in the believer's words and deeds.

If, however, the plural, *dunameōn*, is correct, this swings the balance back towards the interpretation, 'working of miracles'; particularly in the light of the plural in 1 Corinthians 12:28,29, and of the unambiguous miraculous meaning of the word in Romans 15:18 and 2 Corinthians 12:12 where it is joined with 'signs and wonders'. If this is the case, we have to ask ourselves whether there was a well-attested supernatural demonstration of power notable both in the life of Jesus and of the later apostolic age?

Immediately one comes to mind: exorcism. The power of Jesus was signally demonstrated in the casting out of evil spirits: 'with authority and power he commands the unclean spirits, and they come out' (Luke 4:36). Exorcism was regularly practised in the sub-apostolic church, and was highly prized. The early, though inauthentic, Longer Ending of St. Mark lists exorcism among the signs which would follow the preaching of the gospel. The Acts of the Apostles shows it happening. It continued to be a major weapon in the Christian armoury in the sub-apostolic period. Justin, for instance, writes, 'And now you may learn this from what goes on under your own eyes. Many of our Christian men have exorcised (in the name of Jesus

Christ who was crucified under Pontius Pilate) numberless
demoniacs throughout the whole world, and in your city. When
all other exorcists and specialists in incantations and drugs have
failed, they have healed them and still do heal, rendering the
demons impotent and driving them out' (2 *Apology* 6).

Deliverance ministry

This is not the place to examine exorcism in depth. That I have
attempted in *I Believe in Satan's Downfall*. As with healing, this
is a gift long disused, whose value is being recognised afresh in
the Church. We are called not only to cry to the Lord for his
aid, but to 'resist the devil and he will flee'. This is a particularly dramatic spiritual gift, and a dangerous one. In most
churches it is hedged around with many safeguards by the
ecclesiastical authorities, and with good reason. Generally
those who are affected by demonic spirits have a variety of
other problems as well, and a simplistic approach by an inex-
perienced would-be exorcist is a recipe for disaster. Nevertheless, abuse does not take away proper use. And this ministry of
deliverance, of setting people free from evil powers to which
they have subjected themselves (usually by some active involvement in the occult), is a vitally important spiritual gift to find
in any church that is spiritually alive. There is a particularly
close link between God's supplying his Holy Spirit to us, and
the driving out of spirits which are not from God (Gal. 3:5).
We may, I think, be confident that this ministry of deliverance,
together with the more drastic treatment, exorcism, is what
Paul has in mind when he speaks of 'miracles', particularly in
view of its immediate juxtaposition in the list to 'healings'. It
is at times difficult to operate effectively in a modern parochial
situation without the use of this gift. In an age which has
largely rejected God, people have involved themselves to a considerable extent in the pursuit of other spiritual forces, and this
leaves its mark in a trail of broken lives. These evil spiritual
forces need to be challenged in the name of Christ, and then

the power of God the Holy Spirit is seen. Here again I used to be very sceptical. But I have seen, and have often been instrumental in, the immediate transformation of a life when a person suffering from infestation from evil forces has been set free. I have seen a social worker look on in speechless amazement as someone who was ranting and violent became, like the Gadarene, demoniac 'sitting and clothed and in her right mind' as God's Holy Spirit drove out the demonic force under which she had long suffered.

The gift of faith

The third of this group of gifts of action is the gift of faith. All commentators are agreed that Paul is not speaking of the saving faith by which a man believes in Christ. True, this is a gift of God, if only in the sense that without the God-given capacity to trust, faith in Christ would be impossible for any one of us. Clearly, Paul is not thinking of that here. He is referring to the special ability to trust God in the dark when all the odds are against you: the ability to hold on to God in prayer over many years for the conversion of some loved one: the sure perception of the will of God on a particular matter in the future which enables you to act as though it had already happened.

Noah had this gift of faith, in believing God, against all the odds, that there would be a flood, and acting on that belief by building an ark, despite the laughter of his fellows. Abraham had this gift of faith, in believing that God was calling him out of Ur even though it was economic madness to leave his expensive home in that prosperous city and entrust himself to God and to the desert. Hudson Taylor had this gift of faith in founding and maintaining one of the world's biggest missionary societies on a complete absence of financial backing, a refusal to ask for funds, and an unshakeable conviction about the will of God. I remember as a boy having the orphanages bordering the

County Cricket Ground at Bristol pointed out to me by a schoolmaster who was scarcely celebrated for his Christian allegiance: 'Don't laugh at prayer,' he used to tell us. 'You can see answers to prayer in bricks and mortar when you look at those orphanages. George Muller built them on prayer and kept them going on prayer.' It was perfectly true; Muller was another of these men who had been given by God this exceptional gift of faith. The gift is not extinct!

It is obvious why this gift is mentioned alongside healing and miracles (?or 'power'). You cannot heal in the name of the Lord without having faith that the great Healer himself will act. You cannot exorcise in Christ's name without a deep exercise of faith. The faith that moves mountains is a gift of the Spirit, and it is closely allied to action in the power of the Spirit. It is not the same as that fruit of the Spirit which includes love, joy, peace, faith and others. These qualities should increasingly be seen in every Christian life. The gift of faith seems rather to be this clear insight into the will of God, this staking all upon it, this unwavering conviction that God will provide even in the most impossible circumstances, that has marked some Christians in every age who have received that particular gift from the Spirit.

3. Gifts of Knowledge

The last trio of gifts mentioned in this crucial passage, 1 Corinthians 12:6–10, are gifts not of speech, not of action, but of knowledge. They are all God-given disclosures. It remains part of the work of the Spirit to reveal the things of God to those whom he indwells. And this is of the utmost importance. When praying for the Colossians whom he had never yet seen, Paul's first request for them was that they may be filled with a deep knowledge of God's will, along with all wisdom and spiritual understanding: only so would they be able to live lives obedient, pleasing to the Lord (Col. 1:9–11).

The gift of knowledge

'Knowledge' in pagan religion

Let us examine first what Paul means by knowledge. *Gnōsis* is the Greek word employed, and it is used very sparingly in the New Testament, probably because of incipient gnosticism. This was a movement which sought salvation by knowledge. 'Knowledge' might be anything from magic, ranging through the revelations to the initiate in the Mystery Religions, to philosophy. This pagan idea of salvation by knowledge was a particular problem at Corinth, and formed a dangerous antithesis to Christian knowledge in three ways.

Compromise

First, in the sphere of religious practice, it led to compromise. It is clear from 1 Corinthians 8:1ff that Christians tarred with this Gnostic brush were making their 'knowledge' a substitute for obedience. They were too sophisticated to believe in the reality of idols, and therefore were prepared to compromise their Christian position by eating meals in an idol's temple. No wonder they were castigated as carnal Christians in chapter 3 of the Epistle. Keen on knowledge, they were one with the pagans in supposing that salvation was a matter of this knowledge, which they, fortunately, possessed.

Asceticism and licence

Second, in the physical sphere, emphasis on 'knowledge' led to the twin, though opposite, results of asceticism and licence. An important strand in Greek thought, which seems to have affected the Corinthians, held that the body was a tomb, in which the eternal soul lay imprisoned. The important thing was the illumination of that soul and its eventual rescue from the confines of the body; what happened to the body did not matter. Therefore one could run to the extreme of asceticism, mortifying the body by harsh discomforts; or one could indulge the body by rampant sensuality. It simply did not matter. What mattered was the soul. It is against this background that we can understand the rebukes of Paul to the libertines in chapter 6 and the ascetics in chapter 7. Both operated from the same false view of the body as evil (or at best indifferent) and the soul as good (especially when illuminated with knowledge).

Division

Third, their emphasis on knowledge produced a most unhealthy divisiveness. If salvation is primarily a matter of knowledge, those who have it are in a position to look down on others, despise them, and boast over them. That is what happened at Corinth. It accounts for the party strife which we read of in the first three chapters. It accounts for the litigiousness of chapter 6, and for the troubles at the Lord's table in chapter 11 when some would eat and drink to excess while others had none. It accounts for the need Paul felt to insert that superb chapter 13 on love, the gift without which all others were of no avail.

'Knowledge' in Paul

Knowledge, therefore, as understood at Corinth, facilitated religious compromise, emancipated you from the claims of normal morality, and enabled you to look down on fellow Christians who lacked your gift. This background perhaps puts us in a better position to understand what Paul means by the spiritual gift of knowledge. It is important to realise that none of us can be quite sure what Paul meant by this gift, although some people think they know! However, an examination of some of his other uses of the word may give us some clue.

Knowledge of God

First, this is knowledge of God himself, as made manifest in Jesus Christ (2 Cor. 2:14, 4:6). It is not knowledge of heavenly mysteries or recondite intellectual methods of salvation, but knowledge of God. Paul sometimes uses the intensified form of the word, *epignōsis*, which has the nuance of deep or personal knowledge. This knowledge of God is not arrived at by human endeavour; 1 Corinthians 2 is insistent on that. Finite, sinful man cannot possibly arrive by intellectual processes and spiritual striving at God who is both infinite and holy. All knowledge of God must be mediated to us by the Spirit, who searches the deep things of God and reveals them to believers, so that they can be said to have the mind of Christ (1 Cor. 2:9–16).

Holiness

Second, this knowledge is incompatible with an unholy life. The Pastoral Epistles lay an enormous stress on the link between soundness in doctrine and holiness of life, and Paul does the same in his letters to the Corinthians. He claims that he is richly gifted in knowledge, but in the very same verse opens his life up to inspection by the Corinthians (2 Cor. 11:6). As we have seen, he denounces the 'knowledge' which thinks nothing of compromise with idolatry. True knowledge of a holy God must be inextricably linked with holiness of life.

Love

Third, this knowledge is incompatible with a selfish or arrogant attitude towards other people. Hence the emphasis in 1 Corinthians 8 on respect for the other's conscience even when you reckon it is misguided, for this is the way of love. The same goes for chapter 13, of course, and also for chapter 6, where Paul points out that the way of love should encourage Christians even to be defrauded rather than to go to law against each other (6:7). Interestingly enough knowledge is placed between 'pureness' and 'longsuffering' in 2 Corinthians 6:6, as if it were partly at least determined by holiness in personal life, and by patience towards others. Certainly in 2 Corinthians 8:7 loving contribution to others in need is seen as the outcome of 'knowledge'. Indeed, the outward thrust to others implicit in this gift is stressed by the form in which it occurs in the list we are examining, 'the *word* of knowledge': what marks it out as coming from God is not merely its content but its communication. The man who has knowledge of God will not be able to keep it to himself. He must pass it on.

Such is Christian knowledge. It centres on Jesus Christ, in whom are hid all the treasures of wisdom and knowledge (Col. 2:3). And it is something which all the Corinthians were expected to have and to grow in (1 Cor. 1:5).

A 'word of knowledge'

But Paul means something further by the inclusion of knowledge in this list of spiritual gifts. If we compare the passage here with 1 Corinthians 13:2 and 14:6 it becomes apparent that Paul is speaking of some revelatory word from God for the benefit of others. That is why he speaks not of 'knowledge' but of 'a word of knowledge' here. He is thinking not of a settled quality in the person concerned, but of a specific utterance that comes directly from God and cuts to the heart of the recipient. Jesus clearly had, and used, this gift when he perceived the character of Nathaniel as he sat under his fig tree, when he told the waiters at the marriage in Cana of Galilee to bear pitchers of water to the head of the feast, when he looked up into the tree and named Zacchaeus, and when he told the woman of Samaria that she had had five husbands. Peter had that gift when he knew that the heart of Ananias and Sapphira was not right in the sight of God. This seems to be the gift of which the apostle is speaking. It is a God-given disclosure that would not normally be available to the recipient. It is intended not for gratification but for edification. It is a particularly valuable gift for the Christian counsellor, who needs to know the heart of the person to whom he is speaking. It is available today. It has sometimes been vouchsafed to me, and the person concerned has said, 'How did you know that about me?' to which the answer was, of course, that I did not! There are times when such insight does not come by a direct statement, but by means of a vision or picture which brings immediate illumination. When knowledge comes that way, it is very difficult to distinguish it from the picture or revelation which is part of prophecy. Over-precise definition is likely to go astray!

The gift of wisdom

The cult of wisdom

Much that has been said of the gift of knowledge is applicable to the closely allied gift of wisdom. The Greeks were always inclined to think of God in terms of wisdom, and there was a strong tendency to do the same in later Judaism where wisdom was personified and even seen as the consort of Yahweh. Clearly something of the sort had caught on at Corinth. Christianity was seen as the new wisdom. Its teachers were viewed as purveyors of the new wisdom. And they, the Corinthians, were in the position of judges between an Apollos, a Paul, a Peter: they could discriminate between teachers, for they were wise! This utterly misconstrues the nature of the gospel, of Christians, and of their Christian teachers: so Paul, in his First Epistle, has first to destroy, and then to build up.

Christianity is not 'wisdom'

First, he destroys their idea that Christianity is wisdom. It is radically different from the wisdom of this world. The world in all its wisdom never arrived at a knowledge of God: had not God declared in Scripture that he 'will destroy the wisdom of the wise, and will bring to nothing the understanding of the prudent' (1:19)? No, the Christian message is sheer folly, for it centres round a crucified Jesus. Scarcely any wisdom there! A crucified man is a failure, on any showing. And even had he been the most glowing success, ultimate wisdom could not have been found in a particular – every educated man since the day of Plato knew that it reposed in general maxims, ideas and the like, of universal significance. That is how a Greek would have reacted to the preaching of the cross. But precisely because of this misplaced Corinthian reliance on wisdom, Paul determined to preach nothing but the cross: folly, indeed, to men, but to those who had tasted its saving power, the wisdom of God (1:18).

Apostles are not teachers of wisdom

Second, Christian teachers are not teachers of wisdom, as the Corinthians thought. That is to give them at once too high a place, as though they were anything at all in independence of God (3:7ff), and too low a place, as though they were accountable to the Corinthians for what they taught and did (4:1–13). It is to forget that the cross is not something merely to be taught about but to be lived; it is not just the content of apostolic doctrine but the pattern of apostolic life. What arrogance for the Corinthians to assume that the heavenly powers had so come upon them that they had entered on their reign, and could sidestep the way of the cross in the exuberance of an experience of resurrection. The scorn of Paul's rebuke cannot be missed even in translation. 'You have come into your fortune already. You have come into your kingdom – and left us out. How I wish you had indeed won your kingdom; then you might share it with us! . . . We apostles are fools for Christ's sake, while you are such sensible Christians. We are weak; you are so powerful. We are in disgrace; you are honoured' (3:8ff). In other words, the apostles live the way of the cross, and the Corinthians, for all their spiritual gifts, do not.

Christians may not 'judge' their teachers

So Paul turns to their third mistake, to suppose that they could sit as judges on their ministers, just as they would on any wandering sophist who came to initiate them into his particular brand of Greek wisdom. They had no right to judge their leaders, overconfident as they were in the richness of their own spiritual gifts. Paul's biggest problem at Corinth was a band of lawless, charismatic Christians who regarded spiritual gifts as a substitute for the way of the cross, for obedience to Christian leaders, for holiness of life, and for love of the brethren. Is it surprising, therefore, that Paul should dub these gifted charismatics 'carnal', 'babes in Christ'? They regarded others who lacked their gifts as 'psychic' or unspiritual; it was they themselves who demonstrated all the characteristics of people whose behaviour was not governed by the Spirit, despite the amount they talked about him. They were still 'psychic' Christians (3:3), whose daily behaviour was governed by the natural appetites of their fallen nature, not by the unity, humility, love, holiness and teachings of Christ. Therefore Paul tells them that it makes little difference to him how they account of him. It is not their judgment now that he has to face, but Christ's judgment at the last day: and they will have to face it too. They are not the judges, but the judged. And the Lord who knows everyone through and through will apportion praise in the last day. In the meantime, they would be wise to do less boasting about wisdom, and more copying of the apostolic way of living and suffering and dying along the way of the cross, after Jesus.

Authentic wisdom

Any attempt, then, to claim wisdom as a spiritual endowment is a mark of unspirituality. God has not called those who reckon themselves wise, and who, as spiritual people, regard 'psychic' (i.e. ordinary, second-class) Christians as fools (3:18, 2:14). On the contrary, he has called those who know they are fools, to confound the wise (1:26f). For the only source of wisdom is God. He will not have anybody boast in his presence. It was entirely his work that these Corinthians were in Christ at all, and in Christ alone could they find wisdom, right standing, holiness, and redemption (1:30). Any boasting, therefore, was rigorously excluded.

Paul thus goes out of his way to attack Corinthian pride and misconceptions about wisdom. There is indeed a Christian wisdom. But they lacked as yet the maturity to take it in (2:7f). In the verses which follow, Paul goes on to show that it centres on Christ, it embraces the cross, and it is imparted by the Spirit. It is a broad word, this wisdom. In Ephesians, for instance, Paul applies it to the whole mystery of our redemption, our acceptance in Christ, and the riches of God's grace (1:8). He prays that God would give them the spirit (Spirit?) of wisdom in revealing to them more of the Lord, the hope to which he calls them, the wealth and glory of the share he offers them among his people in their heritage, and how vast are the resources of his power open to those who trust him (Eph. 1:17f). Wisdom, this gift of the Spirit, would seem to be, therefore, a many-splendoured thing (Eph. 3:10). It springs from Christ in whom all wisdom is hidden (Col. 2:3), is nourished by the word of Christ learnt and relied on (Col. 3:16) and includes practical wisdom in behaving in a Christian way to those who are not Christians (Col. 4:5).

James also speaks of the practical, peaceful way in which divine wisdom will show itself (3:13). It is a gift that God promises to the believer who asks in faith (Jas. 1:5). And James writes to his readers about it in a way that Paul could easily have echoed towards the Corinthians.

> Who among you is wise and clever? Let his right conduct give proof of it, with the modesty that comes of wisdom. But if you are harbouring bitter jealousy and selfish ambition in your hearts, consider whether your claims are not false. This is not the wisdom that comes from above; it is earth-bound, sensual, demonic. For with jealousy and ambition come disorder and evil of every kind. But the wisdom from above is in the first place pure; then peace loving, considerate, and open to reason; it is straightforward and sincere, rich in mercy and in the kindly deeds that are its fruit. (Jas. 3:13–18)

This seems to be the nature of the wisdom to which Paul is inviting the Corinthians once they have renounced their claims to man-made wisdom and the arrogance to which it gives rise.

'A word of wisdom'

There seems to be little to justify the neo-Pentecostal claim that the wisdom to which Paul refers in his list of spiritual gifts is 'the sudden and miraculous giving of wisdom to meet a particular situation, answer a particular question, or utilise a particular piece of knowledge, natural or supernatural' (Bennett, *op. cit.* p. 163). In the first place, there is no suggestion in 1 Corinthians that this word of wisdom is supernatural and miraculous. Paul was not dogged by any division between natural and supernatural: he saw God as the author of both. All true wisdom comes from him. Second, there is little enough in the New Testament usage to suggest that the gift is sudden. The one verse that could properly be adduced to the contrary is Luke 21:15. Here Jesus promises to give his followers 'a mouth and wisdom' when they have to bear testimony for him in unexpected circumstances. But rather than suppose that this is a sudden gift of wisdom, in contrast to the normal usage of the New Testament, it is surely more likely to mean that our Lord will give us when a crisis is upon us the ability to enunciate the broadly based understanding of his salvation which has been growing in us for years. To be sure, Paul is thinking about something very specific here: it is an 'utterance of wisdom' not 'wisdom' that he is talking about. But there is nothing to suggest it is sudden. On the contrary, both Jesus and John the Baptist are said to have grown in wisdom as they grew in years (Luke 2:40,52). We are therefore likely to be on the right track if we interpret the word or utterance of wisdom as the spoken application to some particular situation of the wisdom God has been gifting us with through his Spirit. That wisdom is a settled disposition of mind, generally to be found in someone who has long companied with the Lord. It is a gift which enables a Christian to draw on a broad understanding of the purposes of

God, the Scriptures, and supremely of Jesus and his cross, and to speak appropriately with wise utterances for the building up of members of the Christian Body. A precious gift indeed.

The gift of discernment

There is one final gift in the Pauline list, the abilities (plural) to distinguish between spirits. This is not just spiritual discernment in the broad sense of the term, but the varied abilities that are needed to discern whether a spirit is from God or not. In a church as charismatically alive as Corinth it was a gift of crucial importance.

Vital for tongues

Take the matter of tongues, for instance. Tongues, as we have seen, can be a vehicle for the Spirit of God. It can also be psychologically induced, and was a perfectly well-known phenomenon in paganism. The Corinthians had probably engaged in it in their pagan days, so we read in 1 Corinthians 12:2. And the hangover from those days remained in church; some people who laid claim to be speaking in tongues inspired by the Spirit were actually calling down a curse on Jesus (12:3). The gift of discernment was needed here.

. . . or exorcism

Or take the question of exorcism. In Acts 16:17 the evangelists Paul and Silas were pestered by a girl who kept on shouting, 'These men are servants of the supreme God, and are declaring to you a way of salvation.' Perfectly true, they were doing just that. But Paul had the spirit of discernment. He realised that this testimony came from a demonic spirit in the girl, and he exorcised her: 'I command you in the name of Jesus Christ, to come out of her,' and it went out there and then. Jesus also showed the same gift of discerning spirits when he refused to accept testimony to who he was from demons, even though they spoke the truth (Mark 1:23ff, 5:7f). This is the gift of discernment which Paul has in mind.

. . . or prophecy

Or take the gift of prophecy. How are you to know if the man who claims to be a prophet is really speaking from God or making it up? David Watson, in his excellent book *One in the Spirit*, gave us three tests to go with this capacity to discern between spirits, three tests, indeed, which inform that capacity of spiritual discernment.

> The tests are clear: (a) Is Jesus Lord of that person's life? 'No one can say that Jesus is Lord except by the Holy Spirit' (1 Cor. 12:3); (b) Is Jesus Christ acknowledged as perfect man and perfect God? 'By this you know the Spirit of God: every spirit which confesses that Jesus Christ has come in the flesh is of God' (1 John 4:2); (c) Is there a measure of true godliness and holiness about the person? 'Every sound tree bears good fruit, but the bad tree bears evil fruit . . . Thus you will know them by their fruits' (Matt. 7:15–20).

Prophecy is clearly a very dangerous gift, and the ability to discern the true from the false is even more crucial in New Testament days than it was among the Old Testament prophets. Anyone purporting to speak direct from God has enormous powers of manipulation. Therefore discernment is crucial. The sheer dangers inherent in prophecy have inclined most parts of the Church to leave it well alone, particularly if they know about the abuses in Montanist days. By way of contrast, in Pentecostal circles, almost anything goes in terms of prophetic utterance, and frequently no attempt at discernment is made. So this gift tends to be abused throughout the churches. But abuse should not take away proper use. St. Paul was acutely aware of the dangers of false prophecy and bogus prophetic pretensions. In Thessalonica someone had prophesied in Paul's name that the day of the Lord had already come (2 Thess. 2:2). Paul's response comes in the verses following where he shows them how contradictory that supposed prophecy was to his actual teaching while he was among them. He urges them to hold fast his own teachings (v. 15). They are to weigh all such supposed prophetic utterances in the light of his apostolic teaching. The same point is made in 1 Corinthians 14:37ff. Nothing can derive from the Spirit of God if it contradicts his revelation in Scripture.

Criteria

There are other criteria that were applied in the early Church. One was, it seems, the length of discourse. 1 Corinthians 14:29,30 imagines a situation in church where one prophet is in full flow while another is sitting by, anxious to have a word. Paul urges 'the others' (perhaps other church leaders, perhaps others with the gift of discernment between spirits) to use their faculty of discernment. And then he goes on, 'If a revelation is made to another sitting by, let the first be silent. For you can all prophesy one by one, so that all may learn and all be encouraged.' Presumably, the longer the prophet goes on, the more likely he is to be talking from his own ideas rather than from the Lord! He is to sit down and keep quiet, so that the brother with a fresh message direct from the Lord can make it known.

A further test which came to be applied, as we saw earlier, in Montanist days, was the willingness to submit to church leadership, and to allow Scripture to be decisive. God is not the author of confusion, and he is not the source of any teaching through a so-called prophet which conflicts with the apostolic testimony about Jesus, nor with duly appointed leadership loyal to that standard. Paul anticipates this test in a piece of biting satire at the end of 1 Corinthians 14. 'Did the word of God originate with you, or are you the only ones it has reached?' he asks, as he upbraids them for their individualism and arrogance. 'If anyone thinks that he is a prophet or spiritual, he should acknowledge that what I am writing to you is a command of the Lord. If any one does not recognize this, he is not recognized' (i.e. by God). Paul goes on, 'So, my brethren, earnestly desire to prophesy, and do not forbid speaking in tongues; but all things should be done decently and in order.' Notice here the supreme place he accords to his own apostolic testimony to Jesus. If a man is truly spiritual, if he is a prophet speaking from God, he will know and respect and abide by the apostolic testimony. The prophet does not add new items of revelation to 'the faith which was once for all delivered to the saints' (Jude 1:3). His is a gift of direct speech from God to console, teach, or evangelise by taking some element in that apostolic revelation and applying it with power to the situation in hand. At the same time, Paul is rebuking them for their unwillingness to abide by his authority as their spiritual leader: charismatic revelations sometimes makes it hard for the recipients to abide by church order!

Exercise of discernment in the Didache

One of the most interesting passages we possess on the discerning of spirits comes in the *Didache*, chapter 11. 'Not everyone who speaks in a spirit is a prophet, but only if he has the behaviour of the Lord. From his behaviour, then, the true prophet and the false prophet shall be known. And every prophet who teaches the truth, if he does not do what he teaches, is a false prophet.' The emphasis on godly living is very strong, and it is also very specific. 'Concerning apostles and prophets, act thus according to the ordinance of the gospel. Let every apostle who comes to you be received as the Lord (Matt. 12:31 seems to be indicated). But let him not stay more than one day, or if need be a second as well; but if he stay three days he is a false prophet.' Clearly, there were wandering Christian teachers claiming to be apostles (not, presumably, apostles of Jesus Christ in the sense that the Twelve were, but apostles sent out by the churches, cf. 2 Cor. 8:23, Phil. 2:25) or prophets, who were on the make for themselves. They got free accommodation and respect, and even tithes from the congregation (*Didache*,

13). But if they stayed on longer than they were needed, it was a clear mark of their self-centredness. The same applied to food. 'No prophet who orders a meal in the spirit shall eat of it. Otherwise he is a false prophet,' is the wise advice which the unknown Christian writer of the *Didache* offers, in order to guard against the abuse of hospitality. The same shrewdness is applied to finance. 'Whosoever shall say in a spirit, "Give me money or something else", you shall not listen to him; but if he tell you to give on behalf of others in want, let none judge him.'

. . . in Hermas

We find much the same shrewd ethical appraisal of those who claimed the prophetic gift in the writings of Hermas. 'Try the man who has the Spirit of God by his life. First, he who has the Spirit of God which proceeds from above is meek, and peaceable, and humble and refrains from all iniquity and the vain desire of this world, and contents himself with fewer wants than those of other men; he does not speak privately (Hermes means, as he goes on to explain, that the true prophet speaks during the meeting of the church, when men offer up prayer to God; then the Spirit fills him, and he speaks to the multitude as the Lord wills) and the Holy Spirit does not speak at the whim of man, but only when God wishes.' On the other hand, 'Hear in regard to the spirit which is earthly, empty, powerless and foolish. First, the man who seems to have the Spirit exalts himself, and wishes to have the first seat, and is bold and impudent and talkative and lives in the midst of many luxuries and many other delusions, and takes rewards for his prophecy.' The conclusion is short and to the point: 'Try by his deeds and his life the man who says he is inspired' (*Mand.* 11).

This is precisely the criterion which Jesus himself had laid down long before. 'Beware of false prophets who come to you in sheep's clothing but inwardly are ravening wolves. You will know them by their fruits . . . Not every one who says to me, "Lord, Lord", shall enter the kingdom of heaven, but he who does the will of my Father who is in heaven. On that day many will say to me, "Lord, Lord, did we not prophesy in your name, and cast out demons in your name, and do many works mighty in your name?" And then I will declare to them, "I never knew you; depart from me, you evildoers"' (Matt. 7: 15–23).

... in Montanism

It is interesting to notice that in its early days, at any rate, Montanism recognised this criterion. Epiphanius tells us that Montanus said, 'Behold, man is like a lyre, and I rush upon it like a plectrum. Man sleeps and I awake. Behold, the Lord is he who throws the hearts of men into ecstasy, and gives to men a new heart' (*Haer*. 48:4,1). In other words, the Spirit is not only the author of ecstasy but of ethics; he arouses the heart, and he gives a new heart. No doubt there is an allusion to those words of Jesus on the true and the false prophet in Matthew 7 when Maximilla, one of Montanus' prophetesses claimed plaintively, 'I am chased like a wolf from sheep; I am not a wolf; I am word, and spirit, and power' (Eusebius, *H.E.* 5:16.17). Nevertheless Maximilla was a wolf after all. One of the criteria for true prophecy was, as we have seen, the difficult one of fulfilment. 'After me,' says Maximilla, 'there will be no more prophets, but only the consummation' (Epiphanius, *Haer*. 48:2.4). The Church used the gift of discernment, recognised that Maximilla was not speaking from the Spirit of God, and decisively (perhaps too decisively) rejected the Montanist movement.[6]

Its importance

There are few gifts of the Spirit more necessary to the Church than this gift of discernment. The Catholic charismatic writer,

---

[6] There is a wise and practical chapter on discernment in spiritual gifts to be found in George Mallone, *Those Controversial Gifts*, ch. 2., Hodder, 1984.

Fr. Kilian McDonnell, writes of this as the greatest problem in the whole movement:

> There is some uncritical acceptance of prophecy and tongues without sufficient discernment as to what comes from the Holy Spirit and what comes from the human psyche. Discernment of spirits is one of the major on-going problems of the renewal. It should be remembered that the final judgment as to the authenticity of the charisma belongs to those who preside over the Church, and to whose special competence it belongs not indeed to extinguish the Spirit, but to test all things, and hold fast to that which is good.

These, then, are the nine gifts of the Holy Spirit which are commonly held among Pentecostal Christians to be the supernatural endowments open to all believers who have been baptised with the Holy Spirit. We have already seen that the category of 'Spirit-baptised Christians' over against ordinary Christians is not one which we can reconcile with the New Testament. We have also seen that the New Testament writers do not distinguish between natural and supernatural gifts by the Spirit. What remains to be done is to examine whether there is any justification for restricting the gifts to nine.

4. CHARISMATIC GIFTS

The number of the gifts

There seems to me to be one overwhelming reason why it is impossible to treat these nine gifts as exhaustive in number and quality. Paul gives various lists of spiritual gifts or functions, and the lists differ. They oscillate between spiritual gifts and spiritual functions, but this should not surprise us if we remember that the various types of ministry in the Church are all called God's gift to his people (Eph. 4:11). Ministers are just as much God's gift to us as are spiritual gifts. The two belong together, for spiritual gifts are meaningless unless exercised by spiritual people, intent on serving the Lord with their gifts.

Paul's first list in 1 Corinthians 12

Paul gives three lists of gifts in chapter 12 of 1 Corinthians: the first in verses 8–10, the second in verse 28 and the third in verses 29,30. The first list contains the nine gifts we have already considered: a word of wisdom, a word of knowledge faith, gifts of healing, miracles, prophecy, the ability to discern between spirits, tongues and interpretation.

Paul's second list in 1 Corinthians 12

There is a second list in 1 Corinthians 12:28. Here Paul gives a special order of importance to the first three, which are apostles, prophets, teachers, possibly because all three involve the use of the mind as well as the other aspects of the personality (and we know that he felt this was very important from the whole argument in 1 Corinthians 14), and certainly because all three are concerned with building up the whole Church in the gospel. Then follow miracle workers, healers, helpers, administrators, and speakers in various kinds of tongues. Apostles, teachers, helpers, administrators have come into the list; interpretation of tongues, faith, discerning of spirits, the word of knowledge and the word of wisdom have dropped out.

'Helpers', 'administrators' (literally 'helps', 'administrations') are interesting. They are not the spiritual gifts that are most frequently sought, because they are unostentatious, and much hunting for gifts is a hunger for the spectacular. But how valuable they are in any congregation! *Antilempseis*, 'helps', literally indicates the role of those who stand in for someone else – to do the very thing that is needed at the time. I think of an Oxford graduate who worked in our congregation for a while before going overseas as a missionary in Brazil. He was the clearest example of one richly endowed with this gift I have ever seen. Modest and self-effacing, he was always there to help, always visiting those in need, always thinking ahead of little ways in which he could make the lives of those around him easier. I think of another who had this gift: she was old lady of astonishing vitality – and deafness! You would find her making tea after a meeting, collecting for the underprivileged, doing good by stealth, cleaning up the church kitchen, putting the books back in order after the service. Little things which everyone else omits to do you would find her doing. She would probably have been amazed to be told this was a precious spiritual gift, but it was. It was given her by the Holy Spirit of God.

The word translated 'administrators' is no less interesting. It may well mean just that, and the gifts of a good administrator in a church, once he is really trusted and set free to act, are incalculable. He is just as valuable as a good preacher and pastor and evangelist; probably more so to the congregation as a whole. Most churches suffer from poor administration, and from the lack of communication which so frequently causes irritation and mistrust. Good administration can change all that, and set the preachers and evangelists free to do the task for which God the Holy Spirit has equipped them.

But there may be a further nuance to this word *kubernētēs*. For he was the 'helmsman' in a ship, the one whose hand on the tiller determined the direction of the whole vessel. Such a ministry is vital in any church that is on the move. The gift of the helmsman is very important. He needs to be equipped by the Holy Spirit to gain a sense of vision, of direction, and to have the requisite power to move the church in that direction. It need not be the senior minister in the church. God may equip any member of the Body with this gift, and if it is someone other than the chief minister, the latter will need to be given a special endowment of humility by God in order to heed what the helmsman is saying! We find this hard because our idea of leadership is by office: Paul's was by gift, by *charisma*. And offices in a Christian church should be filled because the person concerned already has the requisite charism for all to recognise.

When churches operate on that pattern every limb finds its proper task and discovers fulfilment in it, and the whole Body grows in love and effectiveness, because round pegs are not being squeezed into square holes.

So much for the second list of gifts to be found in Corinthians 12:28.

Paul's third list in 1 Corinthians 12

In the next two verses Paul gives a slightly different list. Once again he combines people, i.e., apostles, prophets, teachers, with qualities, i.e., miracles, gifts of healing, speaking with tongues and interpretation. Once again the gifts of wisdom and knowledge, faith and discernment have dropped out, as compared with the first list; so have helpers and administrators (roles not highly prized in Corinth!) as compared with the second; while interpretation of tongues has found its way back. It is beginning to appear very precarious to argue that any one of the three lists is exhaustive and definitive of the gifts the Spirit can bestow.

Three additional lists

In Romans 12:6–8 he mentions several *charismata*, and emphasises both that they are given to us and that they are different. We are to employ them 'by the reckoning of faith', that is to say by recognising that they are loans rather than gifts, and need to be received in faith and exercised in service for others. These gifts include prophecy, practical acts of service to others, teaching, the lovely gift of encouragement, wholehearted generosity, leadership in the church, and 'showing mercy', presumably taking trouble over the disadvantaged, the hurt and the lonely. It is very obvious how necessary such gifts are in every congregation, not only at Rome. But it is noteworthy that of the 'original' nine in 1 Corinthians 12:8,9 only prophecy remains! However, as in Corinthians 13, love crowns them all (Rom. 12:9).

Another list emerges from Ephesians 4:11,12. He is expounding the nature of the Christian ministry. It is Christ's gift to his Church: three times he stresses it. And this ministry is not monochrome. Nor is it a matter of bishops, presbyters and deacons. No, once again it is function rather than office which interests him. He tells us that the gifts of the ascended Christ are apostles, prophets, evangelists, pastors and teachers. All of them are called to equip the Christian Body for service and to help build it up in love. The list is carefully chosen. To be sure, apostles and prophets are always basic in the N.T. understanding of ministry. But the emphasis here on them as gifts to the Church is significant. There should be in every Christian congregation some manifestation of these five charismas. The apostolic role could be seen as two-fold: the uniqueness of apostolic testimony, now enshrined for us in the New Testament; and also the breadth of apostolic circulation, not allowing churches to become self-related and parochial. The prophetic function, too, is needed, both in speaking out to society, the broad sense of prophecy, and also in that specifically Christian understanding of prophecy which we have already considered. There needs to be evangelism, and teaching, and pastoring in every healthy congregation. There is no reason to suppose it must be the same person who undertakes all these roles. It will probably be various people. So the gift of Christ to his Church is a ministry which is *plural* and *variously gifted*. Most churches have a ministry that is a long way from that! But those gifts lie lurking beneath the surface in every church, if only someone will have the courage to set them free.

Peter, too, refers to several more *charismata* in 1 Peter 4:9–11. He understands that every Christian has received a charism, and is called to use it in serving one another in the Christian family. He mentions hospitality without complaining, willing and wholehearted service, and speaking as the oracles of God. Authentic preaching should have that immediacy which marks it out as coming from God. It is nothing to do with human wisdom. It is a particular *charisma* from God.

Just samples!

It is by now quite evident that all these lists are seeking to give samples of what the Spirit will do in the life of the believer, not to make exhaustive lists of gifts, some of which are to be labelled natural and some supernatural. It is of course true that some of these gifts are striking and exciting, such as prophecy, tongues and healing compared with more ordinary and dull gifts like administration, helping people, or teaching. But the same Spirit is active in both. And Paul's estimate of the relative value in the Church of the several gifts of the Spirit is made pretty clear by the fact that in each of the three lists in 1 Corinthians 12 he places tongues and their interpretation at the bottom of the list, whereas the Corinthians would have put them at the top! Moreover, gifted though he was in this direction himself, he preferred to play down the more obviously showy and 'supernatural' gift of tongues in worship and to speak, however briefly, as a Christian teacher so that he could edify not merely himself but others. 'I thank God that I speak in tongues more than you all. Nevertheless, in church I would rather speak five words with my mind, in order to instruct others, than ten thousand words in a tongue' (1 Cor. 14:18f) – a proportion of one to two thousand!

The meaning of 'charisma'

God's love gift

There is another reason for supposing that we would be wrong to imagine that the nine gifts of 1 Corinthians 12:8–10 are the only or even the typical *charismata* which the Spirit bestows. The word *charisma*, which has become common coin among Pentecostals and neo-Pentecostals to denote the gifts of 1 Corinthians 12:8–10 (with particular emphasis on tongues, interpretation, prophecy and healing), literally means a gift of *charis*. And *charis* in Greek denotes God's unmerited love to us. It is instructive to see how the word is used in the New Testament. Do we find it applied to these nine gifts and them alone? Do we find it restricted to a special class of Christian?

. . . used unrestrictedly

The word is exclusively Pauline apart from 1 Peter 4:10, which encourages us to use the gifts that have been given us by God, notably speaking his oracles and engaging in his service (neither precisely to be found in 1 Corinthians 12:8–10). Paul uses it some sixteen times, and in a variety of ways. Above all, he uses it of the gracious forgiveness of God in contrast to Adam's disastrous rebellion (Rom. 5:15,16). To put it another way, men deserve to be paid death for their actions; God, however, makes us a gracious gift, *charisma*, of eternal life (Rom. 6:23). He uses it of the gracious deliverance God gave him from some terrible but unspecified peril (2 Cor. 1:11); of the results of the mutual fellowship he expected with the Christians at Rome (Rom. 1:11); of Timothy's ordination (1 Tim. 4:14, 2 Tim. 1:6); of God's faithfulness towards his rebellious people Israel (Rom. 11:29); and of marriage (or, alternatively, celibacy) as being a gracious *charisma* of God (1 Cor. 7:7). To cap it all, he encourages the Corinthians to long for the best gifts, and in the very next verse begins his hymn to love, thus indicating unmistakably that the greatest of all God's gracious gifts to Christian people is the gift of love, God's very own nature, imparted to us through the Spirit (1 Cor. 12:31, 13:1ff). The charismatic gifts are nothing other than the gifts of God's love.

. . . of natural and supernatural gifts alike

These *charismata*, these gifts of God's love, begin with our creation and redemption. They include the heightening of qualities already latent within us, such as gifts of administration, leadership, teaching, marriage, music and the like. It is important to realise that these natural qualities – or acquired skills, like cooking or typing – can be recognised as charismata, gracious gifts from the Lord, if and so long as they are received from his hand and dedicated to his service for the building up of his people in the strength that he provides. I remember a headmaster in Singapore coming to me once, disturbed that he lacked the gift of tongues. He may well have received it by now. That is of secondary importance. The crucial thing was that he went away that day with a new appreciation of his teaching skills as one of God's *charismata* to him. He came to see that that natural ability could either be used with the professionalism he had been trained to use, or alternatively each day he could lay the whole programme before the Lord in prayer, and say, 'Lord, you have given me teaching skills. I want to use them as your representative today. I want your love and truth to shine through me today in the classroom. I want you to make full use today of the charism you have entrusted to me.' Natural gifts can very properly be called *charismata* if they are seen as God's gift and used in his service. If they are used selfishly, they can be disastrous.

The same is true of gifts which are beyond normal ken, such as prophecy, tongues, discernment of spirits, healing and exorcism. They, too, are not *charismata* without qualification. There is nothing static about them. They too can be either a blessing or a bane, depending on whether they are used for the common good in humility and service, or whether they are used for the pride and gratification of the person entrusted with them. As we saw above (p. 153), *charisma* is inextricably linked in the economy of God with *diakonia* and *energēma*. Charismatic Christianity is seen when the gracious gifts of God are recognised thankfully as such, and used not in assured complacency but in humble dependence on God's power for the service of God's people.

The crown of charisma

But all these gifts, inherent and acquired alike, are brought to their full flowering in love, the greatest of them all,[7] the one which is available to all. For, properly speaking, to be a Christian is to be a charismatic. There is in God's sight no difference between the charismatics and the non-charismatics, between the 'haves' and the 'have-nots' in the one-class community of Christ. For all alike are eternally in debt to the sheer *charis* of God who sought us, rescued us, equipped us with varying gifts, and shared his own nature of love with us through the Spirit which he has lavished upon every one of us who are in Christ.

It would be inappropriate to close this examination of spiritual gifts in the worship of the early Christians without asking how common such gifts were? Paul lists these various gifts in 1 Corinthians, Romans and Ephesians in such a casual and allusive way that I am convinced the worship of the early church

---

[7] It is sometimes argued in neo-Pentecostal circles that love is nowhere said in the New Testament to be a *charisma*. It stands, therefore, apart from the gifts we have been considering. I do not think that this argument will stand. For one thing, 1 Corinthians 13, the great hymn on love, follows immediately upon Paul's injunction, 'be very anxious for the greater (or greatest?) gifts (*charismata*). And moreover I show you the way in abundance (*kath huperbolēn*)'. He then proceeds to show the primacy of love, the very life of God. It is supremely apposite to bring love forward at this point, particularly after having refused, in verses 21–6, to countenance any ranking in gifts. For love means self-giving, not self-assertion: it is the way of service, the way Jesus himself adopted. Paradoxically, therefore, love is the greatest of the gifts which permit of no priorities! A second passage which seems to make plain that love is one of the *charismata* is Romans 12. In verse 6 he recalls that we have *charismata* differing according to the grace given to us by God; and after teaching, leading, giving, acting mercifully, he moves naturally on to love. Irrespective, therefore, of the etymology which suggests love is a *charisma*, Romans 12 and 1 Corinthians 12 assert it.

was far more charismatic than has been true for most of its subsequent history. It is very hard to imagine the need for the
Pauline strictures on the use of *charismata* in any of the mainline churches today. But among the first Christians those warnings and corrections were needed, as they are in many of the
fast growing churches in the Two-Thirds World today. It is clear
from the Thessalonian epistles, from the Acts, from Jude, 1 and
2 Peter and from the Apocalypse that the early Christians were
acutely aware of living in the times of fulfilment, the age of the
Spirit. The Spirit was their key to understanding the Christian
life from beginning to end, and it was the Spirit not as a dogma
but as an experience. When the Samaritans or the 'Ephesian
dozen' received the Spirit it was obvious. There was a manifest
difference in experience. They knew it, and so did other people.
Paul expected his converts to know they had received the Spirit,
to experience his life-changing power, and to use his gifts for
building up the people of God and for winning over those not
yet converted. These are the two aims that resonate through the
treatment of the topic in 1 Corinthians, and they remain worthy
goals for every church.

What is to be thoroughly deprecated is any attempt, as at
Corinth, to assert spiritual superiority on the ground of gifting.
Pride and self-advertisement have no place among Christians
engaged in worshipping the great and holy God. Any *charismata* they may have come from his Spirit and are to be used in
his service and for his glory alone.

11

What are We to Make of the Charismatic Movement?

It is impossible to write on the subject of the Holy Spirit these days without taking full account of the charismatic movement, which during the past few decades has been affecting churches throughout the world and right across the theological and ecclesiastical spectrum. Consideration of the *charismata* in the previous chapter leads naturally on to the three questions which will occupy us in this chapter. Should we expect to see the charismatic gifts in the Church today? What are the strengths and the weaknesses of the movement which promotes their use? And is it possible for 'charismatics' and 'non-charismatics' to live together unitedly and effectively in the same church?

1. SHOULD WE EXPECT TO SEE THE CHARISMATIC GIFTS IN THE CHURCH TODAY?

Have the gifts died out?

Christians in the main line of both Catholic and Protestant traditions have for a long time been very scared of allowing that these gifts of the Spirit of which we read in the New Testament might be expected to occur today. They are supposed to have died out in the apostolic era.

It is much more comfortable to suppose that this is the case, and to look for the contemporary manifestations of the Holy Spirit in the peace and order of the Church of today rather than in the violent irruptions of earlier days. Both Catholic and Protestant camps have been heavily infected by the rationalism of the Enlightenment, and our Christianity has been unduly cerebral (hence its appeal to the educated only). If the Corinthians were inclined to identify the work of the Spirit with the abnormal, we tend to make the opposite mistake, and suppose that he can only manifest himself in moral renewal, spiritual illumination, and through either Bible or sacraments according to our theological reference! This attitude, however, is sheer escapism from exposing ourselves to the Spirit's powerful life. He remains the Spirit of wind and fire; he remains sovereign in the Church, and is not to be boxed up in any ecclesiastical compartment. It is simply not the case that healing, prophecy, exorcism and speaking in tongues died out with the last apostle. Still less can a passage like 1 Corinthians 13:8 ('as for prophecies, they will pass away; as for tongues, they will cease . . .') be adduced to attest the supposed demise of these gifts. They will pass away only when 'the perfect comes', i.e. at the Parousia – not at the end of the apostolic age or the formation of the New Testament canon! There is in fact plenty of evidence in the sub-apostolic days, and periodically throughout Church history, to show that these gifts did not die out, though they were often viewed with great suspicion by Church authorities. I have gathered together some of the sub-apostolic material in my *Evangelism in the Early Church*. John Woolmer has collected more patristic material in his *Healing and Deliverances*. The evidence is compelling. And it is perfectly evident from the widespread growth of the Pentecostal church and the neo-Pentecostal movement in the last hundred years that God has poured out these gifts in rich measure on his people, rationalistic and sceptical though we have been about them.

A place for tongues?

We should, therefore, expect the Spirit of God to show himself as God. We should neither reject speaking in tongues, nor regard it as the be-all and end-all of spirituality. A Catholic charismatic evaluation is valuable at this point: 'It is clear that the issue of the renewal is not tongues, nor an insistence that praying in tongues is in any necessary way tied to the spiritual realities received in initiation. Many outside the renewal attribute a centrality to tongues which is not reflected in most sectors of the renewal. On the other hand, those involved in the renewal rightly point out that this *charisma* was quite common in the New Testament communities. It should neither be given undue attention nor despised. Since it is the lowest of the *charismata*, it should not be a matter of surprise that it is so common!'

The value and the danger

That is a wise and balanced statement of the truth as the New Testament confronts us with it. We should, therefore, rejoice when a member of the congregation discovers that he has the gift of tongues. Of course, we should be wary. The gift of tongues does not edify anyone else unless it be interpreted; otherwise it is for private use in someone's own devotions. But if it is interpreted it can be a valuable form of edification for the congregation. Why, one wonders, does God choose to use tongues-plus-interpretation sometimes, instead of prophecy, which is so much more direct and needs no interpretation? The answer may, as we have seen, lie in the interdependence within the Body of Christ which God is seeking to deepen. And tongues speaker without interpreter is as useless to the Body as interpreter without tongues speaker. Interdependence is crucial.

One has only to mention tongues-speaking in church, particularly one of the mainline churches, for hackles to rise. But why should they, if this is an authentic gift from God? Fear is, of course, one reason, and a very unworthy one at that. Why should we fear what our heavenly Father allows for our edification? Order is another. But that need be no problem either, if the apostle's injunction is obeyed that there should only be two or at most three such messages in a meeting of the

congregation, and that they must not take place without interpretation, and that there should be sensitivity and mutual submission (1 Cor. 14:27,29,40). Of course there is difficulty in
knowing if there will be anyone to give an interpretation, but
that is far from insuperable. If the tongues speaker feels
impelled to give an utterance in tongues, we can be confident
that God will provide someone to interpret. If nobody is forth-
coming, then the worship leader will, after due pause, go on
with the service. Either someone was smothering the impulse to
interpret, or the original speaker simply got it wrong, and
should never have spoken in that tongue in the first place. In a
congregation where spiritual gifts are allowed to operate there
will inevitably be mistakes; and the ability to apologise and
admit we got it wrong is one of the surest ways to grow in
maturity and sensitivity to what God is really saying.

Other problems crowd in. Will not some people feel upstaged
if others speak in tongues in public? Perhaps they may, but not
if there has been adequate teaching on the variety and interdependence of gifts. Not every Christian has been given this gift.
Like all other gifts, it is distributed by the Holy Spirit as *he* wills
(1 Cor. 12:11). So it may well not be given to us *if* we ask for it
(1 Cor. 12:10,30) or *when* we ask for it. When I wrote the first
edition of this book I had asked for this gift, and had not
received it. Instead, God gave me other gifts, even more useful
than tongues, and my task has been to exercise these to the full.
In the course of time he graciously added the gift of tongues,
when I was not even expecting it or asking for it! It is important
therefore to be relaxed about seeking the Spirit's gifts. He
knows what is best for us and when it is needed, and so long as
we are expectant and dependent we can trust him to equip us as
he sees fit for our own fulfilment and that of the Church.

If you have it . . .

If you have this gift, therefore, praise God in ordinary words,
and praise him in tongues; sing to him in ordinary words, and

sing to him in tongues. Do not be embarrassed to dance before the Lord in the joy the Spirit gives. Allow him to rid you of the inhibitions that may for too long have kept you over-cerebral and sub-personal. Be careful not to regard this gift as the mark of super-spirituality on your own part, something that sets you apart. It is nothing of the sort. Muslim mystics speak in tongues; and, as William Sargent has shown in his *Battle for the Mind*, tongues can be psychologically induced in those who have no faith at all. There is a fascinating story from the charismatic movement of the nineteenth century among the Irvingites, of how a young sceptic went to criticise one of their meetings, and found himself speaking in tongues – to his great surprise. In consequence he underwent a conversion from the philosophical position of Hegel and became a Zoroastrian! No, tongues is not an exclusively Christian or even religious phenomenon, so there is no ground for pride among those who possess it.

If you don't . . .

But if you don't possess it, and if after prayer you still do not receive it, do not let that worry you. God has some other gift or gifts for you. It may well be that you do not need tongues, or at any rate, not now. It may be that you need the gift of administrative ability, or of being prepared to act in a subordinate position under someone else's leadership. And, believe me, those gifts to the Church (and they are nothing less than priceless gifts) need just as great an effusion of the Spirit's enabling as does speaking in tongues. Only you will be very careful not to denigrate the gift of tongues which you do not possess. You will neither write off those who have it as extremists nor be secretly jealous of them. For you know that there is one Spirit who gives gifts as he chooses for the building up of the Body of Christ, and you will be grateful for the role he has chosen for you, and the gifts with which he has equipped you.

A place for healing?

It may be that God has given you a gift of healing. Perhaps you will be used to heal regularly in this way, as a man like Oral Roberts was in America. Perhaps God will use you only occasionally. If healing is your gift, rejoice, and use it for the good of those to whom God leads you. But remember the dangers which beset the use of such a gift: the danger of showing off; the danger of supposing that to heal without means is more spiritual than to heal with means – as if God were not the author of all healing, whether through orthodox medicine, acupuncture, hypnosis, psychotherapy, or spiritual healing. You will be tempted to think there is some special property in oil or hands imposed upon the patient. You will be in danger of playing God, and assuring men that they will recover when they will in fact die. You will be in danger of supposing that suffering may not even form part of the permissive will of God, and thereby perhaps underestimate the role which suffering has in keeping us dependent on the Lord's strength which comes to fruition in weakness (2 Cor. 12:9). You will be tempted to think that God is using you because of some special virtue of your own. The Israelites of old had to learn that God had not chosen them because they were great or holy, but in order to show something of his love in them (Deut. 7:7) and the same is true of the election and the gifts of God today. So remember the dangers, while you rejoice in the gift for the good of others. And wise is the church that does not restrict its role in healing to spiritual solace, but allows scope for those of its members who are gifted in this way to exercise their gift with love and humility alongside the more usual medical methods.

More ways than one

There are various ways in which a congregation can pray for healing. I have been in churches where at the mention of a need a group of elders gather round the person and pray fervently in

English and in tongues. Sometimes there is a person who is signally used in healing, and his or her ministry to the individual
while the rest of the congregation pray is the right way to
proceed. Sometimes people keel over backwards and are 'slain
in the Spirit' for a short while when they are prayed for and
hands are laid on their heads. I can remember the first time that
happened to me: I was both amazed and terrified. What had I
done? But I soon realised that I had done nothing at all; it was
simply that as the need had been laid before God, he had elected
to use this method of reaching the person in need. I see this
fainting when prayer is made as God's anaesthetic, so to speak,
while he is doing something unseen deep within the patient.
Normally there is, subsequently, some signal mark of God's
hand on the person concerned.

Another way in which God's healing is sometimes ministered
is in response to prayer with anointing with oil. There is, of
course, a long history of this within the Christian Church, and
it has power. This is hardly surprising since it is done in direct
obedience to Scripture (Jas. 5:14). We have certainly seen
notable healings, both physical and psychological, in our
Oxford church. We occasionally advertised that there would be
prayer for healing on such and such a Sunday, and asked those
who so wished to submit their names and needs either beforehand on paper or at the time. Sometimes as many as seventy
came forward, and the congregation was once kept for hours in
prayer! This is clearly not something that can be attempted too
often, but we frequently gave opportunity during regular Holy
Communion services for people to receive such ministry after
they had partaken of the sacrament. Another way of seeing
God's healing power at work in the congregation was to ask
people to pray for any needs they spotted as they came into
church among members of the congregation, and unite in silent
prayer for five minutes or so for them. This involves the whole
congregation in prayer for healing.

It is very important that those who have been healed in

answer to prayer should have the opportunity of telling the congregation so at the first opportunity. This both gives the patient the opportunity for witness, and also greatly encourages the congregation and heightens their expectancy that God will answer prayer. Every congregation should be a community of 'salvation', that is to say of healing in every sense; and it is to our shame that until recent years we have not really expected God to heal in answer to the united, believing prayer of the congregation.

A place for exorcism?

Demonic forces

Increasing numbers of Christians are finding that they are called upon to perform exorcism these days. This is perhaps because when, as is so common in our own society, God is driven out of the front door, demonic forces crowd into the house by the back door. Did Jesus not warn us of precisely this danger (Luke 11:24f)? At all events, there is a most notable increase in black and white magic and in demon possession. Sometimes this comes about by deliberate surrender to the power of evil, as long ago Faust is reputed to have sold his soul to the devil. Sometimes it comes by mere physical contact with, for instance, a charm brought back from an animistic country where it was offered in worship to demons. Sometimes it may be that a house is troubled by an evil spirit, or a group of youngsters start toying with spiritism. We in the West have too long pooh-poohed the idea of demon possession, and we are paying for our arrogance by a marked increase in demonic activity. Why otherwise should a leading intellectual bishop head a report on exorcism? It is a real gift of the Spirit of God, and it certainly did not die out in the apostolic era – fortunately for us. This is often how the Spirit worked in the early Church when the gospel was spreading so fast. Tertullian, for instance, could say to pagans who mocked at Christ:

Mock as you will, but get the demons to mock with you! Let them deny that Christ is coming to judge every human soul . . . Let them deny that, condemned for their wickedness, they are kept for that judgment day . . . Why, all the power and authority we have over them is from our naming the name of Christ, the Judge. Fearing God in Christ and Christ in God, they become subject to the servants of God and Christ. At our command they leave, distressed and unwillingly, the bodies they have entered (*Apology* 23).

I do not pretend to understand demon possession. But I know that it is real, and have not infrequently been instrumental in the deliverance of those afflicted with it.

Exorcism proper

It is important to avoid evocative language in this matter. The Roman Catholic Church has long ago and wisely recognised that exorcism proper is only appropriate when the fullest investigations have been made, both medical and psychological, and when it is plain that the person concerned has wholly given themselves over to the power of evil. It should only be attempted by the Church's senior leadership, normally the bishop and his colleagues, and is as difficult as it is rare. If it goes wrong, it can cause (and has caused) terrible trouble, and one celebrated instance in Yorkshire led to murder because the problem was incorrectly handled.

Deliverance

But it is not often the case that people have so handed themselves over to evil that there is in them nothing whatever that responds to the offer of freedom; and freedom is what Christ gives. Something less than exorcism, a ministry of deliverance is offered by God to liberate people who genuinely want to struggle free of dark influences (sometimes hereditary) on their lives. Most churches that have been touched by the charismatic renewal have seen people who were bound in this way set free.

Often the person concerned had no idea that a demonic force was active upon them. But once set free they know it very well, and are aware in a fresh way of the spiritual battle in which we are all engaged whether we recognise it or not.

Possession and oppression?

It is sometimes urged that there is a difference between being possessed by a demonic force and being oppressed by one. While appreciating that a strong sense of oppression by evil is not the same thing as having a demon within you, there is, in fact, no basis in the New Testament for distinguishing between oppression and possession by an evil spirit. The word most commonly used is simply *daimonizesthai*, 'to be demonised'.

Ministry to the demonised

There is no one infallible method of getting rid of these demonic influences. You need to be dependent very much on the leading of the Holy Spirit. My advice would be that nobody should attempt to minister in such a situation alone, nor without the backing of prayer. It is important to be utterly right with God oneself, and confession and claiming God's forgiveness are vital for those offering ministry before any attempt is made to help the sufferer. He in turn must renounce any way in which he has become involved in the occult, and he must destroy any images, tarot cards, or the like, in his possession. Then those ministering will claim the authority of Christ himself, and in his name command the evil force to leave. Sometimes this takes place so quietly that only the patient is aware that liberation has dawned. Sometimes there are violent struggles, vomitings, suicidal or murderous attempts. The occult is a dark world, and its prisoners are not lightly released. The thing to remember is that the power of Christ is greater than all the power of the enemy, and ultimate victory is certain if claimed in his name.

A word of caution

But let nobody seek out this ministry. It is spiritually demanding, highly unpredictable, and can be dangerous. It should only be exercised with the utmost discretion, and people can be greatly harmed if it is suggested that they are demonised when they are not. That is why most dioceses are very strict, and rightly so, in allowing only a very few tried and trusted clergy to engage in this delicate and difficult ministry. There is no particularly compelling reason, so far as I can see, why this ministry should be confined to the clergy. It is not only clergy, but every Christian who is bidden, 'Resist the devil and he will flee from you.' But it remains a wise precaution. A lot of harm has been done in recent years by those who, once alerted to the element of the demonic, then sniff out demons under every bush and in every common cold. Very often there are medical, psychological and spiritual maladies all intertwined in a person who is demonised, and it is naïve in the extreme to think the case can be cured by pills or E.C.T. alone, by psychotherapy alone, or by spiritual ministry alone. All three may well be needed. Perhaps the surest test of whether a person is demonised or not is to see if he reacts violently at the name of Jesus. This was a characteristic of demoniacs in the days of Jesus' life on earth; and it still is Christ's name which causes profound disturbance to a person who is dabbling in the occult. 'Every spirit that confesses that Jesus Christ has come (or "is coming") in the flesh is of God, and every spirit which does not confess Jesus is not of God. This is the spirit of antichrist, of which you have heard that it was coming, and now it is in the world already,' declares John (1 John 4:3f). He continues, 'Little children, you are of God, and have overcome them; for greater is he that is in you than he who is in the world.' The power of the Spirit is greater than the demonic forces that oppress and sometimes possess mankind. And we are right to claim his power in casting out evil forces that remain impervious to medical and psychological treatment. The local church should expect some of its members to be equipped by the Spirit to deal with the ministry of deliverance, and they should be supported by the prayers of the congregation, for theirs is a perilous work, as those who have engaged in it know.

Prophecy for today?

Nor is there any reason to suppose that prophecy died with the apostolic era. As we have seen in the previous chapter, prophets were alive and well in the second century, and it was only the less acceptable face of Montanism which drove prophecy into disrepute and assumption under the role of the bishop. It is encouraging that this gift has been recovered in our day, and that men and women do, as the Spirit leads them, give a word direct from God to their congregation, provided that the local church as a whole recognises the validity of the gift, and encourages them to use it. I have written fairly fully on this topic, and its practical use in church, in *To Corinth with Love*. Of course, a person with prophetic gifts needs to remember that it is all too easy for him to be mistaken and confuse his own message with that of the Spirit of God. It is therefore wise if he avoids speaking as from God in the first person. Much of what is put out as prophecy is banal in content and couched in Elizabethan English! He or she needs to be clear that God has no further revelation to offer outside Jesus Christ, and therefore that if his prophecy is genuine it will not be dissonant from the prophetic Scriptures of the Old and New Testaments with their focus in Christ. He will not be averse from having his prophecy tested and verified. Quite apart from the assessment of those gifted in discernment, the Old Testament criterion of a true prophet is demanding enough in all conscience:

When a prophet speaks in the name of the Lord, if the word does not
come to pass or come true, that is a word which the Lord has not spoken.
(Deut. 18:22)

He will not be bemused by the divine source of his gift into
supposing that he is more spiritual than the lady who provides
the tea after the meeting at which he has spoken!

A famine of the Word

But just as the man with this gift needs to beware of dangers,
so does the local church. Let them beware of supposing that
only the person with the dog-collar can speak from God in
their midst. Let them beware of despising a direct word from
God, or fearing to enter into the depth of fellowship where
such things could take place. There is in many churches still
a terrible famine of hearing the Word of the Lord; and that
does not merely mean that the preaching is of an indifferent
standard, and the Bible largely misunderstood or little used.
The really shocking thing is that congregations are expected
(by themselves as much as by the clergy) to keep quiet and
be passive apart from the singing of the hymns. In the
Church of the New Testament, and in many churches today
where charismatic gifts are made welcome, there is an orderly
but real opportunity for those who have a message from the
Lord to share it simply and directly with the rest of the congregation.

Prophecy in the congregation

It may come through direct speech. It may come through a
'picture' which burns itself into the mind of some member of
the congregation. It need not be predictive: much prophecy in
the New Testament was not. It may simply be a much needed
word of encouragement (1 Cor. 14:3). We found in our church
that it was perfectly simple to give a period of quiet reflection
after a time of worship, or before the end of the service, when

contributions were welcomed from the congregation if they were sure that in so doing they would have something appropriate to add to what had transpired already. Sometimes this would be a verse or more from Scripture; sometimes a picture or a direct word to the congregation. St. Paul bids those who offer this gift to be willing to have their words tested, and in our congregation we generally expected those who were presenting some such ministry to let the leadership see it first. This kept the whole congregation together and provided a check on what was said and when it was said on the one hand, but on the other was a healthy corrective against clericalism. Sometimes one part of the message was seen at once to be appropriate, and the rest not so. I recall one such incident when the Archbishop of Canterbury was present and a prophetic word was brought forward. The two of us who were leading the service went over to the Archbishop, and all three of us were clear that the first half of the message was really a word from God and should be read to the people, while the other part, though worthy enough in itself, was not what was needed at that time and probably proceeded from the speaker and not from God. Discernment is very difficult. But it is easy to recall times when a prophetic word has provoked in the whole congregation a conviction of 'rightness'. And those certain times give encouragement on more marginal occasions. There will be mistakes, but granted humility and love and encouragement all round, those who speak and those who hear will alike be edified if room is found for this most useful and beautiful spiritual gift.

In a word, just as the 'charismatic' Christians need to remain humble and not feel that they are on a higher spiritual level, so the 'non-charismatic' Christians, if I may so miscall them, need to heed Paul's injunction, in a context where he has been talking about the exercise of spiritual gifts, 'Do not quench the Spirit. Do not despise prophesyings. Test all things. Hold fast that which is good' (1 Thess. 5:19ff).

2. WHAT ARE THE STRENGTHS AND WEAKNESSES OF THE CHARISMATIC MOVEMENT?

It is a truism that our weaknesses are very closely allied with our strengths. This is certainly true of the neo-Pentecostal surge in the world Church these days.

In the realm of vitality

Life

It is a movement of life, dynamic spiritual life, in the midst of a Church that has looked very dead in many areas. Vibrant, youthful, unco-ordinated life easily leads to excesses in the spiritual realm just as it does in the physical. Yet where would we be without youth? The church that is determined 'not to have any of this charismatic stuff round these parts' may well be putting up a 'Keep Out' notice to the Spirit of life in Christ Jesus. The church at Corinth could certainly be taken to task for its many failings, but thank God for the life and rich spirituality of such a church that made possible such failings! To how many modern churches would 1 Corinthians need to be written at all?

Faith

It is a movement of faith, deep and real faith in God. Belief that with God all things are possible; belief that the promises of God are meant to be claimed today and not regarded as historical bygones to be dissected by theologians. It is a revolt against the strait-jacket of Protestantism, confining the Spirit to an article in the creed, and of Catholicism, confining the Spirit to predetermined persons and sacraments. It is a revolt against the dead hand of theology which can publish endless dreary (if technically correct) books about the Spirit without ever suggesting that the authors know the power of the Spirit in their lives. What an encouraging sign of life this is. But it lays itself open to various dangers. The danger of spiritual naïveté. The danger of anti-intellectualism. The danger of overvaluing the more showy gifts. And the charismatic movement has fallen into all these dangers; but mercifully its leaders have learnt fast, and the intense vitality of the movement is being channelled into healthy growth in these areas where they have been weak.

Gospel

It is a movement of the gospel, the full-blooded call to repentance, new life, and a new lifestyle through conversion to Jesus and reception of his Spirit. To their credit, charismatics have refused to remain content with the traditional Catholic tendency to equate water baptism, *tout simple*, with Christian initiation; or with the traditional Protestant tendency to identify it with intellectual belief in the preached word; or with the typical Evangelical insistence on personal reception of Christ into the life at conversion. They have made it quite clear that you can have all these things, but still remain a pauper in the palace of the King. Unless the Spirit is welcomed as Lord of the life in all his love and power, it is a very sorry Christian life that you will have. And this is a much needed emphasis. Christianity had become practically binitarian and the Holy Spirit a respected and respectable stranger. But with the proper God-centred emphasis of the charismatic movement went an unbalanced rejection of the earthbound, social gospel which has been characteristic of much Christianity in this century. In consequence its record for social concern and political involvement has often been very poor, as friendly critiques, like d'Epinay's *Haven of the Masses* and Hollenweger's *The Pentecostals*, have pointed out and documented.

In the realm of holiness

It is a holiness movement, and sprang from a tradition of such movements. To my observation, many but by no means all of the people who have claimed a 'charismatic experience' have in fact become more loving, more unselfish, more dedicated, more reliable and more prayerful than they were before. But this very fact can give rise to the very same danger that there was at Corinth; of the recipients of certain spiritual gifts (particularly tongues) regarding other Christians as second-raters, and even maintaining that the gift is the gateway to spiritual power and character. Quite apart from the fact that Paul is careful to distinguish the fruit of the Spirit in terms of character from the *charismata* of the Spirit in terms of gifts, even a superficial glance at the Corinthian correspondence makes it abundantly plain that these highly charismatic folk were notoriously weak in holiness of life: party strife, gross immorality, disbelief in the resurrection, disorder at the eucharist, chaos in church, criticism of leaders on and so forth, were all too evident. The arrogance that one finds sometimes among immature charismatic people today is no less distressing. Claiming to be superior and to have arrived, they are often cruelly condemning in their attitude to others and refuse to take advice from anyone who is not of their own type of spirituality. This often springs not from any particularly vicious spiritual pride, but from false teaching to which they have been introduced on the subject of initiation, seeing it as necessarily a two-stage affair; other Christians may have reached stage one, but they have, through a 'baptism in the Holy Spirit' attained *ipso facto* to stage two – a mountain ridge from which they are unable to descend whatever they do (for they are the Spirit-filled folk; they have arrived), a mountain ridge which relieves them of any further necessity to go on climbing. This two-stage initiation theory has already been examined and found wanting. Here it is enough to point to the tragic irony of one of the most loving and effective Christian ministers I know being written off as unspiritual by his son simply because that unstable youth, as he was then, had received the gift of tongues, and his father had not. So long as this arrogance remains among charismatic people they will get and will deserve opposition from within the Church.

In the realm of fellowship

Body life

The charismatic movement is a corporate movement, designed to let the different limbs in the Body of Christ express their several gifts in harmony. It is the very antithesis of the ministerial exclusivism which afflicts churches of all denominations, where nothing can be done without the minister, and where the conduct of worship is a responsibility shared (or fought over) between him and the organist! It aims to allow room for every member to play his part. The hymns may not be the ones the organist would have chosen; the prayers may come from many lips, not those of the priest; the most powerful word of exhortation may come from a bank clerk, not from the preacher. It is a revolutionary, corporate conception of 'Body-life'. This partly accounts for its appeal. The congregation are no longer an audience, but participants. The priesthood of all believers, so long assented to as a doctrine, has become a reality. And when this happens it can cause tremendous problems. Some ministers try to clamp down on it, because they feel threatened with unemployment, instead of realising that if all the congregation came alive in this way, the pastoral work of the minister would be multiplied ten times over! But there are failures on the side of the charismatics too. They may tend to take little notice of the duly constituted ministry in the local church. They either bow to the dictates of the fashionable charismatic guru of the hour, or to their own ideas; have they not arrived? Does God not speak directly through them in prophecy and heal through them? What need have they for the stuffy old minister? It is back to the Corinthian situation once again. Back to the problems which gave rise to the Epistle of Jude or 2 Peter, where arrogant charismatics, who thought they had arrived spiritually, were taking no notice of God's gift to his people, in the shape of the local ministry. It is interesting that 1 Thessalonians 5 does not only need to say (to the cautious 'non-charismatics'), 'Do not quench the Spirit. Do not despise prophesyings,' but also (to the pushful 'charismatics'), 'Respect those who labour among you and are over you in the Lord and admonish you, and esteem them very highly in love because of their work.' Both injunctions are still needed.

Belonging

Then again, the charismatic movement has made fellowship in the Spirit a reality for many to whom the word 'fellowship' had been almost meaningless. The life-giving Spirit of Christ has brought the love of Christ into personal relations for countless modern Christians. Members really do care for one another and are not ashamed to express their love in embraces, their joy in dancing, their concern in praying openly for one another, their trust in open confession and costly reparation to one another. The depth of the fellowship at local level is one of the most moving characteristics of the whole movement. It results in a high level of sacrificial service, generous hospitality, and that caring love for brothers in Christ that finds nothing too hard to do or bear for them.

Ecumenism

On a wider canvas, at a time when the ecumenical movement after more than ninety years is showing some signs of effeteness, the charismatic movement draws its members from every denomination under the sun, and bids fair to become the new ecumenism, but with this difference. It derives its vitality not from the big bosses at the top, but from the common life in the Spirit experienced at local level among believers, be they Catholics or Lutherans, Pentecostals or Methodists, Baptists, Dutch Reformed, Orthodox or Moravian. It is fellowship at grass roots level and in great depth; therein lies its power.

The Spirit gives unity, and the charismatics show it in a degree of love and commitment to one another which is probably unrivalled in any other strand of contemporary Christianity. But in this unity lurks its own special temptation. Fellowship at depth is sometimes restricted to the like-minded, those Christians who have had a similar experience of the Spirit. In many a local congregation the coming of the charismatic movement has spelt an incalculable deepening of fellowship: but in many others the very reverse has occurred. Instead of enriching the fellowship, it has rent the congregation in two. Similarly, on the ecumenical front, it is true that the charismatic movement binds together men and women from all the different denominations in a way the ecumenical movement never began to approach, but it does so at a price. The price paid can sometimes be the virtual exclusion of Christians who do not share the 'charismatic experience', and a tendency to dub doctrine unimportant because it divides, while emphasis on experience in the Spirit unites. If great care is not taken, therefore, experience becomes the criterion of truth, not truth of experience. And the Church which failed because it was too cerebral will give place to the Church that fails because it is too non-rational.

The minus . . .

There is plenty more that could be said. F. D. Bruner in his *Theology of the Holy Spirit* has pointed out, from models in the Corinthian correspondence, three striking contrasts.

Those charismatics were always out for *more*, and Paul was always insisting that Christ and Christ alone was the blessing for Christians. Any doctrine that adds something to Christ, as some charismatics do in their cry, 'Christ, yes, but beyond Christ you need the Spirit', stands self-condemned.

Those charismatics were always out for *power*, they were elated by spiritual power, and were always seeking short cuts to power. It is the same today. Paul's reply is to boast not of his power but of his weakness, through which alone the power of Christ can shine. Paul knew all about the marks of an apostle, in signs, wonders and mighty deeds (2 Cor. 12:12) but he knew that the power of an apostle, or of any other Christian, came from the patient endurance of suffering, such as he had with his thorn in the flesh, or the patient endurance of reviling and hardship such as he was submitted to in the course of his missionary work (1 Cor. 4). The charismatics had a theology of the resurrection and its power; they needed to learn afresh the secret of the cross and its shame . . . which yet produced the power of God (1 Cor. 1:18).

Those charismatics were always out for *certainty*. That is why tongues and healings and miracles were so highly esteemed among them. But Paul knows that we walk by faith while we are in this life, not by sight. There are many times when God calls on us to trust him in the dark, without any supporting evidences.

. . . and the plus

But it would be churlish to end this brief evaluation of the char- ismatic movement on a negative note. I believe it has done much more good than harm. I believe that it has emphases which the modern churches neglect at their peril. It has taught us to believe in God's reality and his ability to break into the even tenor of our lives with the invading power of his Spirit. It has taken the doctrine of the Spirit off the dusty shelf and put the person of the Spirit right in the heart of the living-room. It has taken the formality, the stuffiness, the professional domination, the dreary predictability out of worship, and made it living, corporate, uplifting and joyful. It has recognised the variety of gifts God has given to his people, discovered some which had been forgotten for a long time, and increasingly insists on a structure of Church life where these gifts can be exercised. It has brought together in intimate fellowship men and women of the most diverse backgrounds. It has driven the silent Christians into bearing joyous and courageous witness to their Lord. It has taken seriously the dark element of Satan and the demonic, and has revived among Christians the sense of spiritual battle. It has opened the flood gates to prayer and praise in many a heart that had run dry. In every generation, God raises up some counterpoise to the current weakness and abuses in his Church. In our own day he has raised up this remarkable movement which we call charismatic. It would be tragic if the Church did not learn from it what God wants us to learn.

This leads directly to our third question.

3. CAN ORDER AND FREEDOM BE RECONCILED IN TODAY'S CHURCH?

The tension between order and freedom . . .

Opening up

The traditional churchman is highly suspicious of any pretensions by members of the congregation to direct leading by the Holy Spirit. Such a claim seems a very horrid thing to him, just as it did to the Bishop of London when Wesley made it in the eighteenth century. Order cannot risk allowing the responsibility of freedom to the Spirit. On the other hand, the man who is drunk with his experience of the liberating Spirit of God is tempted to lose patience with the institutional Church and pull out into 'free' worship among like-minded friends. The charismatic distrusts order, and the traditionalist fears freedom.

It would be a great tragedy if charismatics and non-charismatics could not live together in peace and harmony in the same Church; tragic if we have learnt nothing in the centuries since Paul wrote to the Corinthians. Paul prized order in the Church, for order was a mark of the faithfulness of the

Lord the Spirit. Paul equally loved freedom in the Church, for freedom was what the Spirit came to bring us. He knew that order could degenerate into the peace of the graveyard, and freedom turn into the chaos of the revel. The enthusiasts must remember not to do for the Spirit what he does not do for himself, and that is to seek the limelight. The traditionalists must remember that they do not control the Spirit, but that the Spirit creates, indwells and leads the community of the Church. That is why they need not fear to trust him. For the Spirit, at once free and orderly, will not lead the prophets all to speak at once, or the tongues speakers to hold forth when there is nobody present who will interpret. The charismatics must not make the mistake of always identifying the Spirit's activity with the abnormal; nor of supposing that they have a monopoly of the Spirit, for he is no less present through other gifts and other members of the one Body. The more institutionally minded must for their part be patient if the new wine of the charismatics sometimes breaks the old wineskins of traditional Church deportment; be understanding if some aspects of the Spirit's work are for a while given a false perspective; and be prepared to learn from the charismatics renewed zeal, deeper devotion to our Lord, and a willingness to take risks for God and be fools for Christ's sake, if need be, while committing themselves afresh to the preaching of the gospel and prayer.

Making room

In practice it will mean making room within the worshipping life of the congregation for those who have special gifts to exercise them. It is not good enough to approve of the charismatic movement in a benevolent way without making room for every-member ministry, and the gifts of tongues, prophecy and healing to be used in the mainstream of the Church's life for the benefit of its members. It will not do to restrict these activities to a somewhat secretive mid-week meeting for those who like that kind of thing. If they are gifts at all, they are gifts for the Body of Christ, and should be exercised when the congregation meets. How this will be done needs to be worked out locally. Perhaps the most appropriate occasion would be in the context of the Holy Communion. In churches which have a liturgy, there is already room for freedom and flexibility within that liturgy. Generally speaking, much more participation from a variety of members of the congregation is possible than is in fact practised. Naturally, care must be taken not to make too many innovations too fast. It is impossible to overestimate the conservatism of most congregations. But given patient teaching, love, and a gradual introduction of new features, a congregation can be prepared to welcome hitherto unused and unrecognised gifts; the fellowship can be maintained; and order and freedom can fertilise one another. It really should not be beyond the capabilities of men dependent on the Spirit of God to combine freedom and order, provided that both sides realise that they have complementary and partial insights into the nature and operation of the Spirit, who is so much bigger than our apprehension of him. Alone, both emphases distort the gospel; together, they build up the one Body of Christ infused by the Spirit, the one temple of God in which, for all their different emphases, he is pleased to dwell (Eph. 2:22). It will certainly not be easy: but then, who ever promised Christians an easy life?

The tension between order and renewal arises most acutely in three particular areas, the ministry, the Church and Christian initiation.

. . . in the ministry

Charismatics often distrust the settled institutional ministry. It was so in the first century, as 2 Peter and Jude show us; it was a pressing problem in the second century, as the *Didache* makes plain. It still is. And the problem has two main roots.

Clericalism

In the first place charismatics distrust the institutional ministry for a very proper reason; namely that many priests identify ministry with office, and suppose that no effective ministry can be carried out within the church apart from their own official ministrations. In a word, the official ministry, so far from fulfilling its God-given function of building up the saints for their work of service to the Lord (Eph. 4:12) in fact prevents the Body acting as the Body, with all members taking their proper part. Ministry gets concentrated in the hands of the official; and then not only the official but every part of the Body is harmed, because the various members are not allowed to make their contribution. How often have loyal but heartbroken Christians with a special gift for the local congregation told me that they are not allowed to exercise it 'because the vicar does not like it'. Charismatics are right to bemoan the ordained ministry when it misuses its role in this way.

Distrust

But there is another cause for their unrest, which is not so worthy, though it is readily comprehensible. Charismatics tend to distrust the ordained ministry because often the clergy do not seem to share the intense experience of the Holy Spirit which they themselves enjoy. The ministers concerned feel the hurt of being mistrusted, reckon that the charismatics are immature, and perhaps resent the influence they may have in the church. This again is the tragedy of the half truth. The Spirit does not restrict himself to the charismatic, nor to the official. Office is not the enemy of *charisma*. Paul can speak of ordination as a *charisma* of the Holy Spirit imparted to Timothy by the laying on of his hands and those of his fellow presbyters (1 Tim. 4:14, 2 Tim. 1:8). The Holy Spirit can be as really present at (or absent from) a Catholic ordination as a Pentecostal praise meeting. There need be no antipathy between charismatic gift

and catholic order so long as the charismatic does not repudi-
ate the function of oversight to which the ordained minister is
called by the Lord, and the latter does not presume to think that
he and he alone is the 'spiritual' man in the congregation, and
that none of them can possibly have, or be allowed to exercise,
a spiritual gift which he lacks. The way of Jesus, the way of love,
the way of building up the Body, will refuse to allow a wedge to
be driven between order and *charisma*.

. . . in the Church

The second area where this tension between freedom and order
is becoming very pressing is the matter of schism. Since the
church down the road is so manifestly unspiritual, we 'spiritual
people' had better get out, and found one of our own. Alas for
the presumption in claiming to obey the Spirit's leading when
specifically disobeying the Spirit's commands in Scripture to
maintain unity. Alas for the arrogance of supposing that the
ensuing church will be any more spiritual than the one from
which we have seceded. Charles Spurgeon is reputed once to
have answered one such 'spiritual' woman who was in search of
the perfect church, 'You will not find it, madam, this side of
heaven; and if you do find it, don't go near it: you will only spoil
it.'

Secession or renewal?

Secession does not seem to be God's way: throughout the long
history of the Bible, God shows himself as the one who revives,
reforms, and remakes vessels which have disappointed. He is
the one whose Spirit does not scrap the valley of dry bones, but
breathes new life into them. Not even in the Letters to the Seven
Churches in Revelation is there any suggestion that one should
secede from a 'dead' church. It would be ludicrous, were it not
so pathetic and damaging, to imagine that any company of
sinful human beings could exorcise unspirituality from their

midst by the simple expedient of seceding from those they could not easily get on with. What, then, would become of the new humanity, embracing Jew and Gentile, male and female, barbarian and educated, slave and free man – that fellowship of love and unity which was, as we have seen, the Spirit's home in New Testament days? It is through renewal, not secession, that God has purified his people from Abraham's day to our own. When individuals or groups separate, they show that they are not the men and women of the Spirit which they take themselves to be (1 Cor. 3:3).

Life and order

It is generally wrong, therefore, for charismatics to secede from a church because of its lack of spirituality. It is right for the leadership in the church to exercise control over individual charismatics. But this does not mean that in a properly ordered church they will cease to exercise their gifts. Far from it. The Lord who gave a settled ministry to his Church stemming from the Twelve, also gave prophets to his Church who owned no succession. It was the function of the prophets to prevent the Church from identifying her tradition with the will of God without further question. They were, and still can be, God's gadfly, his stinging pointers to the truth, when his Church is in danger of sleeping and growing complacent. They must not be silenced.

Of course, just as the official ministry is in danger of identifying the Spirit with traditional ways of doing things, or with traditionally sacred symbols; so the prophet can fall into the trap of identifying the Spirit with his own interpretation of events and even with his own prejudices. Paul was well aware of that, and he appealed not to any legalistic sanctions but rather to the prophet's own sense of discrimination, and that of his fellows, to curb arrogance and wordiness (1 Cor. 14:29–32). The prophet is no more immune from the temptations of the world, the flesh and the devil than is presbyter or bishop. Sometimes

the word of God will come through the prophetic man; sometimes through the bishop. As Haddon Willmer put it in a most
penetrating article on *The Holy Spirit in the Church*, 'The
bishop may himself be the prophet, and in him the institution
itself may become prophetic – or it may not. It follows that no
lines can be drawn in advance beyond which the prophet may
not go for fear of disturbing the unity of the church.' Often,
indeed, the tension in church circles will be great. I imagine that
there was tension enough at the Council of Jerusalem in the
days of the Acts. The mark of the Spirit's presence, Willmer
continues, is 'not the absence of argument, but its quality. Love
that is patient, enduring all things, hoping all things, keeps in
check that frustration and despairing touchiness which drives
the controversialist to the bitter, boastful and rude extrava-
gances which deprive divisions of the hopefulness characteristic of the Spirit. Love keeps the prophetic spirit from gloating
over other men's sins and leads them to delight in the truth, by
which alone controversy can be made fruitful' (*Church
Quarterly*, April 1971, p. 292f).

. . . in Christian initiation

The third area of tension between *charisma* and order in the
Church concerns the whole subject of what makes a man a
Christian. There has long been tension, even within the same
church, between those who have placed the main emphasis in
Christian initiation on the sacraments and those who have
placed the main stress on belief in Jesus and conversion. Into
this tension has come a further complication. The charismatic
movement has made a habit of speaking of the overwhelming
experience of God which characterises it as 'baptism in the
Holy Spirit'. This has been both perplexing and distressing to
sincere Catholics and Protestants alike, but it should prove to
be a most healthy disturbance. For it reminds us that there are
three ways, not two, of defining the nature of the Church.

Those who have been baptised?

One may think of the Church as an extension of the Old Testament people of God. The Catholic church at large has tended to do this. And there is excellent biblical evidence to support such a view. In the Acts of the Apostles Jerusalem is the centre of the visible Church throughout the world; the Jerusalem church embodies and continues the history of salvation from the days of Abraham onwards. That note is struck on the day of Pentecost when Peter appeals to his hearers to repent and save themselves from 'the crooked generation'. This is an allusion to Deuteronomy 32:5 where the true members of Israel are called upon to show themselves distinct from the crooked generation of apostate Israelites around them. The inference is plain. The Church is the true Israel; unbelieving Israel is the crooked generation; to be baptised and join the Church is to show oneself within the true historic Israel of God. The same point is made in Acts 3:25,26. Believers in Jesus must show themselves to be the true Israel, in genuine succession to Abraham, by joining this community, entered no longer by circumcision but by baptism. It is instructive to see how the Old Testament name for the people of God, *hoi hagioi*, 'the saints', is ransacked by the New Testament writers and applied to the Church (Acts 9:13,32,41 etc.). The Church is the true Israel, and it is entered by baptism. That is the Catholic case in a nutshell. And it is part of the truth.

Those who believe?

Another way of defining the Church is to see it as the fellowship of believers. Protestants at large have tended to do this. Once again, there is excellent biblical evidence that can be adduced in support, and from the very same quarry, the Book of Acts. One might turn to the description of Christians as 'the believers' which comes so frequently throughout the book (2:44, 4:32, 5:14 etc.). This company was entered by repentance and faith (2:38,

16:31). Baptism is the mark and the badge of the believer, for only believers have the right to claim personally what Christ achieved for everyone. That is the prevailing Protestant understanding of the Church. And it is part of the truth.

Those who have received the Spirit?

But a third way of looking at the Church has been staring us in the face all down the centuries, and we have been blind to it. The great characteristic of the New Testament Church is that it consisted of men and women who had received a living experience of the Spirit in their own lives. That is what turned the first disciples from a company of disappointed folk whose leader had died, risen and left them, into a Church – reception of the Spirit. That is what marked out those Christians at Samaria once their initiation was complete – a manifest reception of the Holy Spirit. That is how Peter saw that he must swallow his principles and baptise Cornelius – the man had clearly become a Christian, because anyone could see as clear as a pikestaff that his life was radiant with the Spirit. It is one of the merits of J. D. G. Dunn's *Baptism in the Holy Spirit* that he recognises the centrality of receiving the Spirit in the New Testament definition of the Church. 'What is the distinguishing hallmark of the Christian?' he asks at the conclusion of his book, and continues, 'Our study has given us the N.T. answer to this question with some precision; with remarkable consistency the answer came: That man is a Christian who has received the gift of the Holy Spirit by committing himself to the risen Jesus as Lord, and who lives accordingly.' It is the Pentecostal movement we have to thank for drawing attention to this crucial New Testament definition. It is perfectly possible to be baptised and to believe the articles of the Christian faith, and yet not to have the Spirit in your life.

Not three ways – but one

It is easy to see the abuses in any one of the three ways of defining the Church that we have just considered, when taken in isolation. The important thing is to see that they all belong together in the purposes of God for his people. It was possible for the author of Acts to embody in his account these three quite different ways of looking at the Church, and yet he would have been amazed had he been told that in later centuries these three would have been set in competition against each other. In a truly biblical theology Christian initiation consists quite simply of three actions which belong together, though they may be widely separated in time and may be received in any order. They are repentance and faith by the individual, water baptism by the Church, and the giving of the Holy Spirit by God. There is no room in a biblical theology for any further initiation into the Christian community, whether it be through confirmation by the bishop (as some 'two-stage Catholics' might argue), or by a 'baptism in the Holy Spirit' (as some 'two-stage Pentecostals' might maintain). By the same token it will not do for a man simply to say, 'I am baptised: therefore I am a Christian,' or 'I have believed in Christ; therefore I am a Christian.' The charismatic would very properly point such people to the New Testament where there are clear signs of being a Christian, signs brought about in the life of the individual by the Spirit once he has been welcomed in. There may (or may not) be notable gifts such as prophecy and tongues, but the fruit of the Spirit may be expected in every Christian life. If there is no love, no joy, no peace, no gentleness and goodness, no faith, no self-control then there is no evidence that the Spirit is planted in such a life, no evidence that the man is initiated into Christ, however valid his baptism and however loud his protestations of faith. If there is no sense of wonder and joy at being sons and daughters of God, if there is no compassion and concern for other brothers and sisters in the same family, if there is no prayer, no praise, no love of the Scriptures, no desire to reach others with the good news, then – let us face it – it is not New Testament Christianity that we are talking about any more.

And the charismatic movement has drawn attention to this fact in no uncertain way.

Marks of the Spirit

To return, then, to our quest for order and freedom within the Church, what marks of the Spirit's work shall we expect to see? We should ask ourselves where reconciliation is being effected; where unity is being guarded without crushing spontaneity; where fellowship is deep and honest; where worship is live and real, shared in by the whole Body. We shall look to the place where evangelism has a high place among the priorities of the individual and the congregation alike – for the Lord the Spirit is no less present in the conversion of the penitent than in the tongues of the charismatic. We shall expect to see the work of the Spirit in the interdependence of the Church membership, where love controls attitudes, and where gifts are used for the good of the community, not for the gratification of the individual. Such a Church will be very much concerned with building up its members in obedience to the Lordship of Jesus; for to live under that Lordship is both the Christian's baptismal confession and his undying obligation. In the Church where the Spirit is given freedom, the charismatics will not obtrude their gifts, and the settled ministry will not fear them. Both strands need each other in the corporateness of the Body of Christ; and both will, in the Church where the Spirit is obeyed, resist the temptation of seceding from their sometimes awkward bedfellows. They will guard the unity which the Spirit gives, in the peace, joy and mutual service which are engendered by the same Spirit. Even when they stand together they are not complete. For the Church on earth can never be that. It was a gnostic failing to imagine that the truly inspired man had the fulness of the divine Spirit in him *now*. Paul taught the Corinthians a better perspective. We never have the fulness of the Spirit *in ourselves alone*, but only as we are incorporate in that Body, that temple in which the Spirit demonstrates the varied beauty of his harmony. And we never have the fulness of the Spirit *in this life alone*. For the Spirit does not give us his fulness in the world of time and sense. He is the first instalment of God's future. He is the guarantee of heaven. And life in the Church here and now is at best only a foreshadowing of the unity and service, the harmony and love, the final and complete reconciliation, the unending praise and worship, of heaven itself. This is no 'pie in the sky when we die'. It is the final climax of a reality we already enjoy if we are able to say from personal experience and commitment, 'I believe in the Holy Spirit.'

12

The Holy Spirit and the Future of the Church

1. IN STEP WITH THE SPIRIT

It is just over thirty years since I first wrote this book, and I am grateful for the fact that it has for the most part remained in print and that it has been used all over the world. Many people have told me it has had a real impact on their lives. I have already revised it twice, and now I do so again, conscious of the need to keep in step with the Spirit. For he is mightily at work in our world.

New life in the churches

Movements of the Holy Spirit in Chile, for example, have led the Pentecostals and Evangelicals whose numbers were negligible seventy years ago to become a major factor in society, with small, informal churches everywhere. The explosive growth of vibrant Christianity throughout most of sub-Saharan Africa has been well documented. Everyone is aware of the Christian renewal which is sweeping through the countries once dominated by the U.S.S.R. In China there were less than a million Christians when the Western missionaries were evicted in 1950; now on the records of the Communist government themselves the numbers approach 75 million, and are apparently growing at a rate of some 20,000 a day. I am personally familiar with several parts of South-East Asia where there has been a massive growth of vigorous

Christianity in recent years. It is indeed a fascinating time to be alive.

In revising this book the first time, I found I did not need to make many changes to what I had written about the biblical material. I made no substantial change in the general stance of the original book, which was to build bridges between those who call themselves charismatic and those who do not. I am still totally committed to that bridge-building operation. Christianity is not a two-party state.

But I found that what I had written about the gifts of the Holy Spirit had a curiously dated ring. Substantial rewriting was needed. That was not merely because I had gained and learnt a lot more in the intervening decade. It was because the whole climate of Christianity in the West had improved, and there was a new expectancy, a new freedom, a new vision for outreach, and a new trans-denominational co-operation among the churches. Of course this new vitality was not uniform throughout the country, nor is it now. But the change was real, and it has proved lasting.

I need now to make substantial additions to what I wrote some years ago, and particularly to take a careful look at the so-called Toronto Blessing. But the signs of new life continue to abound and multiply, albeit in the midst of much formal religion that can only be headed for death. You will find celebrations of the Christian faith being held in cathedrals, accompanied by joyous praise, dance and extempore prayer. You will find 'Life in the Spirit' seminars held all over the world, pioneered by the Roman Catholics, to help people into a personal experience of the Spirit in their lives and churches. You will find groups in homes all over the country meeting together for fellowship and praise, for outreach and nurture, and their membership has no relationship whatsoever to denominations, but is determined by life in the Spirit – and life needs life to interact with. You will find churches cancelling their evening services to allow members the chance to meet in homes and discover there the intimacy and the opportunity for mutual ministry which is to be found in the Christian cell. You will find books like David Watson's *I Believe in the Church* or Richard Foster's *Celebration of Discipline* being read and valued all over the Church; and, of course, both of them draw deeply from the springs of charismatic renewal. Indeed the very word 'renewal' has become almost a watchword in the churches. Everybody seems to be for it, whether or not they know what it means! There is nowadays a widespread hunger for the freshness and spiritual power of Celtic Christianity before Roman organisation choked some of the vitality out of the churches of Britain. In just a few years New Wine, a transdenominational movement strongly committed to the renewal, has spread from being a small gathering based in a single church in Chorleywood to a massive organisation, with a network of clergy and ordinands, conferences and the annual fortnight at Shepton Mallet when some 14,000 gather annually in their tents and caravans while thousands are turned away. Soul Survivor, the counterpart for teenagers, draws well over 10,000. I notice that this quest has spread to other countries such as America. It accords very naturally with a postmodern society and its impatience with formalism and hierarchies.

I find that many ordinands in this country and overseas owe their presence in a theological seminary to the influence on their lives of the charismatic movement. Colleges of this stripe are not short of candidates. This is hardly surprising when almost a third of all Christians in the world would call themselves charismatic, and when the vast majority of youth groups, and the increasing number of youth churches have a strong charismatic emphasis. This is worlds away from the situation forty years ago. Whether it has led to more in the way of mindless repetition of songs with shallow words, and an over-personalised faith impatient of structures and history is a moot point. It may well be so. It is also probably true that the majority of enthusiastic young Christians are much weaker in Bible knowledge and have less deep foundations than their counter-parts a generation ago. There is real cause for concern at this point, and yet one cannot but rejoice at the prevalence of so many dynamic groups of young people worshipping God with profound abandon. Without them the theological colleges, and therefore the future ranks of the clergy, would look decidedly thin. My experience is that if someone has zeal, you can impart knowledge to them. If not, they are unlikely to want to go further spiritually, or if they do it may prove to be in search of mere academic achievement and head knowledge. A warm heart and a cool head make the ideal combination, with balanced emphasis on the three great means of growth, the Scripture, the sacrament and the Spirit.

Speaking in tongues is no longer a forbidden subject in the churches. Indeed it has become a fit subject for the study of sociologists. A generation ago 'inner healing' and 'spiritual warfare' were terms hardly known in mainline churches. Nowadays they are commonplace. The songs of the renewal are sung everywhere and in every denomination. In many parts of the world the decline of the ecumenical movement has been replaced by a new sort of ecumenism, the sharing of those who have discovered fresh life in the Holy Spirit – a sharing which goes right across denominational and cultural norms, and touches the place where dogma cannot reach. It is indeed a different world from when I wrote the first edition of this book. Now nearly every Anglican diocese has not only a diocesan exorcist, but a panel of clergy who have gained experience in the ministry of deliverance. Centres for healing have sprung up in various parts of the country, and Christians are no longer surprised when they or their friends get healed in response to prayer and the laying on of hands. You will find abbots and nuns who engage in glossolalia, and some bishops lead their dioceses in healing, celebration of the Holy Spirit, and charismatic prayer. All the major denominations have been forced to evaluate this movement, and to publish their appraisal of it.

Pope John XXIII prayed, 'Renew thy wonders in our day, as by a new Pentecost.' Pope Paul VI affirmed, 'The Church needs an eternal Pentecost,' and it is significant that it is in the Roman Catholic Church, in some ways the most structured and traditional of all churches, that this renewal movement has broken out most strongly and been most influential. Protestants who had treated Catholics with great circumspection all their lives suddenly found themselves praying and praising God together with them in the release of the Holy Spirit. And Catholics who had been accustomed to see the Church as coterminous with Roman Catholicism began to rejoice that the Lord had given his Holy Spirit to Protestant brethren also. This is taking place on an enormous scale in Latin America, where in many countries Pentecostals, together with renewed Catholics, are the fastest growing spiritual forces in a subcontinent that was veering towards Marxism forty years ago. Despite some continuing mutual suspicion these two very different expressions of Christianity are increasingly knit together in a strong fellowship forged by the Holy Spirit.

New style in the worship

Actually, this holds good worldwide. Not only in Latin America, but in most of Africa south of the Sahara, in much of Indonesia, in Singapore and Korea, in China and Russia, there is an amazing flowering of spiritual gifts. Even in our own jaded post-Christian culture of Western Europe it is those churches which are open to the renewing breeze of the Spirit which are growing apace. I think back to the changes which took place in the church where I served in Oxford during the seventies and eighties, and I cannot help being struck by the transformation that decade brought, as we sought to follow the Spirit. From a building that was typically Anglican our church was rearranged so as to facilitate Body life. From a service which was entirely predictable and read from the book, it was freed up and became subject to considerable change: sometimes punctuated by the prayerful commissioning of a missionary or a team going out on ministry for the weekend, or by extempore singing (sometimes in tongues), or by a prophetic utterance.

In the old days the service was led by one person: that gave way to a ministry team leading the worship. A robed choir singing compositions from the past gladly made room for a singing group which led contemporary worship and often created their own songs which they taught to the congregation. The music and the words may have lacked the quality of earlier times: but they were a contemporary expression of God's joyous and empowering presence in our midst, and that had an authenticity all of its own. Before the change, the use of drama and dance in the church would have been exceptional if it happened at all. But as the Spirit's creativity was welcomed by the congregation it became commonplace, and highly valued. A new factor was the eagerness of the church as a whole to pray for healing with the expectation that God would answer. Some remarkable healings took place, although often there was disappointment – we cannot manipulate God. In earlier days the church was very much led by the rector. But as the warmth of renewal spread, it became comparatively unimportant whether he was there or not: indeed it was good for him to be away at times, for then the gifts God had entrusted to other members of the congregation could have freer use. When I came to the church there was only one home group. But as the new life spread there emerged more than thirty, and they proved to be the main pastoral agency in the church, as members got into a depth of relationship with one another, bore one another's burdens and shared one another's joys and sorrows. It was in these groups that spiritual gifts began to manifest themselves and were given the opportunity to develop. All this does not mean that ours was a specifically 'charismatic' church, or that new ways were better than the old. But it is the case that all these changes were brought about by the renewal movement.

There is no doubt that the last thirty years or so have seen an enormous change in the whole climate of church life within the mainline churches.

New forms of the church

The House Churches

Quite apart from its impact on traditional churches, the renewal movement at large is throwing up new ways of being church. Robert Warren has taken a leading part in making churches think in terms of becoming 'missionary congregations', organised and motivated towards reaching society at large and individuals in particular who have little or no contact with Christianity. His books *Building Missionary Congregations* and *Being Human, Being Church* were ground-breaking investigations into how this can be attempted, even in the mainline churches. However, many had grown impatient of waiting for the mainline churches to change, and had broken away to form house churches, which began to grow in numbers and vision during the seventies and eighties. They started in homes (hence the name) but soon outgrew the house and instead hired school halls, cinemas and other natural and non-churchy places in which to worship. The leadership was originally made up of gifted men and women who were not ordained in the mainline churches and had not been given the opportunity to exercise leadership and deploy their gifts. The emphasis on Body life and every-member ministry which came with the charismatic movement led them to leave their churches and start again, free from the traditions that had encumbered the mainline denominations, and free to use their developing leadership skills without having to go through a long training in theological colleges.

Many in this movement would see it as a restoration of New Testament church purity and unity. They believe that God is restoring the spiritual gifts of those early days to his people.

Accordingly it is incumbent on true believers to come out from the denominations and join the one, undifferentiated people of God, arranged in house churches throughout the land. The call to come out originated, I think, with Martin Lloyd-Jones (who was graciously rebuked for it by John Stott in public debate!), but it was taken up stridently by Arthur Wallis. His influential little book, *The Radical Christian*, contains a trenchant critique of mainline churches, however renewed, and issues a stirring call to get rebaptised and come out. Terry Virgo, Bryn Jones, Gerald Coates and John Noble have been among the most influential leaders of this New Church movement. They are impressive in terms of commitment, self-sacrifice and generosity. Their worship is dynamic if somewhat monochrome, and their outreach is exemplary. They tend to appeal to the normal Briton far more than the mainline churches, with their lively worship, humour, risk-taking and unstuffiness. They have a strong social concern, train their own leaders (often very young men and women) and make exuberant celebration an important part of their worship. They take far more risks than the traditional churches, and make free use of the gifts of the Spirit. At first, they were strong in repudiating the traditional denominations. They hankered for the one pure, restored church. But time has shown that this was not a realistic goal. Several divisions have occurred within the house church movement, and they now generally exhibit a much more tolerant and indeed cooperative attitude towards the mainline churches, or at least those within them who share a biblical Christianity!

Spring Harvest

The influence of these New Churches, as they rightly prefer to be called, is far greater than their numbers. They have had considerable exposure in the media. Their leaders (and members) have played a major part in the development of Spring Harvest, a movement which brings together some 80,000 Christians at Eastertime each year. They come in their thousands to one of several Butlin's Holiday Camp sites for a week of teaching, worship, celebration and exposure to a vast variety of seminars. Children and teenagers are catered for separately, and simply love it. The food is good, the accommodation poor and the joy great. It is like a giant family. Large numbers of Anglicans, Baptists and others mingle easily with members of the New Churches, and a remarkable unity is experienced in the dynamic worship, clear teaching, personal ministry and sheer enjoyment. The influence of Spring Harvest on Christian life in Britain during the past two decades or so is incalculable. Whole parishes, whatever their churchmanship, get renewed by taking their members there. You will find Catholics and Protestants, New Churches and traditional churchmen, Anglicans and Baptists joining together in a new ecumenism. It is not much appreciated by the older ecumenists of the W.C.C., because it does not take ecclesial relationships into consideration. But it does bind together an astonishing cross section of Christians in the fellowship and life of the Spirit.

Widespread celebrations

Nor is Spring Harvest alone. Other massive celebrations, usually lasting for a week, have sprung up in different parts of the country. In addition to Soul Survivor and New Wine there is Easter People, which is the Methodist version of Spring Harvest. It was originally discounted by the leadership of Conference, but now gladly acknowledged: it is growing apace. While writing this page I have just had an invitation to speak at another of these celebrations, which draws together 3000 people in a very improbable part of the country! Gatherings like these proliferate, and they do a great deal to foster renewal and encouragement across the board. They are particularly valuable for scattered Christians struggling with unpromising situations. This is an important factor to bear in mind when statistics show a decline in attendance at regular church services. There is new grass growing under the wilting trees. The renewal movement has certainly not run out of steam. It is alive and well, growing steadily, and is influencing the mainline churches more than some would care to admit: many a cathedral now revels in Graham Kendrick's superb modern hymns, for instance. As a result of all this new life and enthusiasm there has been a spectacular growth in events like March for Jesus, a trans-denominational extravaganza organised each year on a worldwide basis. Here again it is the churches in renewal which provide the initiative. March for Jesus is basically a great march through a city by thousands of people praising God and demonstrating joyful and unembarrassed Christian commitment. It is bathed in prayer and often leads to explicit evangelism. I remember speaking at one such march in London, a few years ago. About 90,000 people took part, and the march ended up with hours of exuberant worship in Hyde Park. A policeman on duty was in tears because of the good behaviour of the vast crowd and the impact of the worship and addresses over the p.a. system. Some ten million Christians march for Jesus worldwide on the same day each year, including those in Muslim and communist countries.

Another such public event was a massive Christian concert where some 50,000 people poured into Wembley Stadium for a day-long celebration of exuberant praise. This is all the fruit of the renewal movement, and would be unthinkable without it.

The youth churches

Another form of church which may foreshadow the future is the youth church. A number of these are now operating in Britain, mostly among independent churches, but increasingly among the more imaginative of the mainline churches.

These are churches run by young people for young people. Adult advisers are to hand. They help to finance it, guide the policy and counsel members as required, but the whole leadership and organisation of the church is in the hands of people in their late teens and early twenties. They give the talks, form a band, lead the worship, plan the programme and reach out with enormous enthusiasm to fellow teenagers in a medium that is immediately attractive to them.

I was in one such youth congregation, three hundred strong, recently. The worship had young people lost in wonder, love and praise. Some were in tears, some were bowed to the floor. Several were drawn to Jesus that night and began the Christian life. Outside, sitting smoking on the wall, was a further group of youngsters who had not dared to venture in this time, but were fascinated by it all. Among them moved some of the Christian youngsters who had sacrificed their time of worship in order to be of help to their not-yet-Christian colleagues.

Another youth church runs two big celebrations a month, one for outreach and the other for nurture. They have a number of cell groups, run by the young people for young people: it is here that most of the discipleship training is done. They get into all the schools in the town, take assemblies for grateful school staff, allow themselves to be 'grilled' for their Christianity in R.E. lessons, run an outreach cafe and small groups for those just starting to investigate Christianity. Their relations with the parent church are significantly good. The rapport with the vicar is superb. The support of the P.C.C. for what they are doing is unanimous. The congregation is prepared to take risks in supporting a youth church like this. They are allowed to make mistakes (something not always tolerated in more traditional congregations). Finance is partly shared by the parent church, which has a church planting mentality. It has already planted another congregation on a nearby estate. And it is more than happy to see the youth church as just another plant, and not agitate for the young people to come into the parent church, whose culture would be so different from their own. We shall see many more such churches emerge in future. The mainline influence on the youth of the country, already less than 5%, may well disappear completely. It is youth churches like these that will catch the imagination and meet the needs of the young people of the land.

Student communities

It is more than fifty years since the International Fellowship of Evangelical Students was born. During those years it has shown itself to be one of the most effective of all agencies for furthering the gospel. Its members do not constitute churches as such, but their primary form of fellowship and witness is the student group which is interdenominational and student led – very much the same principle as the youth church. The size of this work worldwide is breathtaking. In Nigeria, for example, more than 35,000 students meet weekly in Bible study groups, and in 1998 they had a Missions Conference drawing 20,000, many of whom are committing themselves to go all over Africa in the cause of the gospel. In Ethiopia, 25% of all students are members of the IFES and meet in Bible study and prayer groups on a weekly basis.

Think of Nepal. Before 1956 there was no church there. Now, despite considerable persecution, there are 300,000 Nepali Christians, and much of that advance has been due to the student work. In Cairo, 1200 students meet every Friday night to worship Christ. They are not allowed to do so on university premises so they need to use their ingenuity. One bright idea was to rent a ship holding 350 and invite their friends for a 4-hour trip down the Nile – during which they presented the gospel in imaginative ways to their captive audience! In India, 60% of all cross-cultural missionaries are the product of the student work. And so one could go on. I have been thrilled to meet courageous Christian students from Russia, Albania, Croatia, Pakistan, Peru, Jordan, the Sudan and many other countries who have been converted and built up by the student witness in their universities. In all but twenty-seven countries of the world this movement has taken root and is growing at a phenomenal rate. It is not a church, since it has no clergy and no sacraments, but it has all the other marks of a church, notable cohesion, and is a community of Christ where his Spirit is wonderfully at work.

Sports ministries

Another initiative of the Holy Spirit in the past thirty years or so is the development of what are virtually churches among the sports community worldwide. A number of prominent international golfers, footballers, rugby players, basketball players and cricketers have been instrumental in setting up fellowships for sporting people in many parts of the world. This is vital because the intensity of training and the team cohesion among top sports people is such that it is almost impossible for them to become part of any normal church, and it is very difficult for non-sportsmen to reach them with the gospel. They have to form their own fellowship.

I think of international surfers I got to know in Hawaii who started a Bible study on the beach and it developed into a lively church of some 300 people which met on a golf course, in the shed where the golf carts were kept! I used to belong to that church. I think of what are in effect Christian cells in the international golf circuit, the cricket world, and widely among the football players of Brazil and elsewhere. This is now a massive international movement, working not only among top professionals but among club players and youngsters. Sports camps, training for deprived children in the inner city, and big outreaches at world sporting events make this a very significant sphere of advance in the Christian cause. It was a major feature in the 1996 Olympics, where I had the privilege of working with its leadership and could assess something of its impact.

When the 1998 World Cup took place, a magnificently illustrated booklet *To Be the Best* was produced and a million copies sold to football fans crowding into France, the host nation, for the competition. It was translated into many languages, and explained the gospel very clearly. Partner churches were set up between Britain and France, and reports indicated a remarkable interest and response to the gospel. In addition many Christian football teams went out to France to play against French teams and to witness to Christ. Best of all, this included Catholics and Protestants working together, all part of the new thing that the Holy Spirit is doing in our day.

Church planting

But by far the most significant mark of the dynamic work of the Holy Spirit is the proliferation of church planting all over the world. New congregations are being planted all over the place, without waiting for finance or buildings, or the say-so from denominational authorities. I have been in a refugee camp in Guatemala where colporteurs had formed more than twenty churches. I came across a church in that country which had planted more than five hundred congregations. I have been in the jungles of Sabah in the island of Borneo and worked with the leaders of church after church that had been planted within the past few years in villages hitherto utterly heathen. It was wonderful to see the zeal of their village headmen, now fully committed to Christ, and to marvel at their unpaid evangelists who went still further into the jungle with the good news of Christ to win fresh villages to his allegiance. The whole conference of leaders from these new church plants was vibrant with the Holy Spirit. It was an enormous privilege to give teaching at it and to learn from their passionate commitment and directness.

Some time ago I came across a superb example of pioneering church planting under the leading of the Holy Spirit. In 1992 the Archbishop of Lagos consecrated Bishop Emmanuel Nglass to a see with no churches, no clergy and no resources. 'I was told to go across the river and to make disciples for Christ,' he said. Six years later the Diocese of Uyo had twenty congregations, twenty-nine clergy and several thousand communicants. It all began, as in the early days of the church, with

Bishop Emmanuel preaching to the people in the town square. They came out of curiosity, and stayed to hear and share the good news.

Nor is this confined to the South. It is happening in the West as well. The AD 2000 movement aimed to plant a church for every 1500 of the population, and came near to achieving that target. One church in London planned to plant 1000 churches in the years leading up to 2000, and only fell short by two or three hundred. These new churches start with a core group, including a leader, an evangelist, and a worship leader. They meet in a home, in a simple shelter, in a hired school room, or even (as with one such church I came across in Chile) under a tree in a residential square! The vibrant worship and fearless witness draws others, and soon there is a congregation.

Of course many of these church plants fail for one reason or another. But far more succeed. I have met leaders of such churches in China. Many of them have had no theological training and are only in their twenties, but such is the growth of Christianity in that land that they are pastoring churches of several hundred. In Chile, I was fascinated to see the approach of the Pentecostals. They start moving down all the streets in Santiago on a Sunday morning singing to the guitar, and end up at the central shrine, having gathered several hundred people on the way, who had no idea what it was all about but wanted to be part of the action! Powerful preaching, passionate worship and personal testimony lead to the conversion of many of them. They are immediately cared for in homes, start witnessing on the streets, and before long have shared in the foundation of another church of *los evangelicos*.

Church planting is proving to be, worldwide, the fastest method of spreading the gospel, and it is easy to do. You only need to build a shelter in a Third World country, or hire a hall in the West, to have an adequate place to meet. Many Anglican parishes are now planting new congregations in halls on estates in a hitherto unreached part of their parish, or in the local pub. But none of the commitment for this sort of thing will be present unless the Holy Spirit has been welcomed, with his love, his gifts, his empowering and his outward thrust. The churches of the future are likely to begin like this. There is more than one way of being church!

Alpha

One of the most remarkable forms in which the Church at large is being revitalised at present is the Alpha Course. It is essentially a twelve-week course based on a dinner each night, relaxed fellowship and laughter, good teaching, the opportunity for any question whatever to be raised in the small groups which make up the main meeting, and, very importantly, a day or sometimes a weekend on the Holy Spirit – who he is, what he does, and how to be filled with him. At the end of the course there is a big welcome dinner to which the members of the group invite their friends. They, in turn, tend to join the next Alpha. And so it goes on and spreads. There are courses in well over 100 countries and they are constantly being expanded. The course is designed to cover basic Christian teaching in the most attractive and accessible form, and is non-churchy, relaxed and open textured. This accords very well with today's postmodern age when nobody is prepared to take anything on authority: they need to work it out for themselves. That is what Alpha enables them to do. They set out on an exploration into God, and vast numbers of them find him. The sheer professionalism of Alpha, with its videos, its leaders' guides and its members' handbooks, is impressive in an age which will not tolerate slipshod communication, dull talks and incompetent clergy. The talks are of the highest standard and technical quality, and the beauty of it all is that you do not need some high-profile speaker to run the course. You just use the video, and then the leader of the group handles the question period which follows. Gradually the fellowship develops, and one by one the members come to put their trust in Christ in their own time, with nobody pressurising them.

The influence of Alpha on the Church worldwide is becoming enormous. It is taken up by the Roman Catholic Church and the Orthodox, as well as all the main Protestant denominations. It is proving both a tool for the follow-up of new Christians and a way of drawing utterly unchurched people into a living faith. Nominal churchmen discover Christ, unbelievers are won over, regular church members are instructed properly, and sleepy Christians are awakened. Many get the passion for helping others to faith. The rumour gets around that Christian life is attractive and that it is cool to go to something like Alpha. That represents a massive change in attitudes. Something like a quarter of a million people are currently going through the course in Britain, and there are nationwide initiatives to reach the whole country – significantly, with considerable media support, which is rare for a Christian enterprise. Overseas the impact is incalculable. New nations are taking it on daily.

Alpha is not a church, but it enables people bored with church or unfamiliar with church to discover Christ and in him to find a warm fellowship within the small group. Indeed, many who have been through the course are loath to leave it at the end, and want to continue this cell-like form of gathering to worship, to share joys and sorrows and to develop Christian lifestyles and gifts. It will be interesting to see where all this leads.

Cell churches

This leads to at least a mention of the cell church, about which Ralph Neighbour and Bill Beckham have written so powerfully. This is another development in church life which is growing rapidly in some parts of the world, especially in countries where the profession of Christianity is dangerous such as China, Cuba and some parts of the Middle East. But it is also making headway in Singapore and Sabah as well as the U.S. and Britain. The basic principle is that every church member is also a member of a cell, in which the majority (or all) of his Christian fellowship and service takes place. The members may come together occasionally in some large celebration, but essentially they belong to the cell. The leaders are properly trained and there is a system of careful oversight. But small is beautiful – and flexible. As a result these churches, untrammelled by buildings or tradition, tend to grow and multiply very fast and the minister's main problem is how he can train enough leaders fast enough for the expanding work. I was recently in Sabah with an Anglican clergyman who has no less than 320 cell groups in his church, and it is with them that the action lies. This places a high emphasis on every-member ministry, on versatility and on training. It gives room for the Holy Spirit to be freely at work encouraging, teaching, revealing hitherto unsuspected gifts and ministries. In denominations where the administration of Holy Communion is restricted to the ordained clergy alone, a church of this sort obviously provides considerable problems. But even here it can be done. The church in Sabah which I mentioned has its celebrations of the Holy Communion centrally, though practically everything else is done in the cell. Those who would like an insight into what is happening among cell churches in different parts of the world might like to turn to a book I have edited, *Church without Walls* (Paternoster, 2002). There is talk, too, of 'Liquid Churches', loose networks of believers meeting in their natural fellowships, and Alpha groups which do not want to disband are in some places becoming small churches.

All these different expressions of church are emerging at a time when the traditional churches are struggling. Who can tell what will emerge in the next half century? One thing is certain. Wherever the Holy Spirit is welcomed in a church, and allowed to guide the people, there will be life and growth and impact on secular society all around. But what if there appears to be too much Holy Spirit? What if things get out of hand – as maybe they have at Toronto?

The Toronto Blessing

Randy Clark, the founding pastor of the Vineyard Church in St. Louis, was hungry for a deeper experience of God and more fruitfulness in his ministry. He was powerfully touched through the ministry of a South African evangelist, Rodney Howard-Browne, and shared what had happened with the Vineyard National Board in October 1993. There was a limited outbreak of unusual phenomena at that meeting. Among those present was John Arnott, pastor of the Airport Vineyard in Toronto. He invited Clark to come to his church, which was small and unpretentious, in January 1994. Two days of meetings turned into a continuous ministry every night except Mondays to a packed church. These meetings continue to this day. When I went there must have been 4000 present, from many countries, and many hundreds of clergy and ministers had been having a training seminar there all day.

The worship is very ordinary North American stuff: band, worship songs, address – and is accompanied by much noise from the aircraft. There appeared to me to be little attempt at hype, although there were markings on the floor to ensure that those who fell did so in an orderly fashion! The pastoral team were self-effacing and remain amazed by what has happened and by the plane loads coming in from all over the world, as people determine to see for themselves what is going on.

The phenomena are mainly shaking, falling to the ground, 'drunkenness', weeping, laughter and revelations (dreams, prophetic words, while under the Spirit's influence). Sometimes people are unconscious for a long time, and often they have no knowledge of what has been going on, or why it should have happened to them. Others realise that God has been dealing with a specific area of their own needs. The outcome seems generally to be a greatly enhanced love for Jesus and for other people, coupled with a deep sense of joy. The note of love was the main thing that impressed a colleague of mine who went there for a whole week to experience it in person. But inevitably questions arise.

Are these phenomena biblical?

They certainly form no part of Christian theology or ethics as found in Scripture, and therefore they are in no sense normative. However the Bible reveals a wide variety of experiences which God's people have sometimes had under the impact of the Spirit of God. *Ruach* in the Old Testament frequently has this sense of God's violent invasive force (see pp. 21,22). The Lion of Judah is no pussy cat.

Thus *falling* before the Lord, a noteworthy aspect of this experience, is not uncommon in Scripture (Deut. 9:18, Ezek. 1:28, Dan. 8:17, 10:9, Rev. 1:17 etc). It is a reaction to the perceived presence of God (John 18:6 is an interesting parallel).

Trembling, another common phenomenon at Toronto, and the many other places throughout the world that have experienced similar phenomena, is also to be found in Scripture, though not often (Ps. 2:11, 119:120, Jer. 5:22, Dan. 10:8–10). It cannot be ruled out as an appropriate response to God.

Drunkenness, or being so full of the Spirit that the limbs are uncoordinated, is also to be found in Scripture (Jer. 23:9, Acts 2:13, Eph. 5:18). So, of course, are *weeping* and *laughter*. Both constitute release of the emotions, which have often been kept in check both in home and church, by our desire to maintain control and our emphasis on the intellect. Nehemiah 8:9, 2 Chronicles 34:27, Acts 2:37, along with Psalm 126:2, Ecclesiastes 3:4, and John 17:13 are examples of the spilling out both of tears and laughter. I wonder what Peter meant by 'joy inexpressible' (1 Pet. 1:8)? Is not laughter precisely that – a joy which words cannot communicate? And of course *revelations* occur frequently in the Bible, and

St. Paul expected them to be one of the contributions in worship (1 Cor. 14:26).

Are these phenomena unprecedented in church history?

By no means. Here are some examples.

Jonathan Edwards writes: 'Many have had their religious affections raised far beyond what they had ever had before. There were instances of some people lying in a sort of trance, remaining for perhaps 24 hours motionless, and with their senses locked up. In the meantime it was as if they went to heaven and there was a vision of glorious and delightful objects.' Again, he writes: 'I had not spoken for more than a quarter of an hour when an awful solemnity seemed to settle upon them; and the congregation began to fall from their seats in every direction and cried for mercy. If I had a sword in each hand I could not have cut them down so fast. Nearly the whole congregation was either on their knees or prostrate.'

John Wesley writes: 'Immediately one that stood by (to our no small surprise) cried aloud with the utmost vehemence even as in the agonies of death. But we continued in prayer until a new song was put in her mouth, a thanksgiving to our God. Soon after, two other persons were seized with strong pains and constrained to roar for the disquietness of their hearts. These also found peace.'

George Fox writes: 'The priest scoffed at us and called us "Quakers". But the Lord's power was so over them and the word of life was declared in such authority and dread to them, that the priest himself began trembling and one of his people said, "Look, the priest trembles and shakes. He is turned Quaker too."'

Jonathan Edwards, operating as he was in a time of marked spiritual revival, has some words on laughter and tears. 'It was very wonderful to see how persons' affections were sometimes moved when God did open their eyes to the greatness of his grace, the fullness of Christ and his readiness to save. Their joyful surprise has caused their hearts as it were to leap, so that they have been ready to break forth into laughter, tears often at the same time issuing like a flood, and intermingling loud weeping ... The manner of God's work on the soul, is very mysterious sometimes.' It is indeed! But we would be unwise to write off such phenomena, strange though they seem. They have all happened before.

What is the point of these phenomena?

For all the current talk of revival in some circles in England it is clear that we are nowhere near approaching the classical concept of revival. The wick of faith burns low, on the whole. But these phenomena do seem to indicate a time of refreshing from the presence of the Lord, a sign of God's manifested presence in our midst. They are a rebuke to the this-worldliness of current Christianity. They are a rebuke to the rationalism that has dogged much of our theology for two hundred years, and a reminder that our God is the living God! They are a challenge to us to allow God to have his way with us, not to retain the control which we hold so dear. One way of understanding 'falling' is to see it as God withdrawing from us the strength in which we trust. When people fall to the floor they seem to be receiving something from God deep in the soul, of which their minds may remain totally unaware, but whose fruits soon become clear.

'Manifestations,' wrote John White, 'while they may be a blessing are no guarantee of anything ... Your fall and your shaking may be a genuine expression of the Spirit resting upon you. But the Spirit may not benefit you in the least if God does not have his way with you, while someone who neither falls nor trembles may profit greatly.'

What are the criteria of authenticity?

These are dangerous waters, and the Bible has plenty of warnings for us. 'False Christs and false prophets will arise and show great signs and wonders, so as to lead astray, if possible, even the elect' (Matt. 24:24). 'Even Satan disguises himself as an angel of light' (2 Cor. 11:14). 'Do not believe every spirit, but test the spirits to see if they come from God' (1 John 4:1). Perhaps three main criteria could be brought to bear.

First, does it honour Christ and exalt him? Jonathan Edwards in the days of the Great Awakening made Christology the first criterion of authentic phenomena.

Second, does the character of those involved withstand scrutiny? It is apparent in the discussion of spiritual gifts in 1 Corinthians 12 and 14 with chapter 13 on love coming between them, that character was crucial in St. Paul's eyes. Character is more important than charisma.

Third, what about the results of a particularly impressive spiritual experience? Does it produce more prayer, more likeness to Christ? Does it manifest that prime fruit of the Spirit, love? If not, it can safely be discounted.

Is this 'blessing' spreading?

It certainly is. From all over the world they have come to Toronto, and still pour in. And all over the world one hears reports of similar phenomena, albeit on a much more restricted scale. Some 6000 churches in Britain alone have been profoundly influenced by the happenings at Toronto. And there are major outbreaks of the power of God's Spirit with similar phenomena in many countries. Sunderland, in the North East of England is one of the roughest cities in the whole country. But in the 1990s something very similar to Toronto took place. Thousands have been blessed by it. At times 600 poured into the church nightly, in an area so tough that the building required unbreakable glass and had to be surrounded by a perimeter fence and protected by security guards. Here large numbers of ministers were renewed. Many people found Christ here. Membership doubled, and lives were transformed. One person put it like this: 'God has done for me in six weeks what counsellors have tried to do for ten years.' Dramatic healings were experienced, and the love of Christ pervaded it all. It was, moreover, entirely transdenominational.

But the most notable recent outbreak of the Holy Spirit took place in Pensacola, Florida in 1995 and continued for many months. The minister, John Kilpatrick, tells the story in his book *Feast of Fire*. Some 65,000 people professed faith in Christ in 14 months. 2000 people were coming to the church every night to receive from God. The manifestations of the Spirit were similar to those at Toronto, and the start of it all was just as unexpected. There was a strong emphasis on personal morality. The county sheriff visited one night to find a huge container stacked with illegal substances, weapons and pornographic magazines which had been 'donated' by the audience that evening. He observed, 'Up till now I thought that the major impact on the community lay in the traffic jams. Now I know differently.'

Other churches in Pensacola have also been involved, and as in Sunderland there appears to be no hint of pride or selfishness about Brownsville, the church where it all began. They do nothing to court publicity, and never announce a visiting speaker before he comes. People fall backwards as is common at Toronto, but also forwards in repentance before the altar. Manifestations are no big deal to them. Their concern is the salvation of the lost and the holiness of the Christians.

So yes, this powerful movement of the Spirit which was seen a few years earlier in the ministry of John Wimber, is certainly spreading far and wide. It is breaking out in many parts of the world that have never heard of Toronto. Often it is merely the intensification of the quality of spirituality already present. I have quite often over the years known people to go out like a light and 'rest in the Spirit'. In Asia it is commonplace, not least in mainline churches like the Anglican. When people are prayed for they often slip to the ground without anyone laying a finger on them. There is no way in which it could be manipulated: one does not even know it is going to happen until it does! It seems that God wants to do something deep in the heart of the person concerned, and afterwards they generally know what it was. At all events Toronto is only the occasion – not the essence. It was, I think, part of the divine humour to stage a large scale movement like this out of a shop front church at the end of a runway that nobody had ever heard of!

What is the fruit of all this?

That is the important question. As the Archbishop of York once said to me, in a memorable phrase, 'I don't mind them falling down. I want to know if they are any good when they get up!' That says it all. The result seems to be that they generally *are* some good when they get up, in a number of ways. There is a prevailing sense of joy which tends to remain for some time. There is almost always an intensified love for Jesus. There is frequently a substantial measure of healing and reconciliation associated with this experience. Many people discern a fresh area of service and are empowered to undertake it. A good, though not massive, number of new conversions emerge from such meetings. A significant number of lapsed people return to the church. And there is a sense that God is preparing his Church for the future, whatever that may hold.

There are many attractive features in all this. The Toronto Blessing reminds us that Christianity is not an ideology: it is the power of God. It reminds us that the Church is in constant need of renewal. Christianity is not at all legalistic at Toronto. They are totally disinterested in making money. They do not lionise their leadership. They are very generous to the endless stream of visitors, and church members quite literally live to serve others. The whole church seems to embody the love of God.

However, there are criticisms that can legitimately be made. The quality of preaching is often weak at Toronto: emphasis on manifestations of the Spirit can detract from the power of

God's revelation, for Word and Spirit belong together in God's economy. The sacraments do not figure highly. It would be fair to say, too, that there is a danger of a reductionist view of the Holy Spirit, seeing his work mainly in unusual phenomena rather than character and mission. There is the danger of spiritual pride, and a certain self-absorption has been noticed among the members of the church and their leadership. In Toronto, as in many similar situations, the danger of anti-intellectualism is not entirely avoided. It is as if the Spirit is only really present when something unusual is happening. I sense that many of the locals go along several times a week for their spiritual 'fix': and I doubt whether this is healthy. In the New Testament spiritual manifestations never take centre stage, nor indeed does the Holy Spirit. He is shy, and always points to Jesus Christ. I hope this is true at Toronto, but I have yet to be convinced. Tom Smail, who has had extensive experience of the renewal movement, is concerned about 'charismatic people whose whole talk is of words of knowledge of deliverance from evil, of being slain in the Spirit, of tingling hands and high emotions at great charismatic meetings, till one is left wondering to what extent such preoccupations bring us nearer to the heart of the New Testament gospel, and to what extent they distract and divert us from it'.

Those are some of the dangers which high octane spiritual movements tend to run, in Toronto or anywhere else. There will always be hype and showmanship. There will always be hysterics seeking a stage to perform on. There will always be the tendency to unchurch those who do not have the same experiences. There will always be a proportion of crazy things happening and purporting to come from the Holy Spirit, such as roaring and growling at Toronto. There will always be spiritual flotsam and jetsam on the edges of the rising tide. Good pastoral care is essential. Discernment, firm leadership, biblical norms and wise counsel are the most important requisites when any spiritual gifts occur.

All in all, I rejoice to live in a day like this. There are dangers, but the dangers of life are infinitely preferable to the dangers of death.

2. A GROWING MATURITY

When the first edition of this book was written, the charismatic movement had only been in operation in this country for a dozen years or so, and showed much of the immaturity of a young movement. There is reason to believe that in the years since then there has been a growing maturity, though this may well be accompanied by a decrease in zeal. Here are some of the areas where I have sensed growth.

Less stress on secondary issues

In the first place there is less emphasis on the differentia of the sub-culture. Every organisation develops its own way of doing things, and tends, when immature, to look askance on any other way. This was true of the charismatic movement. If you did not speak in tongues you could not be baptised in the Holy Spirit. If you did not raise your arms in worship you were not released. If you did not repeat a song several times you had not really learnt to worship. And so on. It is one of the weaknesses of mankind to erect the secondary into the primary, and the charismatic movement was no more exempt from this failing than anybody else. But now I sense an indifference as to whether or not arms are raised in praise: hearts are certainly raised, and it is common to see people 'lost in wonder, love and praise'. It has a profound effect on a congregation, and those coming in from outside are often deeply struck by it.

Less insistence on 'the baptism'

Second, there is less of an insistence (in Britain though perhaps not in the U.S.A) on the term 'baptism in the Holy

Spirit' for the experience of revitalisation to which charismatics refer. It never was a good word, partly because it has little linguistic backing in the New Testament, and partly because it is essentially divisive. After all, baptism is the decisive and unrepeatable sacrament of Christian initiation, and if you say of someone else, 'Poor thing, he has not been baptised in the Holy Spirit,' you are inevitably carving out a great chasm between you. The doctrine of Spirit baptism was derived from classical Pentecostalism, and they got it from the holiness movements of the nineteenth century; indeed, it goes back in essence to Wesley's doctrine of perfection, the doctrine of entire sanctification, perfect love, or simply the second blessing. It is much more widely appreciated nowadays that the reviving power of the Holy Spirit is quite distinguishable and distinct from the Pentecostal wrappings in which it burst upon the world early in the last century, and that the three strands of water baptism, repentance and faith, and the gift of the Spirit are strands in the one Christian initiation, and may occur in a different order with different people. There is, accordingly, much less tendency to put down other Christians who have not had a second climactic experience of the Holy Spirit, but have gradually come alive to God and his generosity. This is mirrored in the language which is increasingly being used to describe the taste of new wine: not 'baptism in the Holy Spirit' so much as 'release in the Spirit' or 'a new filling with the Holy Spirit' or the like. Such linguistic change, unimportant maybe in itself, is very important as a mark of increasing humility and love towards other brothers and sisters in the same family of God.

Less stress on rebaptism?

I wish I could say that there is a widespread growing maturity over the question of rebaptism in charismatic circles. In many parts of the country there is. People recognise that there is one baptism into Christ, and no more. They do not urge rebaptism in water on those who have experienced a filling with the Spirit, any more than wise Evangelicals urged rebaptism on those who had come to repentance and faith. However, the Baptists have always done it. The house churches do it. And there is a constant trickle of people who have been helped by the charismatic movement and want to seal it by entering into the waters of baptism by immersion. I see this as an inking in of a pencilled commitment, which some people feel they need either for psychological reassurance or in obedience to what they take to be the normative pattern in the Acts of the Apostles. Certainly as a paedobaptist I freely admit the grave abuses of infant baptism which encourage rebaptism. We have allowed it to be a formality. We have allowed it to be a social nicety. We have baptised children where there is not the least glimmer of Christian faith and commitment in the family. And we have been wrong to do so. I do not blame people who feel that such a baptism was no baptism. I do not agree with them, but I understand them. We have not allowed sufficient room for the public profession of faith in Christ which is so important a part of baptism; it has been hidden away, in most denominations, in some rite of confirmation which is often as culture-bound, formal and meaningless as the ceremony of baptism was before it. I deplore rebaptism: how can the sacrament of the once-for-allness of the Christian life be repeated? But I have sympathy with those who feel driven to it by the abuses of Christian initiation to which they and those around them have been subjected in the mainline churches. Mercifully, I find that many who have come to faith subsequent to baptism and confirmation, many who have become alive in the Spirit, are happy not to be rebaptised but to take an opportunity in church to give a public testimony to Christ and explain something of the difference he is making to their lives. And to be willing for that modification of rebaptism bespeaks a growing maturity!

Less pride and prejudice

There was, I noticed, in the early days of the charismatic move-ment a strong tendency to think of oneself more highly than one ought to think, and to think less highly of others, particu-larly those whose way of worship and expression of the faith was different. There was more than a touch of arrogance: 'I've got it: you haven't.' This was very offensive. But so were the rebuffs and rejection which were handed out to the charismat-ics by those who felt threatened by them. The result was divi-sion, and this marred the early days of the charismatic movement in the mainline churches of this country. I hear very little of this now. There is a new humility, a new readiness to listen to others and learn from them as well as contribute to them, a new recognition that we are called to stand and live and love together. In a word, censoriousness and divisiveness are in retreat in the current manifestation of the charismatic move-ment. Long may they so remain.

Closely allied to this touch of arrogance which often marked early charismatics in Britain was a sniff of that perfectionism that has always lurked under the surface in two-stage initiation theologies and attitudes. It was almost as though the 'Spirit-filled' inhabited a plateau which others could not reach except by precisely that same route as they themselves had, and from which they could not slip down whatever they did. So there was a good deal of minimising of sin to be found in early charis-matic circles, even some libertinism. I have met a good many who claimed that in such spiritual believers as themselves there was no room for sin. Well, experience proved the folly and the blasphemy of that, and it is fortunately rare to come across per-fectionism in charismatics these days. They have grown out of that particularly unpleasant heresy, and there is often now in charismatic circles a readiness to acknowledge sin and failure individually, as a Church, and as a nation, which I find attains a depth and a sincerity which I have rarely met with elsewhere.

Less preoccupation with gifts

One of the early shibboleths was that the mark of being baptised in the Holy Spirit was the ability to speak in tongues.
Everyone should have their 'prayer language' if they were real
members of the family. Such was the mythology. It sprang, of
course, from the classical Pentecostal background, where it so
happened that all the handful of people in the Azusa Street
awakening in Los Angeles in 1906 did in fact speak in tongues
as a result of that experience. But of course approximately half
of all Pentecostals today do not speak in tongues, so surveys
show. And the belief that tongues is the badge of being baptised
in the Spirit is as false to the New Testament (and experience)
as the notion that baptism in the Spirit is a second initiatory
experience. Many people who are manifestly alive in the Spirit
do not speak in tongues. Many whose spiritual life is very dim
and unimpressive do speak in tongues. And many in the charismatic movement receive tongues some years after receiving
other gifts. I did myself. It is neither an authenticating badge
nor an initiatory experience incumbent upon all 'Spirit-filled'
Christians. There is an increasing readiness today to see that the
gift of tongues is simply one of the many gifts that the Holy
Spirit gives at his discretion, and that we cannot claim it as a
right. Least of all is it to be treated as an essential credit card,
without which one's ministry is suspect. This has led many to
counterfeit the gift in order to get accepted, and then, of course,
the gift itself gets brought into disrepute.

In the early days of the charismatic movement in this country
there was a preoccupation with internal matters within the
groups, the fellowship, the worship and the gifts. Nowadays
there is much more of a concern with evangelism, and people
understand that gifts are not given for our delectation but for
our service of God in a needy world. I think it would be the case
that the most charismatic groups and churches at present are
among those who are most concerned with evangelism.

A break with triumphalism

There was in the early days a naïveté, almost a romantic escapism from the banalities or horrors of daily life. This was particularly the case with respect to healing. It was hinted, indeed often openly taught, that God always wants the health of his people, and that if they do not enjoy it it must be because of sin or lack of faith either in the person concerned or those ministering to him. This imbalance sprang from a theology of the powers of the resurrection without taking into account the complementary truth of the fellowship of Christ's sufferings. It was a triumphalism as foreign to authentic Christianity as the apathetic acquiescence which preceded it. We should expect God to heal. And we should realise that he is sovereign, works mysteriously, and cannot have his arm twisted by charismatic healers or anyone else. I notice an increasing awareness of these two paradoxical truths among modern charismatics. They do pray expecting God to hear and to answer; and they do not make the mistake of supposing that they know what is best for the person concerned and that it is their duty to persuade God to take their view. David Watson, by the manner of his dying, gave the Christian world such a stirring example that this lesson is coming home to many of the triumphalists. David had the best medical care available; he received dedicated ministry from some of the leading charismatic healers in the world; he was more prayed for than any man has been for decades – and yet he died. But his death was glorious. He was on the edge of heaven while he lingered here, and to pray with him and hear him pray for me and my family shortly before his death brought tears to my eyes and is one of the abiding spiritual experiences of my life. His death was not defeat, it was victory. But the fact remains that he who had brought healing to so many was not himself healed, except by death. And that is a solemn warning against a shallow triumphalism such as had often been found in circles which had begun to experience the healing power of God in answer to believing prayer.

Retreat from anti-intellectualism and pan-demonism

There are other areas where maturity is coming to the movement. There is less theological immaturity than there was, less fixation on the Holy Spirit to the neglect of the Father and Jesus Christ. There is less anti-intellectualism than there was, and a growing recognition that the God who gives us his Spirit also endows us with reason. There is less pan-demonism than there was; the attitude which saw most spiritual struggles as a battle between God and the demonic in human life, wherein the individual Christian was almost a spectator. It led to a dangerous abnegation of responsibility, and a dangerous dependence on some fellow Christian to come and minister deliverance – when what was really needed was a resolute crucifying of the flesh rather than ascribing everything to the devil. There has without doubt been an over-fascination with the devil as a result of the new awareness of spiritual battle which is part of the charismatic experience. It is a danger that is still with us, but I believe it to be on the wane. In all these ways it is possible, it seems to me, to discern a remarkable growth and maturity during the past few years in this astonishing movement which has swept the Christian world in our time. It is not mature yet, but the growth in that direction is phenomenal, and I would like to think it is matched by those parts of the Church which look on the renewal movement with fear, disapproval or disdain.

3. A Lasting Contribution

Is the charismatic movement finished?

There are those who believe that the charismatic movement is finished. I believe that it has hardly started. In many parishes there is still deep peace – the peace of the graveyard. The emphases of this movement are desperately needed all over the world.

They are needed in Western Europe, where the faith is like an ancient heirloom that nobody wants to give away but nobody knows quite what to do with in this postmodern age. Christianity seems to be a matter either of folk religion, of ethics, of comparative religion, or the phenomenology of religion to be studied in universities. It is not customarily seen as a dynamic way of life in which the power of the living God is exhibited. But that is just what the charismatic movement does believe, and at its best, does exhibit. There is credulity and showmanship, immaturity and exhibitionism to be found in this movement, alas; but there is also the power of the living Christ, transforming men and women. It was a joy to take part in a conference for renewal in Belgium some time ago, where Protestants and Catholics met to share in Christ and celebrate him together. There was a unity, a love, a spiritual power in that conference which was very different from the normal lifestyle associated either with the Roman Catholics or l'Eglise Réformée. The members of the conference, Catholics and Protestants alike, visited the homes of that town and together told people of the living Christ, and then preached him together in the local Catholic church. To say that the inhabitants were amazed is an understatement! It is much the same in Ireland. We hear the constant headlines of sectarian hate and killings. But when the Holy Spirit is allowed access all that changes. One of the unsung glories of Ireland is the celebrations of the faith when thousands gather to worship the Lord, Catholics and Protestants alike, and are prepared to lay down their lives for one another and care for each other in ostracism and injury. That quality of authentic Christian life makes ordinary denominational allegiance pale into the pathetic thing it is, and demonstrates the power of the living Christ to transform an otherwise intractable situation.

Some years ago I was privileged to speak at a conference for the bishops of Nigeria. West Africa at that time had never experienced revival. Churchgoing was widespread but a little formal. There was no expectation that God could heal. And so when Christian people were really in need or trouble they would often resort to the prayer houses of syncretistic animism or the corybantic Christian subculture, such as the Cherubim and Seraphim, for help, because the churches had not led them to expect that the Spirit of God is really active to heal and to give them his gifts. I was saddened to see the results of the powerless, rationalist Western Christianity that we seem to have exported to them. As it happened, God gave us two remarkable healings during that conference, and now of course Nigeria is in the forefront of renewal and mission worldwide. The number of Anglican dioceses has doubled in recent years, and there are now more Anglicans (not to mention other Christians!) worshipping in Nigeria than in all the Anglican churches of England, North America and Australia combined. In the last decade of the twentieth century their numbers more than doubled from approximately eight million to nearly eighteen. That is what can happen when the Holy Spirit is given free rein in a church.

I fancy that what we have seen of the work of the Spirit through this movement hitherto is merely the tip of the iceberg of what we may prayerfully expect.

A signpost for the Church at large

No movement in Christendom should exist for itself. If it does so, it deserves to die, and it will not long be of service to the wider Church. A spiritual movement is a signpost to what the whole Church should be like. Thus Catholicism should not be a denomination or a party, but a powerful exhibition of and pointer to that wholeness which Christ wills for all his people. Evangelicalism should not be a party within Christendom, or a subculture spanning the denominations. It is, at its best, a pointer to that loving outreach with the New Testament gospel of Christ which should characterise all God's people. Equally, the charismatic movement has little to offer if it is just a body of enthusiasts at a particular stage in history, but everything to offer if it demonstrates to the Church universal that dependence on the grace of God, that expectancy of his active intervention, which marked the earliest Christians but is all too rare nowadays. The future of the charismatic movement lies not in itself but in its faithfulness in so embodying the charismatic life of the Spirit that this overflows into the whole Church. It seems to me that the Fountain Trust was a paradigm of this. The Fountain Trust was set up to enable the growth of the charismatic movement in Britain during the sixties and seventies. And then, when it was having a remarkable influence in all sorts of areas of the nation's spiritual life, the Fountain Trust disbanded itself. I wonder how many organisations would do that? But it was a superb example of being willing to die as an institution in order to allow life to flow out. 'Unless a corn of wheat . . .'

Lasting contributions

But what are the lasting contributions which the charismatic movement will have contributed to the Church at large, when the very name of charismatic may well be forgotten?

In his valuable book *Keep in Step with the Spirit*, Dr. Jim Packer offers us a considered evaluation and critique of the charismatic movement, and with it a recall to the values of the Puritans, at whose feet he has sat for many years. He looks beyond the charismatic renewal to true revival, that sovereign work of God which nobody can organise, but which nobody can mistake when it is present. He summarises its characteristics as follows: God comes down, God's word comes home, God's purity comes through, God's people come alive; and when this happens, outsiders are drawn in. He validates this analysis from the Scriptures and from Christian history, and then turns to compare this with the charismatic renewal. He rightly declares they are not the same thing, and analyses the charismatic contribution to the renewal of the Church as follows:

1. Rediscovery of the living God and his Christ and the supernatural dimensions of Christian living, through Spirit baptism or the Spirit's 'release'.
2. Returning to the Bible as the inspired Word of God, to nourish one's soul upon it.
3. Habits of private and public devotion designed to bring the whole person, body and soul, into total, expectant dependence on the Holy Spirit (glossolalia comes in here).
4. A leisurely, participatory style of public praise and prayer.
5. A use of spiritual gifts for ministry in the Body of Christ by every member of Christ.
6. Exploration of the possibilities of ministry through a communal lifestyle.
7. An active commitment by this and other means to reach out to the needy in evangelism and service.
8. A high level of expectancy that the hand of God will again and again be shown in striking providences ('miracles'), prophetic messages to this or that person, visions, supernatural healings, and similar manifestations.

He compares these things with what historically has been experienced in conditions of revival, and he makes two observations. One I believe to be true; the other is more questionable. The truth he points to is the lack of awe and reverence coupled with excessive informality which marks much charismatic worship, together with an element of egoism and showmanship which can also be discerned. Alas, that is not infrequently the case, and needs to be rooted out. What is less true, it seems to me, is Packer's claim that a strain of supernaturalism runs through the renewal movement which is alien to revivals, and has always been seen by them as a mark of spiritual immaturity. I do not believe that to be true. Every revival from the days of the Acts of the Apostles onwards has been the power of God revealed in healings, in miracles, and in the awesome conviction of sin brought about inexplicably in large numbers of people. Most of the supernatural experiences of the current renewal were there in Wesley's day and Finney's day, often more markedly than at present. In revival God shows his hand. The current charismatic renewal is not revival, but is a remarkable rekindling of embers by the Spirit of the living God, and we should not dismiss his acts of power as 'marks of disturbing immaturity' (op. cit. p. 247). The Spirit in our day has been bringing before us afresh gifts that he knows we need for our mission as a Church: we must not be gullible and uncritical when people profess to exercise these gifts, but we cannot affect to do without them. God does not give his gifts to be spurned.

Jim Packer ends his book by pointing to some challenges which keeping in step with the Spirit will pose to the Church. He lists reality and vitality in worship and Church life, radicalism in Church order and organisation, reaching out in love to others, hunger for revival, and a spiritual realism which is willing to face and act upon the unpalatable sides of ourselves and of our Church. Christ, he points out, hates pretence and unrealism, and will expose it. These are all important points. I believe they are foremost among the lessons which the charismatic renewal has to teach the Church. I myself would select the following as challenges put by the charismatic movement to the Church at large, challenges which have a lasting relevance.

A challenge to institutionalism in the Church

First the charismatic movement offers a challenge to institutionalism in the Church. Far too often the Church is seen as, and indeed *is*, the club for those who like that kind of thing.

The Church is seen as an organisation, whose local branch is to be seen in bricks and mortar (or mock Gothic stonework) down the street. But that is not the Church. It is merely a meeting place of the Church. The Church is people alive in the Holy Spirit! It is immaterial where they meet, so long as the Lord is in their midst. The Russian church, estimated at something like 60 million, knows this truth full well. They were only allowed a tiny number of churches in the days of the Soviet Union, and much of the worship took place in woods and on mountain sides in the middle of the night, as believers gathered together in secret homage to their Lord. The movement of the Spirit always poses a challenge to the conservatism of the institution. Somehow the Church of Christ must embody both charism and order, and the renewal movement will remain a lasting challenge to those who exalt institution over life.

A challenge to intellectualism in the Church

Second, the charismatic movement is a challenge to intellectualism in the Church. As we have seen, the movement is often weak on the importance of the intellect, and has undervalued it. That is a serious error and is hopefully being rectified. But the traditional churches are guilty of an even more serious error. They have so intellectualised the Christian faith that it seems beyond the reach of ordinary people. The theologians are largely out of touch with the people in the pew, and seem to live independent lives rather than seeing their work as serving God's people in understanding and applying the faith. Christianity seems all too often to be a matter of intellectual assent (or doubt), of churchgoing, and of middle-class mores. It makes very little difference to life, and those who go to church are not readily distinguishable by their lifestyle from those who do not. But nobody could say that of the charismatics. You could call them mad, enthusiasts with religious mania, and the like. But they embody something different. And the *ruach adonai*, the Spirit of the Lord, *is* something different. He is not to be intellectualised or tamed. The charismatics know this. They give the impression of having found something life-changing, and that is a quality which authentic Christianity always needs to have.

A challenge to one-man leadership in the Church

Third, the charismatic movement has placed a lasting question mark against monarchy in the Church. For centuries, and in whatever denomination, there has been the tendency to identify charism and order and to see it as resting in the hands of one man (or very few). Whatever the denomination, monarchy tends to reign. What the priest or minister or pastor or leader wants, goes. He is the professional. He is supposed to know. But the charismatic movement refuses to allow this. One of its prime discoveries is the Lordship of Christ in his Church, and his desire to give charisma to every member of his Body so that they can contribute to the good of the whole. Not some, but all, are called to serve. Ministry is the privilege of all, not the pre-serve of the few. This recall to lay ministry to every-member ministry, to shared ministry is incomparably more revolution-ary in the Church than is the gift of tongues, and incomparably more important too. There are signs that it is taking off in many different denominations. The danger is that the current lay movement may simply ecclesiasticise the layman, not set him free to serve the Lord in the Church with the gifts God has entrusted him with. If the charismatic movement can, in the providence of God, impress on the institutional captivity of the Church the truth that every member is called to serve, that lead-ership exists to equip the saints for their God given work of service, and should be both plural and pluriform, then that alone would render it one of the most important movements the Church has ever known.

A challenge to unbelief in the Church

Fourth, the renewal movement has come at a time when unbelief in the Church has reached epic proportions. As one who has spent most of my life teaching theology, I know the scepticism which underlies many of the books the theological student has to study. Some who write these books do not believe in a personal God, nor in the incarnation of God in Christ, nor in his miracles or resurrection. They are avowedly non-interventionist. Their God, if he is anything more than the smile which remains after the Cheshire Cat has disappeared, is impotent to interfere in our world. But this is precisely the period in history when God Almighty laughs. He sends this movement of his Spirit into the world on an enormous scale, in the most unlikely places and denominations as if to say, 'I am alive and well, thank you!' The charismatic movement is a constant reminder that God is not dead, nor is he absent. This movement has done an enormous amount to kindle and rekindle faith in the living God who delights to answer prayer, to build his people into one, and to equip them with his gifts.

A challenge to introversion in the Church

Finally, I shall continue to value the renewal movement because it is a standing protest against the introversion of the Church. The Church is not for insiders. It is for the whole world. It is far too good news to keep quiet about. To be sure, many other movements in the history of Christianity have stressed the outward thrust of the Christian gospel. But this movement which is so intimately concerned with the Holy Spirit has, when it has been faithful to its calling (as it sometimes has not) made it abundantly clear that the Holy Spirit is given us for service and for mission, for love and for worship. He cannot be muzzled or contained. For the Spirit is the foretaste of that day when the earth shall be filled with the knowledge of the Lord as the waters cover the sea (Isa. 11:9). That is an eschatological prophecy, and the Holy Spirit is the eschatological gift who enables us here and now to enter into some experience of the end-time, God's future. The supreme importance of the movement which in our day celebrates the presence and power of the Holy Spirit is to lift up our hearts in expectancy to God's future, of which the Spirit is the pledge and guarantee.

Bibliography

The literature on this subject is immense, and I append only a sample. I have divided them into serious theological studies (marked with an asterisk,*) and books, paperback or otherwise, which are designed primarily for the general reader. In some instances I have put a few words of comment after the title for the guidance of those who may feel lost in the extensive and wide-ranging plethora of literature on the subject. Books which derive from Pentecostal or neo-Pentecostal sources, or are sympathetic to the charismatic movement are indicated thus †.

* Gary Badcock, *Light of truth and fire of love* (Eerdmans). A major theological appraisal, designed for a learned readership.

* C. G. Baeta, *Conflict in Mission* (S.C.M.).

* C. K. Barrett, *The Holy Spirit and the Gospel Tradition* (S.P.C.K.).

  K. Barth, 'The Christian Life: Baptism as the Foundation of the Christian Life' in *Church Dogmatics* IV. 4 (Clark).

† Dennis Bennett, *The Holy Spirit and You and Nine o'Clock in the Morning* (Kingsway). Theologically unreliable, but exciting reading and highly influential.

  James Beverley, *Holy Laughter and the Toronto Blessing* (Zondervan). An investigative assessment by a leading Canadian theologian.

*† Arnold Bittlinger, *Gifts and Graces* and *Gifts and Ministries* (Hodder). Thoughtful charismatic theological writing.

† Wallace Boulton ed., *The Impact of Toronto* (Monarch). A preliminary investigation into the 'Toronto Blessing.'

* Raymond Brown, 'The Paraclete in the Fourth Gospel', *New Testament Studies*, 1967, pp. 113–32, and *The Gospel according to John* (Anchor Bible).

* F. D. Bruner, *A Theology of the Holy Spirit* (Hodder). A major theological appraisal of Pentecostal claims, but lacking in empathy.

* J. H. Charlesworth, ed., *John and Qumran* (Chapman). See especially A. R. C. Leaney's article 'The Johannine Paraclete and Qumran'.

† Larry Christenson, *Speaking in Tongues* (Coverdale). Lutheran charismatic study.

* J. G. Davies, *The Spirit, the Church and the Sacraments* (Faith Press) and 'Pentecost and Glossolalia' in *Journal of Theological Studies*, 1952, pp. 228–31.

† Leslie Davison, *Pathway to Power* (Fountain Trust).

*† Williamm DeArteaga, *Quenching the Spirit* (Creation House). A powerful theological and historical rebuttal of anti-charismatic writings.

F. W. Dillistone, *The Holy Spirit in the Life of Today* (The Canterbury Press).

A. L. Drummond, *Edward Irving and His Circle* (Clarke).

*† J. D. G. Dunn, *Baptism in the Holy Spirit* (S.C.M.). Perhaps the most influential treatment of the Spirit in modern times, particularly concentrating on Pentecostal theology, its strengths and weaknesses. Also 'Spirit and Fire Baptism', *Novum Testamentum*, 1972, pp. 81–92. 'Spirit Baptism and Pentecostalism', *Scottish Journal of Theology*, 1970, p. 397ff. '2 Corinthians 3:17 – The Lord is the Spirit' in *Journal of Theological Studies*, 1970, p. 309ff – an unconvincing article. 'John 6 – A Eucharistic Discourse?' in *New Testament Studies*, 1970, p. 328ff – strongly anti-sacramental.

* J. D. G. Dunn, *Jesus and the Spirit* (Westminster). A major

and controversial study of the relation of Jesus to the Holy
Spirit.

† S. Durasoff, *Bright Wind of the Spirit* (Hodder). An indifferent documentary of modern Pentecostalism.

C. L. d'Epinay, *Haven of the Masses* (Lutterworth). A
study of Pentecostalism in Chile by a sociologist.

*† Gordon Fee, *God's Empowering Presence* (Hendrickson).
The most careful and exhaustive study ever undertaken of
the Spirit in the Pauline letters by a deeply spiritual (and
Pentecostal) and profoundly learned N.T. scholar. The
most important book on the subject, meticulous in its exegesis.

*† Gordon Fee, *Paul, the Spirit and the people of God*
(Hodder). A simplified and applied version of the above.

J. E. Fison, *The Blessing of the Holy Spirit* (Longman).

* Ernst Fuchs, *Christus und der Geist bei Paulus* (Leipzig).

* R. H. Fuller, 'Tongues in the New Testament', *American
Church Quarterly*, 1963, p. 162ff.

† J. Goldingay, *The Church and the Gifts of the Spirit* (Grove
Books). A brief but careful and balanced interpretation of
1 Corinthians 12–14.

Billy Graham, *The Holy Spirit* (Collins). The most careful
and well documented and balanced book Dr. Graham has
written.

* R. H. Gundry, 'Ecstatic Utterance (NEB)' in *Journal of
Theological Studies*, 1966, pp. 299–307.

M. P. Hamilton, ed., *The Charismatic Movement* (Eerdmans).

* N. Q. Hamilton, 'The Holy Spirit and Eschatology in Paul'
in *Scottish Journal of Theology*, Occasional Papers 6, 1957.

† Michael Harper, *None Can Guess, As at the Beginning*, and
Spiritual Warfare (Hodder). Descriptive of contemporary
neo-Pentecostalism.

* G. S. Hendry, *The Holy Spirit in Christian Theology*.
Highly suggestive.

* D. Hill, *Greek Words and Hebrew Meanings* (C.U.P.).

*† Peter Hocken, *One Lord, one Spirit, one Body* (Paternoster). A wise book from a Catholic charismatic priest of theological acuteness and spiritual depth.

* L. Hodgson, *The Doctrine of the Trinity* (Nisbet).

† A. A. Hoekema, *What about Tongue Speaking?* (Eerdmans).

*† W. J. Hollenweger, *The Pentecostals.* A massive, critical and sympathetic consideration of classical Pentecostalism.

† H. Horton, *The Baptism in the Holy Spirit* and *The Gifts of the Spirit* (Victory Press).

* J. H. E. Hull, *The Holy Spirit in the Acts of the Apostles* (Lutterworth).

* W. James, *The Varieties of Religious Experience* (Longmans).

* Nils Johansson, '1 Corinthians 13 and 1 Corinthians 14', *New Testament Studies*, 1964, pp. 383–92.

* E. Käsemann, *Essays on New Testament Themes* (S.C.M.).

* L. E. Keck, 'The Spirit and the Dove' in *New Testament Studies*, 1971, pp. 41–68.

* R. A. Knox, *Enthusiasm* (O.U.P.).

* Hans Kung, 'The charismatic structure of the Church' in *The Church and Ecumenism*.

* Kirsopp Lake, *Beginnings of Christianity* 5, Notes 9 and 10 (pp. 96–121).

G. W. H. Lampe, Two notable articles on the Holy Spirit in The Interpreter's Dictionary of the Bible (Abingdon Press) and in Hastings' Dictionary of the Bible (revised edition, Clark). Also **The Seal of the Spirit* (Longmans), *'The Holy Spirit in the Writings of St. Luke' (in *Studies in the Gospels*, ed. Nineham, Blackwell), **St. Luke and the Church at Jerusalem* (Athlone Press) and *God as Spirit (O.U.P.), the Bampton Lectures, his last great work.

* E. Lombard, *De la Glossolalie chèz les premiers chrétiens et des phénomènes similaires: Etude d 'exégèse et de psychologie* (Bridel, Paris).

* R. F. Lovelace, *Dynamics of Spiritual Life* (I.V.P.).

*† F. MacNutt, *Healing* and *Power to Heal* (Notre Dame).

† George Mallone, *Those Controversial Gifts and Furnace of Renewal* (I.V.P.).

* R. C. Moberly, *Atonement and Personality* (Murray).

C. F. D. Moule, I have been greatly helped by two of his unpublished papers, *The Gift of the Spirit to the Church* and *The Holy Spirit in the Church*. **Christ and Spirit in the New Testament*, studies in honour of C. F. D. Moule (ed. Lindars and Smalley, Cambridge) is a mine of useful material. Also *The Holy Spirit* (Mowbrays).

† W. Nee, *The Normal Christian Life* (Victory Press).

* L. Newbigin, *The Household of God* (S.C.M). A seminal work showing the strengths and weaknesses of Catholic, Protestant and Pentecostal conceptions of the Church.

† E. D. O'Connor, *The Pentecostal Movement in the Church* (Notre Dame).

* J. E. L. Oulton, *Holy Communion and Holy Spirit* (S.P.C.K.).

* J. I. Packer, *Keep in Step with the Spirit* (I.V.P.).

* E. M. Pattison, 'Behavioural Science Research on the Nature of Glossolalia' in *Journal of the American Scientific Affiliation*, 1968, p. 73ff.

† Graham Pulkingham, *Gathered for Power* (Hodder). The story of a church reborn.

R. Quebedeaux, *The New Charismatics* (Doubleday).

*† John Richards, *But Deliver Us From Evil* (D.L.T). One of the major books on this subject.

* H. Wheeler Robinson, *The Christian Experience of the Holy Spirit* (Nisbet). A classic from 45 years ago.

W. J. Samarin, *Tongues of Men and Angels* (Macmillan).

Dorothy Sayers, *The Mind of the Maker* (Methuen). Original and creative work.

* W. R. Schoemaker, 'The use of RUACH in the Old Testament and of PNEUMA in the New Testament' in *Journal for Biblical Literature*, 1904.

*† E. Schweizer, *Spirit of God* (Black), being an abbreviation of his article '*Pneuma*' in the *Theologisches Wörterbuch zum Neuen Testament* (ed. G. Kittel) and *Church Order in the New Testament* (S.C.M.). Both of these works are invaluable.

* E. F. Scott *The Spirit in the New Testament* (Hodder).

† J. L. Sherill, *They Speak with Other Tongues* (Hodder).

† David Shibley, *A force in the earth* (Word). The charismatic renewal and world evangelism.

† Sam Shoemaker, *With the Holy Spirit and with Fire* (Harper).

† T A. Smail, *Reflected Glory* (Hodder).

* S. Smalley, 'Spiritual Gifts and 1 Corinthians 12–16' in *Journal for Biblical Literature*, 1968, pp. 427–33. 'Spirit, Kingdom and Prayer in Luke–Acts' in *Novum Testamentum*, 1973. pp. 59–72.

* N. H. Snaith, *The Distinctive Ideas of the Old Testament* (Epworth).

J. R. W. Stott, *The Baptism and Fullness of the Holy Spirit* (I.V.F.). A careful biblical dissuasive from the charismatic movement.

* B. H. Streeter, *The Spirit* (Macmillan).

*† Jean-Jacques Suurmond, *Word and Spirit at play* (S.C.M.). An open theological approach to the charismatic movement, emphasising the importance of play in Pentecostal worship.

* J. P. M. Sweet, '"A Sign for Unbelievers": Paul's attitude to Glossolalia' in *Journal for Theological Studies*, 1966, pp. 240–57. A significant study of a very difficult passage.

* H. B. Swete, *The Holy Spirit in the New Testament* (Macmillan). Old, but invaluable and cool examination of the N.T. material.

* Bengt Sundkler, *Bantu Prophets in South Africa* (O.U.P.).

J. V. Taylor, *The Go-Between God* (S.C.M.). Superb, imaginative, poetic, but not adequately enough based in Scripture.

* L. S. Thornton, *The Doctrine of the Holy Spirit* (Epworth).

*† Simon Tugwell, *Did you receive the Spirit?* Able Catholic charismatic work, which, however, evades the basic issue of baptism in the Spirit.

† A. Wallis, *The Radical Christian* (Kingsway). Highly influential book urging radical withdrawal from the mainline denominations.

Rob Warner, *Prepare for Revival* (Hodder). A well researched examination of some of the physical responses across the world when people meet God.

† D. C. K. Watson, *One in the Spirit* (Hodder). Perhaps the most balanced short and positive evaluation of the charismatic movement.

Douglas Webster, *Pentecostalism and Speaking in Tongues* (Highway Press).

† John Wesley, *Journal* (Epworth).

† John White, *When the Spirit comes with power* (Hodder). Practical research into Vineyard and other expressions of charismatic Christianity by a missionary psychiatrist.

† D. Wilkerson, *The Cross and the Switchblade* (Hodder).

* E. W. Winstanley, *The Spirit in the New Testament* (C.U.P.).

* J. E. Yates, *The Spirit and the Kingdom* (S.P.C.K.).

† Bruce Yocum, *Prophecy* (Ann Arbor).

* A Report of the Special Committee on *The Work of the Holy Spirit* to the United Presbyterian Church in the U.S.A., 1970. A most careful evaluation of neo-Pentecostalism.

*† *Statement of the Theological Basis of the Catholic Charismatic Renewal*, ed., Fr. Kilian McDonnell, 1973.

The Church Quarterly, April 1971 (various articles).

Evangelism in the Early Church

by Michael Green

'I cannot conceive how anyone could read this book without having his evangelistic vision renewed and zeal kindled.'

John Stott

Michael Green combines his undoubted talents both as evangelist and theologian as he focuses, with numerous quotes from the primary sources, on evangelism 'in the strict sense of proclaiming the Good News of salvation to men and women with a view to their conversion to Christ and incorporation into his Church.'

This is a comprehensive evaluation and reappraisal of the main aspects of evangelism in the early church, concentrating on the New Testament period but also providing a topical treatment of evangelism up to the middle of the third century.

This revised edition introduces the reader to the latest finds and developments in scholarship.

'A notable achievement.'

Church Times

'The indispensable basis for a consideration of modern evangelism.'

I. Howard Marshall

Kingsway Publications